Amanda
HOLDEN

No Holding Back

**SIMON &
SCHUSTER**

London · New York · Sydney · Toronto · New Delhi

A CBS COMPANY

First published in Great Britain by Simon & Schuster UK Ltd, 2013
This paperback edition published by Simon & Schuster UK Ltd, 2014
A CBS COMPANY

3 5 7 9 10 8 6 4 2

Simon & Schuster UK Ltd
1st Floor
222 Gray's Inn Road
London WC1X 8HB

www.simonandschuster.co.uk

Simon & Schuster Australia, Sydney
Simon & Schuster India, New Delhi

A CIP catalogue record for this book
is available from the British Library

ISBN: 978-1-47112-574-4
ebook ISBN: 978-1-47112-572-0

Typeset by M Rules
Printed and bound by CPI Group (UK) Ltd, Croydon, CR0 4YY

To my precious girls, Lexi and Hollie.
This book is for you. I want you to be able to read it
when you are bigger and make different choices
to your Mama.

You know I love you both to the moon and back but here –
in black and white – is the life I led before you changed
it for the better.

Mama xxx

Contents

Prologue

'Dare to be happy,' I tell myself.

On my knee, baby Hollie gurgles happily, safe in my arms. To an outsider watching us building sandcastles on the beach, I know we must look like the perfect little family – Mama, Dada, Lexi and baby Hollie, enjoying the sunshine. Little do those people know what we had to endure to get here, but one thing the last year has taught me is that every family has its own quiet story, that things aren't always as they seem.

This is my 'happy place' – Shutters hotel in sunny Santa Monica. The rooms here are small and overpriced, but this beach, this vast expanse of sand, is literally what dreams are made of. The one where my miraculous little family – Chris, my darling husband, and my two beautiful girls, Lexi, six, and Hollie, six months – are playing together now and where we are finally a complete family.

In my head, it's never not sunny here and nothing changes – the dining room with its retro diner booths, the crisp white tablecloths and the hotel's happy hour frozen margaritas with salt around the rim. (I remember how one of my midwives, Jackie, knew I was craving a margarita all through my pregnancy with Hollie. On the day I went into hospital she sneaked a cocktail mix into the fridge in my room so we could finally celebrate my long-awaited baby. We had no idea that the margarita would have to wait a long time until after my precious daughter was born and we were both safe . . .)

We come to our home here every year. It's full of memories. I've holidayed here for five years and during every pregnancy – I have pictures of me and my best friend Jane, bump to bump, two years previously. Memories that are precious, but also incredibly painful.

I have craved this moment for nearly six months, and now, as the sun starts to set, I pull on my shades, scoop up Hollie Rose Hughes (HRH) and head back to the hotel. My feet are bare and the sand is boiling hot, making me dance like I'm on hot coals like a nutter across the beach. I look like a total wreck and hope there are no paps to ruin this moment, when I am just like every other mother.

I burst into the dining room, as glamorous as Worzel Gummidge with my hair in a windswept blonde Afro. The room is full of perfectly coiffed women with big LA blowdries and the snooty receptionist, as always, looks down her nose at me and only barely lets me in. I sit at my usual table, Hollie on my lap. After three years and three pregnancies I smile into my baby's blue-green eyes. Behind my shades, tears start to fall freely down my face and I finally allow myself to let go and feel some joy. God, I'm so happy.

Hollie stares at me intently, wondering what the splashes are that fall on to her chubby cheeks. She's not used to seeing Mama cry. It's as if she can see right into my heart and beyond.

The yellow light pouring into the dining room gives the afternoon an Instagram glow and I gaze out across the beach. The events and tragedies of the past few years feel like an out-of-body experience and every time I have, apparently, bounced back – smile on my face, one-liner at the ready – to business as usual. I'm finally a mother of two and I have a longed-for sibling for my gorgeous elder daughter Lexi. I never wanted the age difference – it used to break my heart watching her play alone on holidays, or taking my hand and shyly asking if I could introduce her to nearby children. 'Stay with me, Mama, until I get used to it,' she'd say. Of course, I needn't have worried so much. Lexi is so happy. Being an only child for so long has given her an inventive and imaginative mind. She is robust and creative, and old enough now to be my nappy slave! She is the big sister of HRH and my little helper, and it's amazing to watch them together. Hollie cannot take her eyes away from Lexi and laughs at everything she does. They are so connected.

Chrispy – my pet name for him as his mail is always addressed to Chris P. (Paul) Hughes – has stood by my side and shared every atom of the pain and joy we have endured. He hates any public attention – I still can't believe he married me! – and he has carried us through every storm, giving up so much of his privacy along the way.

Hollie catches hold of a strand of my hair and studies it. I hug her closely – hoping she won't tug too hard and pull one of my extensions out. I risked everything to have her and she is so worth it.

I felt like I'd been away from myself for so long but our weeks in California have brought me back into my own skin. On this sun-drenched shore, every ounce of who I am is beginning to soak back into me. I feel strong again, emotionally, mentally and physically. The laughter is back and the darkness is gone and I feel back to my naughty self, full of bad jokes and mischief. Chris had said I was beginning to be stubborn and argumentative once more. He never thought he'd be grateful for that – but that tenacity is what saved my life, and now for the first time I believe he's right.

My forty-one years have been filled to the brim – with laughter, hope, despair and, now, with happiness. At heart I am a risk-taker although I confess to being less of one now – life has frightened me a bit. Because the truth is that when you nearly die all you can think about is dying. It's not easily shaken from your mind. You look around at all the good things – the sun, the landscapes, the flowers in your garden, the blue sky, your children – and the shadow passes over you as you remember those words. *You nearly died, Amanda . . .*

It's a big thing to be asked to write a book. To go back and delve into the corners of your mind and pull out memories you thought lost. Private things you never thought you would share even with close friends may now be read by the world. Watching my family playing freely and happily on that boiling hot beach in Los Angeles that day, I decide it might be a good thing to do. I decide that I will write it for my girls – to them. The thought of very nearly not being here to actually tell them in person is never going to leave me, so I am going to turn it into a positive force and give them my story so far, so they can know. In years to come, when I am old and cracked (Lexi uses this phrase to describe wrinkles), I will pick up this book and read it to my grandchildren.

So I do what I've always done when I'm happy. I start to sing:

Hollie Rose has got ten toes, got ten toes, got ten toes;
Hollie Rose has got ten toes and a tiny button nose.

With lyrics like that, I think Adele's safe!

Chapter 1

The Lying, the Kitsch and the Wardrobe

It always annoys me how everyone goes on about being 'urban' – especially people in the media. I mean, what's that all about? It's like you're a better celebrity if you come from a hard impoverished background; that if you throw on a hoody and an accent it will make you more famous, or prove you're cool and authentic.

Well, I've never tried to be anything I'm not. But appearances can be deceptive. Although I have a posh accent, am very camp and don't wear sportswear (hoodies don't suit me – but I am quite partial to a bit of Juicy Couture), the house where I grew up in Bishop's Waltham was a modern housing estate home. Back then it was a really sweet, suburban, well-kept neighbourhood that people took pride in (all the houses were painted different colours, the mums had a babysitting circle and we'd think nothing of popping next door for a cup of sugar), but these days it's a lot more run down – I even saw a burnt-out car there on my last visit. So I guess if 'urban' is where it's at, that makes me more 'urban' than most!

That house was the last place you'd expect to find a ginormous old mahogany wardrobe with dressing table to match. They were right out of the war – I think we'd inherited them from my mum's Auntie Lotty. But the wardrobe was a brilliant hiding place. I used to creep inside and pretend one side was my mum and one side was my biological father Frank (more of him later; all you need to know now is, after all the drama and soap-style storylines he has created in our family, we call him 'Fraaaaank' – after Frank Butcher from *EastEnders* – and for dramatic effect do the *EastEnders* drum riff whenever he's mentioned. *Dooff dooff dooff dooff dooff derder doooff*!). With the door closed, I'd have 'chats' to him and my mum. As I look back, I'm fascinated about why I did this, because the irony is that Mum always had time for us and was around to talk to in person back then.

Mum was always playing when we were small, and she gave me and my sister Debbie a lot of freedom. We were as close as sisters could be. I mean, I had the usual older sister jealousy where I would have rules and the same wouldn't apply to Debbie at the same age, but we were only fifteen months apart, and growing up we always played together. We looked after our dollies together (all mine were called Claire, for some reason) – Mum used to stand outside our bedroom door and listen to us playing with them and doing all their voices. We played at being grown-ups together, when I'd hang a tablecloth over the dining-room table to make a house and tell everyone who walked past to 'shhh' so they didn't wake the dollies. And we took bubble baths together – Mum would turn the light off and let the streetlight cast the bathroom in orange light. Mum was really relaxed back then and didn't mind us making a mess – she even let us bury her crockery in the garden.

She says now it was to keep us quiet, but I'm not sure I'd go to those lengths with my girls now . . .! We once dug up a forgotten stainless-steel teapot buried who knows when and gave it to my grandad for his birthday (he must have been thrilled). Long days playing out would always end with hearing her call us from the house, 'Debbie, Amanda! Come in, your tea's ready!'

Mum never let on how poor we were when I was a little girl and, at the time, I had no idea. Even though we didn't have a father around much at first, I think of my childhood as blissful and blessed. Mum was very proud and worked hard to keep it all together. She found jobs packing straw and dog food and later became a secretary at an engineering firm – she even rented out the box room for a bit of extra cash. She often went without herself so we didn't have to, even sometimes not eating. There were very few mod cons in our house – we had one of those old school top-loading washing tubs that you had to turn yourself, and Mum made all our mince by hand, using a mincing machine. She'd put the meat in one end with one hand and turn the handle with the other, and it would come out like a pile of worms!

Mum was a creative and thrifty cook – even now she'll look into what I would consider an empty fridge and make something out of it! – and could rustle up loads of things with braising steak or mince. We would have a Sunday roast every week (I loved the smell and the way the heat of the oven steamed up the windows because it meant I could draw pictures with my fingers in the condensation) but she wasn't really into making puddings, other than the odd apple crumble. I remember I used to stand on a chair and 'help' her make it – which generally consisted of me eating all the skin off the cooking apples. (Lexi does the same thing now. She'll eat the skin, though not because she likes it – she just likes the history of it!) Mum used to try and peel them all in one go and I'd make a wish if she managed it without a break. But crumbles were a special treat. Mostly she'd say, 'If you're still hungry then you can fill up with bread and jam.'

Every summer we helped bring in some extra money by picking strawberries, apples, blackberries and pretty much anything else that could be picked. I'm not sure how profitable it was for the farmer, though, as we operated on a 'one for the punnet and one for me' basis. Those were some of the happiest times of my life: endless summers of red-stained fingers.

Unlike Mum, Frank was hardly ever there. He was a petty officer in the Navy and between visits I couldn't really remember what he looked like. In fact, Debbie has no memories of him at all. There wasn't a single photograph of him around the house and when he wasn't there the only proof that he actually lived there were three scratch marks in the bath Mum said he'd made with his watch while climbing into the tub. I'd sometimes trace the line of them with my fingers when I was having a bubble bath. There was also a large iridescent shell that he'd brought back from a trip to the Far East, which sat in the middle of our glass coffee table and which I'd put to my ear to listen to the sea and imagine faraway lands. But for us, Frank's long absences were normal and I suppose the novelty was when he was around. For Mum, it must have just been a whole world of pain.

Mum and Frank had met when he was a handsome naval officer (all the nice girls love a sailor!). She had had a loving but repressive upbringing and has since admitted she was looking for a way to escape when she became pregnant with me. They rushed into marriage and with so little time together who knows how well they even knew each other? They were both so young.

Not that Frank's early life had been a bed of roses. Frank's mother died when he was a baby. His older sister Joan was expected to look after them all – including him and his twin – but she refused. Instead, she dared to choose to get married and have a life of her own, and so for a while he and his five siblings were put into care and Joan became the black sheep of the family. Mum says now that she was actually the only normal one, and certainly the only one of them who ever gave my mum any support. Frank's father, who was from Liverpool, worked as a banjo player and later a psychiatric nurse. His female colleague at the hospital had a married sister who offered to foster Frank and his twin sister. He later married his colleague (another nurse) but never took Frank and his twin sister back to live with him and his new wife. Early in the 1990s, his second wife died. Later he became engaged, but before he could marry committecd suicide. Shortly afterwards, his fiancée committed suicide as well. That wasn't a happy background to have come from.

It must have been so hard for Mum, coping with two little girls, all the financial pressures of bringing up a family on a paltry income and an absent husband who, when he *was* home, spent all his available cash on booze and was only focused on where his next drink was coming from. Not only that, but he was impossible to live with in every way. He would leave home for hours at a time, often staying out all night and returning drunk the next day. I was shocked to find out while writing this book just how awful life was for my mother with him as her husband, but she is reluctant to discuss that even now. It's incredible to me that she managed to keep this hidden from me and my sister so well, and that we weren't aware or affected in any way by it. It must have been a huge strain on her.

One day, however, after Frank stayed out for a couple of nights, it all got too much even for Mum. She told him she needed a break and went to stay with her parents in Gloucester for the weekend (she must have been desperate, to leave me and my sister behind). I don't have any recollection of her being away but I do remember how pleased I was when she came home – and her face as I ran down the garden path and into her arms. She looked horrified. We were unwashed and dirty, in the same clothes she'd left us in. Mum told me later that the house – which was normally spotless – was full of my father's drunken mates, empty bottles and cigarette stubs everywhere. But even after that, I don't really remember my parents' marriage breaking down or remember them arguing much. It shows what a strong woman Mum is that she kept so much from us.

One of my strongest memories of Frank is the way he always smelled of alcohol. And the day I think he left. In my memory, I am bouncing happily on my bed. My bedspread was brown with large white daisies with orange centres and I'd invented a game where I had to avoid the flowers. (I used to kneel on that bedspread in the late summer light when I was supposed to be in bed and watch my mum walking up and down in the front garden, mowing the lawn with our old hand mower. She took care to avoid the orange African marigolds, the only plants other than grass – they were cheap and they grew fast!) But that day, somewhere downstairs, 'Save All Your Kisses for Me' by the Brotherhood of Man was playing so I was bouncing in time to the music when Mum came into the bedroom with Frank. I bounced into his arms for a cuddle and smelt the alcohol on his breath. Then he set me down without a word, turned around and walked out of the room.

There are two sides to every story but I can only give mine. Frank was a drinker and craved what he thought was the high life. He loved his booze more than he loved us and abandoned his children, pure and simple. He may have been young but he left us with nothing – not that we had much to start with. Whatever tales he has since spun, that much is true. Frank moved a hundred miles away to Plymouth and never came to visit. Even though the court allowed him weekend access when Mum divorced him on the grounds of his unreasonable behaviour, he never bothered to come.

One day a few years later, my sister and I were out riding our Tomahawk bikes (the cheap version of Choppers!) when a car stopped in our street and the driver beckoned us over. Mum had always warned us not to talk to strangers but for some reason we didn't think twice about this one. He was sitting in the driver's seat smoking a cigarette with a woman at his side. He rolled down his window and smiled.

'Hello, girls. Do you know who I am?'

We shook our heads.

'I'm your dad.'

I looked at Frank but felt not a single flicker of emotion. I remember thinking, 'So? What are you doing here?'

He talked to us for a bit and introduced us to the woman next to him but it was all very one-sided. While he was talking, for some reason Debbie reached in through his open window, took some tissues from the dashboard and started cleaning his windscreen, dropping the dirty tissues on the grass verge as she wiped. I remember being really annoyed – not that she'd dropped the tissues, but that she'd cleaned the windscreen for him in the first place. We didn't owe him anything! When he eventually drove off, we cycled home and ran into the house to tell my nan who was staying with us. 'We've just seen Frank!'

She stopped and stared at us for a moment and then she said, 'That's nice. Did he give you any sweeties?'

I looked at Debbie and Debbie looked at me and we shook our heads. 'No.'

Nanny turned away knowingly and got on with her ironing while my sister and I stood there, our bubble burst. Maybe seeing Frank wasn't so newsworthy after all, if we didn't even get a single sweet out of him . . .

After the divorce, he was rarely mentioned – unless I did something naughty. 'Oh, you're so like your father,' Mum would say. Or, 'That's the Holden in you!' Part of me felt ashamed, but part of me was curious to know more about my 'bad' heritage. But to Mum's credit (and this is a miracle, as she isn't normally one to hold her tongue) I don't remember him being bad-mouthed at all, even though after they split he and his family totally abandoned her. The only one who stayed even vaguely in touch with her was my Auntie Joan. But at the time, Frank's family left Mum absolutely on her own.

Not that Mum let on any of this to us. In fact – on the surface, anyhow – life carried on pretty much as usual after he left. Our neighbourhood was embroiled in gang warfare (see, I told you I was urban) – girls v boys – and it was serious stuff. Us girls had our own den in the fields behind our estate, in a hollowed-out area behind a bush, with everything we needed including rocks for seats and useful items made out of twigs. Everything was neat as a pin. I was like Martha Stewart with OCD – I even swept the bush clean! But I was also a bit of a tomboy and I made my own bows and arrows out of pampas grass and string.

The gang warfare ended with my first marriage (not many people know that I'm technically now on my third). It was to Eric Austin from next door – since he was both available and handy – and took place in our back garden. I wore the frothy, lacy wedding dress that Mum had worn to marry Frank when she was pregnant with me and Debbie was a bridesmaid, in something pink, polyester and very definitely a fire hazard. (My poor sister – she had to go along with it. I was the older sister and very bossy.) It was the stuff of pre-school fairy tales, but the wedding was about so much more than just me and Eric. Our marriage ceremony brought together the two gang leaders and single-handedly ended the neighbourhood's gang rivalry just like that.

It was around then that I started gymnastics at a local club. I had to wear knickers and a vest to audition – Mum wouldn't spend the money on a leotard until she was sure I'd got in. I was so embarrassed about it and refused to try out until she encouraged me to! After that, gymnastics became my life for the next ten years.

But with Frank gone, Mum now had to juggle two or three jobs to make ends meet. I hated her leaving for work – I'd run after her to the back gate and scream for her to come back. The babysitter, Beryl, used to walk me back in and practise disco dancing with me to take my mind off it. Poor Mum, she must have felt wretched – and guilty. Even then, I could tell she was deeply unhappy. Debbie and I would go to bed at seven, just before *Coronation Street* (that theme tune still reminds me of bedtime) and then Mum would go to bed too. I could hear her crying through the bedroom wall and I'd get this sinking feeling in my heart, like I'd just gone down in a lift too fast. The weird thing is, I didn't go in and comfort her or ask her what was wrong. I think I knew she'd be devastated that I knew. Instead, I hid under the covers so I couldn't hear her any more. In the morning, I'd shower her with love and cuddles to try and make her unhappiness go away.

From the moment he left Frank did little or nothing to help us and his departure left us even worse off than before – at one stage, money was so tight that we almost lost our home. My mum received a letter from the building society to say the mortgage hadn't been paid for three months (Frank was supposed to pay), they were brilliant and let her pay those months off gradually and, eventually, the Navy deducted a certain amount of money from Frank's salary each month

I was always determined to make Mum smile whenever I could. Every time I ran an errand for her I'd buy her a cheap gift with the change. She always said how sweet I was to think of her but she told me years later she was gutted, because she needed the cash much more than some present from the corner shop. (I once stole a fruit salad from the penny chews from the same shop and proudly showed my mum. She was furious and marched me back to confess, even though I could barely see the lady over the cash register – but I apologised anyway!)

But something had to give, even for a woman as strong as my mum. One day I went to the shop on the way home from school, like I always did, and the woman I vaguely knew behind the counter told me, 'You'll be coming home with me after school today, Amanda.' I had no idea why, but I was a good girl, so I did as I was told until my mum's parents, my nan and grandad, arrived to pick me up. They told me my mother had fainted in the shop and been taken to hospital. (It was only years later that I came to understand that it was actually a very different and heartbreaking story. Things had finally got too much for her. She hadn't fainted at all. It was a huge cry for help that we have never talked about since. She must have been at her wits' end to do that – she loved us so utterly.)

Of course, Frank leaving must have affected both Debbie and me too, but I think it resonated with my sister a lot more profoundly than it did with me. Debbie and I are very different – Mum always says that at the first sign of trouble I will run into it and handle it, whereas Debbie will run away from it. I can remember Mum having to come and pick Debbie up from school because she was being bullied. And as a child, Debbie had nightmares about livers and kidneys – apparently this can mean you are suppressing feelings of anger – and would sleepwalk. She has since confessed that, even though we later had a great stepfather in my dad Les, when Frank left she felt this great loss and a huge hole in her life. I couldn't comprehend what she meant – we never really knew him and were three and four when he left, so how could she miss him?

Years later I now get it – but it took meeting someone that I love and having children myself. There IS a weird black hole that no amount of love can fill, and I realise I have searched to fill mine subsequently in relationships, as has Debbie (at the time of writing this, she still hasn't been lucky). I then poured everything I had into my dreams and ambitions. I turned it into a positive, whereas Debbie has always seemed a little more lost.

Back then, though, I guess hiding in the wardrobe in the darkness was somewhere I could be myself. Out in the real world, where I didn't want to add to my mum's problems, I felt like I had to plaster a smile on to my face so as not to upset her, that I should ignore my feelings and just get on with it.

Little did I know that it would all prove to be a good grounding for the future. Or that a part of me would always feel that way . . .

Chapter 2

The Golden Years

Mum worked so much that she had no choice but to leave us with her parents and we spent a lot of the school holidays with my grandparents at their house in Gloucester. They played a huge part in my upbringing, and some of my most treasured childhood memories are of things that happened with them. And some less treasured, too – like their stinky old cat, for example. There are many things you might like to think your parents named you after, but a mangy old maggot-ridden moggy with matted fur is probably not one of them. However, my mum did just that and chose to call me Amanda, the same name as Mandy, my nan's ancient old cat. She says it was after a character in her favourite sitcom at the time, *Not in Front of the Children*, but I'm not so sure. (My sister, however, was named after the much more glamorous Debbie Reynolds!) The origins of my middle name, Louise, are slightly more salubrious – there's supposed to be some French royalty (wishful thinking!), the Thomases, on my mother's side dating back to one of the Louis kings. My nan says we have Gaelic blood and that both her father and grandfather were called Louis because of it. But whenever anyone calls me Mandy (Chris does it to be annoying and it has stuck) I think of that stinky cat.

My nan and grandpa – known to us as 'Papa' – were lovely, honest, people, the kind who, if they made you a promise, kept it. They lived in a modest new house built not long after the war, a comfortable three-bedroom terrace house in the outskirts of Gloucester. I still think of it as my childhood home. It is immaculately kept by Nan, who is now in her nineties. The ornaments are still the same, as is the smell – a mix of polish and cooking. Their orange swirly carpet that I learned to crawl on was only changed recently. Upstairs the two little single beds Debbie and I used to sleep in have been replaced with just one, and a wardrobe – not big enough to hide in, but containing precious gifts we both made for my grandparents, which include handpainted plaster casts of Miss Piggy and Kermit and a knitting needle case! (Lexi loves to run upstairs to hold them and see what I did when I was her age – she enjoys nostalgia.) I used to love hiding in what seemed like huge conifers at the bottom of the garden, but now I realise they weren't as big as I thought.

Nan and Papa so obviously loved each other. I'd watch them dancing cheek-to-cheek or kissing as if they were never going to see each other again, even if one of them was just nipping down the shops.

Papa was a Welshman, a director of a builder's merchant and proud to be from working class – there were no fancy French connections for my Papa! He was very spoilt emotionally and grew up well-mannered but serious and a little bit self-important (his elder sister Lavinia had died at eighteen months so his mother became an overprotective worrier). He was tall with thin grey hair, which went thin from the age of twenty. He was handsome, with grey/blue eyes (and a 'drinker's nose', which was odd as he was teetotal!). Like many men of his generation he always wore a tie and aftershave. He had some sort of nervous disorder before the war which left him blind in one eye and meant he couldn't go to the front so he served in the pay corps instead. They gave him a medal but he handed it back because he didn't think he deserved it.

It was during the war that he met my nan. He walked into a café, saw her and told his friend, 'That's the girl I'm going to marry!' When she left he ran down two flights of stairs to chase after her and ask her out. From that moment on, Nan was my Papa's life – he adored her. It was all about my nan – he never even really wanted kids. He had his electric razor faithfully plugged into the wall of their bathroom, got up at the same time every morning and shaved in the bathroom – even after he retired – before splashing on his Old Spice. I'd wake up to the comforting buzz of his electric razor and the smell of his aftershave and know that life was alright.

Papa was a huge influence on me and, without doubt, the person who nurtured my love of music – he was fanatical about it. He played record after record, although we were never allowed near his prized player. Like all Welshmen, he thought he had the best voice in the world (no one dared tell him he was a bloody terrible singer!). It was him who introduced me to opera, musicals, orchestral pieces and the Mormon Tabernacle Choir (which really wasn't me – the clue's in the title. I was too polite to say no . . .). He'd tape the tunes I liked the most on his reel-to-reel tape recorder, which was the height of technology then, and give me copies to take home. He'd also conduct Radio 4-style interviews with me in his thick Welsh accent that went something like:

'So, Amanda, this is Jim Harrison from Gloucester on 5 April 1978. Are you happy to be at Nanny and Papa's?'

'I sure am, Papa!'

'So, do you have a song for us today?'

'Yes, Papa. Here it is.' (*Cue music and me singing . . .*)

'Well, that was a lovely song and a lovely tune. Thank you. This is Papa signing off.'

If he ever made a mistake he'd say, 'Ignore that bit. It'll be OBLITERATED.'

Mostly though, he was the quiet one and my nan was the sociable one. Any friends they had were her friends. My nan is very tactile and often saucy – always pinching your bum as you go up the stairs in front of her! She's the life and soul of the party and at the centre of everything, dancing on tables. She was a strong, loving but strict mother to my mum and my Aunt Vivienne. I don't mind saying, though, that Nan is also a pain in the arse and stubborn to the point of unreasonable. She's from that generation who don't want to be a burden or to make a fuss. She's also opinionated and searingly – and often unnecessarily! – honest. She'll say, 'I'm sorry, I have to tell you . . .' and you know it's going to be something you don't want to hear. I always think, 'Why do you have to tell me, Nanny? I don't need to know – I know it's going to hurt my feelings!'

We call Nan Mrs Bouquet, because she is so proper and a bit of a snob. She has always laid out all the breakfast things the night before – the place settings, vitamins, her pills and Papa's pills – and she'd always tell me that you should make sure your husband saw you in lipstick first thing in the morning! Back in the day she would perch on the edge of Papa's special seat at 11 o'clock, which was always milky coffee ('Half milk, half water, dear!') and have a cigarette. She never inhaled it, though – it was just to keep him company. Although she lived on a Gloucester housing estate, she was like the Queen and kept all her cereal in labelled Tupperware boxes. She always bought Robertson's marmalade (which I love) but she kept the jar in a special silver pot so you couldn't see the label, with a proper marmalade spoon. If you ever went into the marmalade with a knife not the spoon, she'd go nuts!

We'd have to help her with the chores – making beds, tidying up – but once we'd finished she'd come to play with us, and it was FUN. Every day would be a trip out – boating, rowing, to the swimming baths (where we challenged her to jump off the high board – and she bloody did it!), to South Cerney pools or Bourton-on-the-Water for a picnic. We sat on scratchy Paisley towels, eating warm sandwiches with sand in and home-made fruit cake and drinking tea that tasted of the flask. That taste of tea from a Thermos will always remind me of my grandparents. No matter how posh the flask, there is a weird taste – it is the best taste in the world and takes me right back to my childhood. Papa used to make the sandwiches – they were so good, but only because he put such a lot of salt and vinegar in. They'd literally be wet with vinegar (our poor arteries!).

Nan is a massive Tom and Jerry fan and for years my sister and I would buy her Tom and Jerry presents every Christmas and birthday. In fact only a few years ago she found a soap we'd bought her when we were little – it was all mouldy, flaky and cracked but she hadn't wanted to throw it away and had ended up keeping it for thirty years!

Nanny would buy us clothes and things we needed for the summer and when we got home we'd stage a fashion show that poor Papa would have to sit through as we tried it all on for him. Their shed was used as our beloved Daisy Chain Cottage. This was a 'hotel' that regularly served mud pies and water tea. Later it was promoted to a cruise ship. The menus – which are still safely stored in my Nan's house – offered gammon with pineapple rings pretend curry. (Hilarious – when would I have had a curry at that age?) Nanny would be receptionist with a birdbath for her desk. We'd make up Papa's workbench like a bed. I sometimes wonder at my children playing in the garden and cannot believe I was a child there once too, using the same lion statues as guards for my dollies.

At my nan's house I also used to write plays. I did shows at home, too, but in my nan's back garden I only ever used to do the 'professional' things, like *Annie*, or plays specially written for Gloucester, which were more 'polished', for 'a bigger audience'. I would obviously have the starring role as the beautiful princess and Debbie would be the witch. I'd get all the kids in the street into the back garden so that I could sing my head off for them. (Of course, now I'd give anything to be the witch – it's a much better part!)

Nan worked at Wall's and, to get on her nerves, Mum used to train us to say that Nanny's job was to put the sticks on the lollies – in actual fact she worked in the accounts department. The best thing about her job, in our eyes, was that she always had a freezer full of ice cream, which she bought wholesale and which we thought was a huge luxury. I still think Cornettos are a treat! Her own special recipe for milkshake consisted of vanilla ice cream, sugar and milk. Debbie and I were so competitive that we'd fight over everything and we even complained if one or other of us had the tiniest bit more milkshake in their glass, so Nan would measure the height of the froth in each glass with a tape.

Every night at bedtime Nanny read us stories with warm sweet milk. She would kiss us and say, 'I love you and don't you forget it,' then in a sing-songy voice call for Papa to come up and say goodnight. He would arrive and test us on the capitals of the world – I used to know them all! We felt safe, warm and happy at their house. They could be strict but we had so much respect for them.

Nan is now in her mid-nineties and lives alone in the house she and my Papa shared all those years. I'm sure she still has that tape measure, and I'm certain that her cupboards are still stocked for World War III (though since we lost Papa in 2007, it makes me sad to see her set out breakfast – place setting, pills, vitamins and all – just for one). She's still the life and soul of any party. I can take her anywhere. When Papa died, she told me she was living for *Britain's Got Talent* and that the series was getting her through a very hard time. So I sent a car to bring her to the finals, and she came to the Dorchester afterwards and stayed up in the bar for hours drinking cocktails with me and Simon. It got to the very early hours and she said, 'Sorry, dear, I don't want to spoil your fun but it is five o'clock in the morning!'

When we were little and Nan and Papa came to visit our house, Mum would make us eggs and bacon for breakfast with tinned tomatoes, which seemed so exotic. We spent every Christmas and Easter with them, too, and Nan would sneak me a sweet martini with lemonade ('I'll make it weak, dear!'). We'd always get a doll or toy, we'd have Christmas dinner with roast turkey and a real tree and one of our Christmas family rituals was to watch *The Wizard of Oz* together. Mum still does a brilliant Wicked Witch of the West laugh. (Hers isn't far off and neither is mine – my nan, however, laughs like Mutley. We all have hideous laughs – it's a gene thing.) Another favourite was *The Sound of Music*. I used to sing along to songs like 'My Favourite Things' and convince myself that I sounded just like Julie Andrews.

Alongside gymnastics, I studied ballet for a while and also took it very seriously. I was constantly going over my routines and my parents were consistently encouraging and supportive, although my mum also made fun of how earnest I was. Once, I was halfway through rehearsing a dance in the living room when she ran into the room dressed in a blouse and tights with a tea towel stuffed down her knickers like bollocks to look like famous male ballerina Rudolf Nureyev. (Another time, when Debbie and I were older, we were sitting watching *Top of the Pops* and she and Dad burst in dressed as Meat Loaf and Cher and belted out 'Dead Ringer for Love'. Mum was wearing a purple corduroy jumpsuit with poppers, which she ripped open as she started headbanging. That time, we sat there with blank faces like the teenagers from Harry Enfield – the only response we gave them was to sulkily ask them to get out of the way of the telly.)

I gave ballet up in the end, because I was 'too busy putting on my own production of *Grease*', in which I obviously gave myself the part of Sandy, resplendent in my Mum's hooped clip-on earrings. Performing helped me fund gymnastics, which was still my first love. I roped my sister in to shows in our garden at home and we'd raise money for the club. I would make little posters, cover them in cling film and me and my sister would go round the whole estate and stick them on to the ubiquitous wooden telegraph poles of the time to advertise it. (For some reason the poles would always ooze tar in the summer heat and I used to love picking it off when it had dried.) Before each performance, my mum would serve sausages on sticks and lemonade out of the kitchen window, and my friend Denise would be at the gate to punch tickets. I can only now apologise to those poor neighbours whose quiet afternoons I must have wrecked.

Even when I wasn't performing, I sang nearly all the time and though it was Papa who definitely fuelled my love of music, it's always been such an important part of my life that Mum says I came out singing. I loved 'Puff, the Magic Dragon' and anything by The Carpenters, especially 'Sing'. I had a tape recorder and stopstarted my Papa's tape recordings, writing the words down, until I knew all the lyrics from *My Fair Lady* and *West Side Story* off by heart. I made up a whole dance routine for my mum to one of her records, Frankie Laine's 'Jezebel' (having no clue as to its meaning). Showaddywaddy was my favourite pop group. I loved 'Under the Moon of Love' and had a major crush on the lead singer Dave Bartram, to the point of kissing the TV every time he was on it. (Recently, after he read an interview in which I confessed this, he asked me to write the foreword to his book – which I did!) I watched the Brotherhood of Man win the Eurovision Song Contest in 1976 with 'Save Your Kisses for Me' and learned their entire performance including the dance steps. Randomly I sang it in a Cockney accent. I don't know why – it's just the way I sang!

My mother said she always knew I was happy if I was singing. And I sang pretty much all the time. I'd lie in bed, scratching at the woodchip wallpaper until whole areas were picked clean, sucking my middle fingers (never my thumb) and tapping my nose with my forefinger while I hummed. I also sucked the corners of clean hankies and picked at my pink blanket to make little balls – singing all the while. The few times in my life when I haven't sung at all, friends and family knew I wasn't happy simply because I had stopped.

I read a lot too and was so gripped by Enid Blyton's storytelling that I'd hide under the bedclothes with a torch, turning the pages way past bedtime. A lot of our books were second-hand (as were our toys), but that didn't matter to me – I liked nothing better than to lose myself in an imaginary world and devoured all the *Famous Five* stories. (I still have my original copy of *The Magic Faraway Tree*, with its Land of Topsy Turvy, Land of Spells, Land of Do-as-you-Please and Land of Dreams, and every time I read it to Lexi we both love to sniff it – she loves it because she says it 'smells of old'.) I read the whole *Malory Towers* series over and over, about the girls' boarding school in Cornwall. Those books always used to lift me if I was ever feeling down.

I had a much-loved teddy bear my grandparents gave me when I was born and a little rag doll called Scraggy Annie that I took everywhere with me. My favourite toy, though, was a rabbit in a blue skirt known as Miffy who doubled as my pyjama case. I called her 'buddy' because I couldn't say bunny.

But I was transfixed by my mum – I thought she was the most beautiful person in the world and I loved to watch her do her make-up in the mirror. I'd sit behind her and watch her every move as she applied Astral cream and foundation. Then she'd suck her cheeks in, dollop blusher from a stick on them, apply her trademark green eye shadow and then finally her favourite orange lipstick that I'd copy her puckering up for. She had long, thick, natural chestnut hair which she curled in Carmen rollers but she was forever losing the pins – it was my job to hunt for them. Once her hair was done, she piled it on top of her head. I used to say, 'Mummy, you look like a cottage loaf with your hair like that.'

If she was going out somewhere, she'd put on her one and only best dress, a yellow maxi dress with floaty cap sleeves bought for her by her best friend from school, Pat, when she came to visit one time and realised Mum didn't have anything special to wear. I thought Mum looked like a movie star and when I look at photographs of her back then I do indeed see a beautiful young woman, one who was still hopeful about the future.

My nan has good genes, too, and always smells of a comforting combination of baking, Silvikrin hairspray, Oil of Ulay (as it was then) and Charlie perfume. I think of her whenever I smell them. (Her bathroom cabinet is still full of them. I continually buy her more expensive perfume for Christmas and birthdays, but they go back in the cupboard and out comes the Charlie!) She has the softest skin and I have watched her gracefully age from fifty, when my mum persuaded her to go 'au naturel' and stop dying her hair. (FYI, my mum shows no signs of giving up highlighting her own hair and is now aged sixty-four herself!)

I liked to play with my nan's make-up and can still remember the taste of her pink lipstick and the cold weight of her powder compact in my hand. She had a dressing-up box and she'd let us look at her small collection of jewellery. There was one brooch I especially loved that had a purple stone with little pearls around it, and in the back was a tiny plait of dark hair trapped under glass. I liked to imagine it as a secret token from a long-forgotten relative who'd cut off a lock of her hair as a keepsake for her one true love, but I've since been told that it is a Victorian mourning brooch and the hair would probably have been taken from someone who'd died. I find that fascinating.

My nan and Papa were classy, and proud, and we always looked well turned out and cared for. Papa could be a bit of a tight-arse so they had separate bank accounts, as do I. (I never rely on a man for money – I would bankrupt Chris!) Nana would always be saving up for something. On 'big' birthdays we would always be given something that was meant to last – a 'proper watch' on my thirteenth birthday, for example, or a 'decent' suitcase on my eighteenth – and they always managed a holiday.

I knew no matter what that I could trust and rely on them. Along with my mum, they have always believed in me and gave me the best childhood they knew how. But little did we know it was all about to get better, with the arrival of a very important new member of the family . . .

Chapter 3

'Les' is More

I was, unwittingly, the one to make my mum's relationship with my dad Les public. They started dating and from then on he came to our house all the time. One morning, our milkman Graham (his best friend from school) dropped the bottles as usual on the doorstep, where Debbie and I were sitting playing with our dolls in our nightdresses.

'Where's your mum?' he asked.

'In bed with her boyfriend,' I announced.

The news flashed round the village and soon afterwards Les moved in. He never left. Almost overnight, he brought stability and joy to our lives. I loved him completely and unconditionally from day one. I especially loved that he made Mum so happy.

Debbie and I accepted their relationship immediately. It seemed like the most natural thing in the world to me and now – more than thirty years later – it still does. He says that when he first spotted what he describes as our 'beautiful mother with her two beautiful girls', Mum pushing us in our double buggy, he fell in love with us all instantly and sought Mum out at the pub in Bishop's Waltham where she worked behind the bar in the evenings.

Up until that moment, Leslie Collister had been a good-looking bachelor who had a nice life doing up cars in the local Spratt's garage and playing football at weekends for Swanmore club. I thought he was wonderful. Not only was it good to have a man around the place but Les was a brilliant handyman who fixed all the things that needed fixing (mostly my mother!). He even mowed the lawn and brought a dog with him, a beautiful Golden Labrador called Elsa, named after the lion in *Born Free*. It was a question of 'Love me, love my dog' – so we did! On one of Debbie's birthdays, he bought her a gift and then gave me a colouring book ('So you don't feel left out') and I treasured that blue colouring book until it fell apart. One Christmas, we asked for a big white plastic Sindy house, but we didn't have the money for one so he made us ski lodges, which were much better. They were amazing. Me and Debbie played with them for hours, doing Sindy voices while Mum and Les listened outside the door. Eventually, I sold mine – I'm still gutted about it and look back on that decision with total regret. I used the money to buy clothes at Moonaz, the local fashion boutique, which sold tie-dye skirts and cheesecloth tops – my village's idea of high fashion!

Seven years later, on 29 October 1982, aged eleven and dressed in a blue velvet ra-ra skirt with white tights and black patent shoes, I was the proud chief bridesmaid (even though I hated my outfit), as Les promised to love and cherish my mother 'til death them did part. They were married in the local registry office followed by a church blessing and a reception in the Jubilee Hall. Mum wore a knee-length red dress and a red hat with red feathers at the back that my nan insisted cried out for an enormous black ostrich feather, so she nicked one out of another hat in the shop when the shop assistant wasn't looking to glue into my mum's (even though it tickled everyone's faces!). Although on that day Mum became Judith Collister, I never felt the urge to change my surname. Dad did offer to adopt us but in the end I think Mum thought it would be too much trouble to get Frank's permission. Amanda Holden I was born and Amanda Holden I would remain.

Les's name changed though. Debbie and I obviously had some strong morals because it was only on the day that Mum and Les became 'official' that (despite thinking of him as our father for all the time they'd been together) we started to call him 'Dad'! But from the moment he was Dad, Mum says we never slipped up. He was the only dad we knew and the only one we will ever know.

Dad was conceived in the war and never knew his own father, but had a stepfather who was unkind to him. He endured unreasonable punishment and resentment from this man who wasn't his father for years until he was finally able to escape to an aunt's house. I think that's why he was determined to take such good care of us. It must have been a bit of a shock to his system though – to begin with, my dad was not one for communicating. Suddenly, he found himself in a family of three girls, always giving him cuddles and loving him so openly, and my mum asking questions and prising things out of him. Then one day, when we were driving to Blackgang Chine for a weekend in the Isle of Wight, he suddenly stopped the car and said, 'Judy, I'll have to pull over, I can't drive.' He was paralysed from fear or panic or something – but whatever it was, he literally couldn't go on. My mum still hadn't passed her driving test at that point, but she had to drive us all home.

After that, he became nervous and emotional, and for months refused to go out anywhere. He'd get really cold and shivery and cry, then go to bed for days at a time. He became even quieter than normal and I can remember my mum tiptoeing around him a bit. She'd get us to give him even more cuddles than normal. Looking back, he'd had some kind of anxiety attack but so little was known about mental health at the time that when he went to the doctor's about it he was told to take aspirin! Mum says we must have loved the pain of his upbringing out of him – being in a happy family and having a stable life after his own terrible upbringing – and it manifested itself as some kind of breakdown.

The whole episode changed him and after that he became much more forthright and outgoing, and very emotional. *Very* emotional! After years of living with us all he now wears his heart on his sleeve and he can barely talk to me about anything without crying. His eyes fill up all the time – he's a wreck! Bless his heart.

Around this time, repeated tonsillitis meant the doctors finally admitted me to hospital to have my tonsils out. I hated it there, I didn't want to stay in for three nights and couldn't wait to come home. Unfortunately for me, though, some of the kids in the ward were found to have some sort of hospital virus and the entire hospital was placed under quarantine. No visitors were allowed at all to begin with and then only in what looked like space suits (it was like that scene at the end of *E.T.* when they're all wearing forensics) and I lay in my bed crying and crying for ten days. The mother of the infected kids tried to cheer me up by giving me a pack of Refreshers but I thought it was such a rubbish gift that it only made me cry more. While I was there, I had an encounter with a really dodgy doctor (as I realised with hindsight). I was asleep on my tummy and woke up and found someone looking at my bum. I distinctly remember thinking, 'My tonsils definitely aren't down there'! (And anyway he should have been checking for foot and mouth disease, not foot and bum disease!)

Mum had always ridden a blue and white bicycle to and from work but, with me in hospital and Dad unwell, she suddenly had to learn how to drive. She drove Dad's car to see me after work every night with her L-plates on – and if she couldn't find another driver to come with her, she came alone. Other times she'd bring her sister-in-law, whose daughter's party trick was to hold her breath until she went blue, which she did repeatedly on the back seat. My mother would be a nervous wreck by the time she got to hospital and then she had to go through the faff of putting on a special suit just to hold my hand.

When I finally left hospital, Dad's mother Nanny Winnie did a high tea for me, including towering jellies that actually wobbled. All the kids from the street were in my house, welcoming me back. There were Jackie and Susan Cox (we played with them for mercenary reasons – they had a Sodastream!) and Jill Dark. Jill and I used to go looking for chewing gum stuck to the walls or floor and – this is so disgusting, I can hardly bear to write it – we used to pick it off and eat it. Classy!

As the older sister, I was used to ordering Debbie around at home and was always boss of the street, but Mum said Debbie tried to take over when I went to school – sadly for her, it didn't work. Thank God there's only one gobshite in the family!

We didn't have exotic holidays when we were little, but they were always great fun. We went camping in Cornwall, or once to the South of France. I didn't get on a plane until I was sixteen and my mum was thirty-two – until then we'd only travelled overseas by ferry. Wherever we were, I thought it was hilarious to stalk Debbie into the bushes and take a picture of her having a wee. Every holiday album has a picture of Debbie squatting in it – we have pictures of her doing it all over the UK! (Some years later Sarah Parish and I continued this tradition in Montepulciano, when I got caught short and had to go for a pee at the top of a hill. Sarah then took a picture of it flowing down the road! T.M.I!)

At school, my crowd was made up of two Amandas, two Lucys and two Clares. Without doubt, I was the gobbiest of us all, but a close second was my friend Amanda, whose mum and dad were best friends with my parents. She was known as 'Fig'. (We're still in touch and I still always want to call her Fig.) We wore luminous socks and Frankie Goes to Hollywood T-shirts and Mum called us 'The Jam Tarts'. It was because of Fig that I became a vegetarian. Fig was crazy about The Smiths and we were both slaves to Morrissey's 'Meat is Murder' campaign. We had badges with the slogan all over our denim jackets. Giving up meat was an easy option for me – I'd never been that fond of it and often hid pieces in my mouth to spit into the loo after a meal. My mother was annoyed at first that she had to make me special meals until Dad announced that he didn't much like meat either, and then Debbie said the same, so we all became vegetarian.

Sometimes, we'd go to Mum's office after school. By then she was a secretary at the engineering firm Husband & Co, which operated out of a big Georgian mansion close to Fig's house. Her mum worked there too, so sometimes she'd come as well. There was a beautiful cedar tree in the garden that I loved to climb – my very own Magic Faraway Tree. The house was stunning and had a sweeping staircase. I used to walk down those grand stairs pretending I was an actress.

It must have been moments like these that made Mum realise I needed an outlet, but without much money she had no idea what to do with me. She had seen me perform at school, in theatrical productions and on a float in the annual Bishop's Waltham Carnival. She and my nan had kept every programme from every production I'd been in, and so she knew how passionate I was about singing, too. I'd written my own song for a band at school based on the movie *E.T.* The chorus went: 'He came from another planet. He was totally alone. E.T., phone home.' (More great lyrics!) For costumes, we went to the launderette and bought bin bags that cost 10p each, cut holes in the sides and wore them as dresses.

Mum even sent me for acting lessons to a lady called Estelle Westcomb, the solicitor who'd handled Mum and Frank's divorce. Estelle had once been in the theatre so as well as becoming my vocal coach she taught me drama and deportment – like how to pull on a pair of gloves and balance a book on my head (which came in very handy later on. . .!). I was very enamoured with her – she introduced me to Shakespeare, Dickens and T. S. Eliot, and ultimately fired my ambition to become a serious actress.

So when a woman named Angie Stanley moved to our village and decided she was going to set up a local amateur dramatics group, it seemed to be the perfect answer, and I joined the Bishop's Waltham Little Theatre. Angie was considered proper 'showbiz' because she used to work with an illusionist, Will Ayling (a member of the Magic Circle, you know!), and was good friends with Billy Dainty, one of the last great music-hall performers.

Mum and Dad not only encouraged me to join, they volunteered to help out – Dad made a lot of the scenery while Mum ran the bar. Debbie did theatre too but, like all little sisters, she tended to trail around after me, which I found really annoying. She followed me into gymnastics and then theatre. Instead of understanding that she was just looking up to her big sister and wanting to do the same things, I thought she was copying me and, I'm ashamed to say, I found it irritating. In fact, my sister couldn't have cared less about theatre – all she was interested in was horse riding, which I'd secretly wanted to do as well, but after my mum kept telling

Debbie silly things like she was always in my shadow, I decided not to pursue that so she could have her 'own thing'.

In my first production, *Babes in the Wood*, I was a fairy and had to sing 'May You Always'. (It was a very grown-up song for an eight-year-old and I didn't want to sing it at first, so I put up a great fight – until Angie told me I had to do it!) I was doing fine in the dress rehearsal until my 'boyfriend' Clifford Culver walked into the back of the hall and my nerves got the better of me. With his eyes on me standing centre stage, I completely lost my voice and had a fit of coughing and clearing my throat. Poor Clifford, he was only nine years old. I don't know who was more embarrassed, him or me. But things went much better during the actual performance and whilst I'm not sure that when I sang you could have heard a pin drop, as Angie tells it, certainly the moment that I heard the applause is when something clicked inside me. Angie says that, standing in the wings, she saw a glint in my eye and she thought, 'She'll go far.' I'd definitely got the bug . . .

By this time, I'd been a member of the gymnastics club for years. I represented Bishop's Waltham in competitions and the vault became my speciality. I was very disciplined and went to practise three times a week – on Tuesdays, Thursdays and Sunday mornings. Gymnastics definitely set me up for my life in terms of my shape and my fitness, and also in terms of my work ethic. It was very disciplined and stood me in good stead for the rest of my life. Gordon Larkham, who'd known me all my life, ran the gym at Ridgemead Junior, my second school, and made me appreciate Simon and Garfunkel, which he used for our warm-up music (the opening bars of 'Cecilia' still make me want to do the splits or stretch). I trained with Gordon until I was thirteen years old, when the club ran out of finance. After a stressful time, it closed and we all had to filter off into other clubs. To be accepted, we had to be able to compete strongly on the beam, floor, vault and bars. The bars had always been my weakness – because I was so skinny I was constantly bashing my hip bones. (I had to shove polystyrene down my leotards to do them, so they'd never been my favourite!) Now, though, the bars let me down totally and I was unable to filter into another club. My ten-year gymnastics dream was over.

Gordon phoned Mum one night to tell her that I wasn't going to get into Southampton, and I lay on my bed and listened to her response outside in the hallway. 'Oh, she'll be heartbroken!' she told him. She was right. After she came into my room and told me, and gave me a hug, I cried myself to sleep, but by the time I woke up in the morning I'd reached a decision.

Stubbornness runs in my family, along with pride and dignity. I didn't want to look like I'd failed – I would have found that humiliating. If I wanted to do something, then I had to make it happen. That was just how it had to be. Nobody else was going to do it for me. Not being accepted for gymnastics was my first big rejection but it opened a new door for me. I put my heart into acting, instead. These days Chris moans at me that I have no hobbies. But that's because my hobbies turned into dreams, and my dreams turned into my job.

Chapter 4

I Have a Dream

I became obsessed with performing and was like Bishop's Waltham Little Theatre's answer to Rachel in *Glee* – ambitious, driven and demanding every lead. I must have been a nightmare. For me, though, it was all about the buzz of being on stage and becoming an actress – I had no comprehension of money, or the effects of fame. Back then, there was no celebrity culture and certainly no sense of becoming famous just for the sake of it – you did something because you loved it. There were no real celebrity magazines and, although there were shows like *Opportunity Knocks* and *New Faces*, they were completely out of reach for the likes of us. (The closest I got to them was on special occasions when my mum would call me back down after bed to let me watch the Benny Hill dancers and the Roly Polys doing their tap routines!) Mum and Dad wanted me to have an education to fall back on but there was never a moment they didn't believe in me and make me believe that things were going to happen for me.

My amateur dramatics theatre director Angie Stanley was my champion. I think she recognised the ambition in me even before I knew it myself. She certainly seemed to understand me. She says now that she could see that I had 'it' (whatever 'it' was) and she wanted to encourage me as much as she could – 'there is nothing as sad as wasted talent', she says. However, there is also nothing quite so political as 'am dram' and there were other girls who wanted the lead roles, so one year Angie gave the lead role in *Aladdin* to another girl, 'to be fair'. I was so angry. I remember thinking, 'This is not how the business works.' (I was thirteen – as if I knew anything!) And so one evening, my mum dropped me off at Angie's house to have this very conversation.

Angie opened the door and I just burst into tears – I was beside myself and could hardly get my words out, I wanted that part so badly. Eventually I sobbed, 'You get somewhere with an audition, you don't do it to be fair.' She was very sympathetic, if unmovable, and even gave me a sherry to calm me down! (You'd never have that now, but back then it seemed quite normal to be having a medicinal glass of sherry with my theatre director!) She explained that I couldn't do it every year because it wasn't fair on the other children and said that it was better I had my first taste of rejection now, when I could go home to my own bed and my mum and dad, rather than in years to come when I was in London and had nowhere but some grotty bedsit for comfort. I, of course, wasn't convinced, but had no choice but to accept it. She gave me the second part, the part of the handmaiden, and I decided to front it out. I was like, 'Okay, I can handle this.'

Someone less focused might have been put off by that but, far from putting me off, the whole experience just fuelled my determination even more. When I wasn't rehearsing or performing, I pored over magazines like *Look-in.* I loved Collect-a-Page, the back page that featured a different singer or pop band member every week, and I'd read it over and over, pretending I was being interviewed and rehearsing my answers so that I'd be word perfect when my time came. You can imagine . . .

'What's your favourite song?'

'"Dancing Queen",' I'd reply (to myself).

'And your favourite pet?'

'Elsa, our dog, who I believe is reincarnated from Marilyn Monroe.'

Yes, I was totally nuts about Marilyn Monroe and I was convinced she was related to Elsa. This was proved beyond any doubt when I used to shout 'Marilyn' and Elsa would come running. (Any more of this and I'll get carried away in a straitjacket before the end of the book!)

I loved school. English was my best subject and I loved making up stories – in fact, if I ever had a Plan B in my plans for the future, then it was to be a writer. Not that I was ready to settle for anything less than Plan A at that point. As well as 'am dram', I volunteered for several school theatrical productions including a musical called *Dracula Spectacular*, directed by my teacher Miss Pearce, in which I played a character named Miss Nadia Naïve. My mum had a beautiful polka dot dress made for me by a lady in the village and then she, Dad and Debbie came to see me on the opening night. We've still got pictures of it – Nan and Papa didn't just keep every programme, they had every photograph and newspaper cutting of everything I was ever in, too.

At school, I used to do impressions all the time – Ruth Madoc as Gladys Pugh from *Hi-de-Hi!* playing the xylophone and announcing, 'Morning, campers!', Margaret Thatcher, my teachers . . .

The girl I looked up to the most in the world at that age was sixteen-year-old Lisa Dolson, who was picked to play the lead in

our production of *My Fair Lady*. She was my first close-up heroine.
Night after night I sat mesmerised as she sang her heart out.
Unfortunately for me, I was four years younger than her and a
mere broad-bean peeler dressed in rags. But she was everything I
wanted to be, and it suddenly struck me that I could do everything
I wanted to do, too.

Once Dad went back to work my parents had two incomes to
rely on and we were able to move to a bungalow in Waltham
Chase, two miles from Bishop's Waltham. My mother had always
dreamt of running a guesthouse but they couldn't afford to buy
anything large enough at first. I didn't care – I thought the bungalow was the best house we'd ever lived in. To supplement the
50p pocket money Mum gave us every week, Nan collected her
loose change in an old toffee tin under the bed. She'd take the tin
out and rummage around in it to give us something to buy treats
at the corner shop. I loved sweets: penny chews, Parma Violets,
necklaces on elastic, cola cubes and pear drops, which I'd split my
tongue on by sucking them so hard. (These days I'm a Haribo
Tangfastic girl.) Even so, I never had as much money as my friends,
although I hid it well. I remember once we got the bus into town
and I bought a blue and silver double eyeshadow. We all went for
a pizza and I deliberately didn't have much to eat because I knew
down to the last penny what I had in my purse. It wasn't that I
cared much about money – if you've never had it, you can't miss
it – but I think I pretended I wasn't hungry or something just to
save face.

A lot of our clothes were second-hand and inherited from my
cousin, but we were always grateful for anything new. That was
until the day I was given a Victorian-style dark blue coat with puffy
sleeves. I thanked Mum and told her I loved it (because I knew she
couldn't afford a new one), but secretly I hated it and took it off as

soon as I left the house. I'd rather have frozen to death than be seen in it, so I draped it over my arm instead. I even dragged it over a bush to tear the lining in the hope of getting a new black donkey jacket like the ones all my friends were wearing. On my next birthday, that's exactly what Mum had bought me. She must have saved up and kept it hidden at work because it smelt of photocopier fumes. I loved that coat so much I wore it until it was hanging off me.

I had big lips, a cowlick and a gap between my front teeth as a little girl but thanks to my mum and dad I'd never felt anything other than beautiful, so I didn't mind at all when, as I became a teenager, I had braces fitted to my teeth – not least because my friend Fig had them, too. Fig had massive boobs, big hips, skinny legs and a bubbly personality, and the boys loved her. (Although I developed early and was wearing a bra by eleven, sadly my cup size didn't develop much from the age of twelve!) I tagged along with her and thought she was really cool, so I thought her braces were in, too. Fig was also really into Madonna. I wore lace fingerless gloves, threaded lace through my perm and bought my first pair of red stilettos in homage to her (Madonna, not Fig).

This was about the time that boys – scarce since I married Eric Austin in the garden – made a reappearance in my life. After my short-lived relationship with Clifford Culver (at nine!), my first boyfriend was Matthew Bishop. I thought he looked like Bobby Ewing from *Dallas*. I used to listen to Radio Luxembourg at night and made Lionel Ritchie's 'Hello' 'our song'. (He, of course, knew nothing about it, but to this day when I hear 'Hello' on Magic FM even Chris says, 'Awww, Matthew Bishop – get over it, Mandy!')

I also got my first weekend job, at Hylands fruit shop in the village, for £13 a day. Of course, I spent it all on clothes and No. 7 make-up. (I adored fashion and I'd pick up bargains in Snob and

Chelsea Girl in Southampton.) That job gave me my first taste of exotic fruit. Seedless grapes were a treat in our house, but they were abundant there – not to mention star fruit and kumquats, 'which go very nicely as a sauce with duck', as I'd tell all the customers, even though I had no clue what I was talking about – I only knew because Ken Hyland, the shop owner told me!

Sometimes, after school and work, I'd go to Spratt's garage where Dad worked and watch him working on a car in his oily overalls. We called the owners, Chris and Jimmy Spratt, 'the Ewings' because they lived in a huge house ('Southfork'!) and were married to two – very glamorous – sisters. The best car Dad ever did up while he was there was a beautiful blue-grey Morris Minor 1000 with red leather interior, which I fell in love with and hankered after for years. We had a Morris Traveller on the drive that my sister learned to drive in (aged ten, in secret – until she flooded the engine!) and we all loved it until it finally gave up the ghost and sat at the end of the drive covered in moss, looking like an old tortoise. A Morris Minor remained my dream car and from then on I always wanted to own one myself.

Years later, I worked at Spratt's as a petrol pump attendant for a while and used to ask if I could write out receipts for the clients for a bit more so I could have the extra in tips! I loved to dip my hands in the tub of Swarfega hand cleaner gel – that smell will always remind me of my dad. It was also there that I first listened to *Steve Wright in the Afternoon* on Radio 1 blasting across the forecourt. I love going on Steve's show and never dreamt I would as that young girl.

I learned how to play the piano to Grade 5 (with Distinction) but I scraped by on the sight-reading by listening to my teacher and simply copying her. After a while, I couldn't get away with that any more and as I couldn't be bothered to learn to read music properly

I gave it up to concentrate on the things I loved more. We have a piano at home now, but it's as if I never played – I should really take it up again.

With both parents working, Debbie and I were 'latchkey kids' and were used to letting ourselves in and out of the house. In the mornings, I used to get myself up, put my heated tongs on, listen to Terry Wogan on Radio 2, tong my perm into my hair and spray clouds of Silvikrin and Shockwaves hairspray. I'd have a cup of tea and a bowl of cereal, make my own packed lunch, sort my home-work, grab my satchel and run outside to meet the friend's mother who took me to school. (I know this makes my mum sound redun-dant – but she's terrible at getting up in the morning. She'd get up with minutes to spare and cycle like crazy to get to work on time!) I'd hate you to think I wasn't being looked after though – she was amazing. It's just that I was very independent, which I think was good – and definitely set me up for the future.

Debbie and I would then let ourselves in after school using a key hidden under a brick in the front garden (great security!). It was our job to peel the potatoes and lay the table for supper but we'd race each other to sit on the heating vent by the TV – first one in got the hot spot! – and watch Grange Hill. Debbie got chilblains from winning too often and I told her it was God's punishment. (My great-grandmother used to get them and soak her feet in her own pee. Luckily Debbie never resorted to that . . .) Mum always came home to make the tea and as soon as we heard her ancient Vauxhall Viva (an upgrade from the bicycle) chugging down the street we'd run around like crazy doing all the things we were meant to have done already.

I was a good girl until the age of about fifteen, when I developed opinions and started to exercise some control in my own life. Suddenly, overnight it seemed, the closeness between my mum and I disappeared. It was difficult and unsettling for both of us and, like a lot of mothers and teenagers, we spent too much time arguing. Her favourite threat was, 'I've got my spies, Amanda,' implying that somebody was watching me. It worked, and I felt constantly self-conscious and paranoid. The first time I said the word 'bloody' in public, my face went bright red because I was afraid one of her spies might have been listening. But as time went on I decided that the only spy she could possibly have would be poor Debbie, which my mum never denied, and which made me resent my sister and only increased the adolescent gap between us. Instead of sharing secrets like textbook sisters should, I hid things from her – sneaking a miniskirt or a better pair of shoes to school to change into or borrowing outfits and make-up from my friends, and never inviting her along with me. (I found out years later that she'd done exactly the same thing! If only we'd been better friends ...)

I was such a well-behaved student at Swanmore Secondary School I was made a prefect, along with all five of my friends. The only time I got into trouble at school was when my friend Claire Butler brought in a birthday cake laced with whisky which we shared between six of us, washed down with some beer. The following day we were in class when our teacher Mrs Shotlander announced that a 'little bird' had told her that some of her pupils had been drinking. We looked guiltily at each other but hoped nothing more would come of it – I think we probably thought, 'They'll think it's Jamie Flook.' (He was a bit naughty – wonder what he's doing now!) Also, Fig was super smart and headed for Oxford and you couldn't rock the boat if you were in that stream. But as it turned out, there was no such luck for me. Mrs Shortlander called out my name and despatched me to the strict Welsh headmistress whose only previous contact with me had been to stop me in the corridor and tell me off for rolling my waist-band over to hitch my skirt up, wearing electric blue eyeliner, or those luminous socks.

This time I didn't get off so lightly. She took my prefect badge away, added that she'd never wanted me to be one in the first place because I was too 'feisty and outspoken' and then made me stay behind and clear out the school bins. I went home that night absolutely terrified, but eventually told my mum the whole story. 'There were six of us, but I was the only one picked on!' Mum was so cross she went to the school to complain that I'd been singled out – I was reinstated, I got my prefect badge back and my mum was a hero!

Mostly, though, my relationship with Mum was far from harmonious and we seemed to be constantly at loggerheads. I used to write little ditties about tits, bums, willies and the 'F' word in the back of notebooks and on bits of paper for a laugh. One day she found some of these, as she termed them, 'rude poems' in my wardrobe and confronted me. I was mortified.

'Wait until your dad gets home!' she warned.

I was terrified all day. (I don't even know why, because Dad had never once hit us or even raised his voice. He always took Mum's side but he didn't play us off against each other – anything for a quiet life!)

When he got in from work he came up to my room with a kind of weary resignation and had a perfectly reasonable chat with me.

'I can't really tell you off as this kind of thing is all part of growing up,' he said, 'but your mum's upset and you're still only a girl so best not look at that kind of thing in the house, eh?'

Although I always acted the leader, inside I was really self-conscious. I was desperate to be older and feel more worldly-wise. Although I was really into boys, I was a good girl, and at sixteen I was the only one of my friends who hadn't yet lost her virginity. Eventually, I decided I needed to do something about it. I was 'going out' with an older boy, Derek, nicknamed Snowy, who I thought looked like Billy Idol – at least, he had sticky-up, peroxide blonde hair. I was a massive Billy Idol fan at the time and used to get ready to 'Mony Mony' and 'White Wedding'. Snowy lodged with the village spinster, Maggie Crawford (who also took part in amateur dramatics with me – we used to call her Miss Jones from *Rising Damp* because she spoke with an affected posh accent and looked just like her). Up to that point, our relationship was all very innocent, but I trusted him and felt comfortable with him, so after giving it a lot of thought, I plucked up the courage and wrote him a letter pretty much saying, 'You're the one, shall we?' I think I even suggested a date and a time – I was so naïve! Anyway, just as awkwardly, he agreed that yes, he thought it was time too.

I can't remember much about it apart from the embarrassment of him having to buy some condoms and it all being a bit fumbling and quick, and me being incredibly nervous. It was hardly romantic, though, and it didn't exactly make me feel instantly sophisticated and grown up, so as soon as I could get away, I legged it straight to The Crown in Bishop's Waltham to meet the girls. (We went there because we looked older than we were and, in typical village pub style, they served us.)

They were all already there when I arrived, and I could hardly wait to tell them, so before we'd even ordered a drink we all crammed into the loo together so I could reveal my momentous 'secret'. Once in there, though, shyness got the better of me and I almost couldn't get the words out. They surrounded me, urging me to tell them, and finally, breathlessly, I told them what had happened – that I'd finally lost my virginity. They were all suitably impressed and eventually, after much hugging and squealing and congratulation, we came out giggling excitedly. It didn't last long, though – there was no way I was going to have sex again, so I had to chuck Snowy not long afterwards and he was really upset – he said he felt used. Up to this point I hadn't thought of it from his point of view, and it was a bit of a shock – I had no idea he might actually have had feelings for me!

The kind of snap decisions I was making at that time were largely shaped by the fact that my parents had finally achieved their lifelong dream of owning a guesthouse. They'd saved and saved and bought a nine-bedroom Edwardian property in Bournemouth which they named Chase Lodge: 'Yes, that's right – as in chase me!' Mum used to tell people when taking a booking. But when they first announced that we were moving, I was heartbroken and threw huge, dramatic strops to my parents. Debbie felt the same way but was allowed to stay for six months with Dad's mother, Nanny Win, in Bishop's Waltham, to finish her GCSEs. At the time this made me envious of her, but now I just think of my poor sister being split up from the rest of the family.

By then, I knew I badly wanted to be an actress and the only experience I had was am dram in our local theatre. It had become my life, and with us moving it all suddenly seemed out of reach again. As we left the bungalow behind, it felt like my world was ending.

Chase Lodge was mortgaged to the hilt and my parents had taken a big risk in buying it, but Dad was a talented handyman and he and Mum did it all up themselves. To begin with Dad commuted because he couldn't give up his day job. Then he found work as a van driver for the *Bournemouth Echo* to bring in a regular wage while Mum ran the business. They were a great team. Mum is a brilliant cook and catered for the guests (she even gave up serving tinned tomatoes with breakfast and served posh grilled ones instead). My job was to strip the beds and put the sheets in the wash and then Dad helped out too when he got in from work.

Mum researched local universities and discovered that Bournemouth and Poole had one of the best A level Drama and English courses going. There was a space available as someone had dropped out, but it was tough to get into. I was auditioned by Terry Clarke, a gruff, opinionated bear of a man who was to have a big influence on the next two years of my life. After a very embarrassing interview at which my mother insisted I 'do my Marilyn Monroe impression', I miraculously got in. I was a proper drama student at last!

But that was the only upside of the move. I went from having the biggest room in our bungalow to sharing a much smaller bedroom with my sister when she came down to Bournemouth at weekends. And I missed my friends. Our new house felt chilly and jaded compared to our last cosy home. When we first moved, it always seemed to rain in Bournemouth and being by the sea made the whole place feel even more depressing in the grey and wet. I hated it.

The weirdest transition of all for me, however, was having strangers in our house, which was even harder to get used to as a self-conscious teenager – I was going through enough change at that time anyway! I never got used to having to sit down to breakfast each morning with people I'd never met.

At no time was this better highlighted than Christmas. Christmas is a favourite time of year for me, and Mum and Dad always helped to make it special for Debbie and me – but that first Christmas in Bournemouth with my parents and their guests was different, to say the least. My friends and I were lured along as Christmas entertainment. Me and Nan were in Mrs Christmas costumes that we'd been pressganged into wearing, even though my sister had some-how got out of it and was wearing normal clothes. (Nan must have been in her seventies at the time – she still had a cracking pair of legs though!) As we handed round Christmas crackers to complete strangers I felt that we'd lost all sense of family. It was fun – ish. But behind my cheery façade, I was filled with a huge sense of sadness. Looking back, that guesthouse killed our family and though, even-tually, we'd never been so financially well off, the fun and the sense of family that we'd had when we were young and had no money had been lost for ever. There had been massive changes in my life – something I was going to have to get used to.

Before then, though, I was about to fall head over heels in love . . .

Chapter 5

Taken for Granted

In the space of a few months my life turned upside down. As well as coping with the strange new situation at home, I was studying for my A levels, trying to make new friends and having to adapt to a completely new environment. Back in Bishop's Waltham, I was Amanda Holden who wanted to be an actress, but here I was only one of a thousand talented people at university, many of whom wanted the same thing as me.

Worst of all, my mum and I weren't getting along. Looking back, it's maybe no surprise – I was growing up, and out of her control, and she was setting up a new business. Dad and my sister were still based in Bishop's Waltham, finishing off work and school, and I wasn't adapting well to sharing a building with strangers and no longer having my own privacy. It was me and Mum against the world, and we clashed frequently and horribly. Eventually things got so bad that one weekend, after an almighty row, I left.

It didn't take long for the enormity of what I'd done to hit me. I was just seventeen and was in a relatively new place. It was scary, but I felt like I had no other choice – the way things were, I certainly couldn't go back to Mum. Instead, I went round to the house of my new best friend at college, Dionne. She used to sing and do Lena Zavaroni impressions, and we had become inseparable from the first day. Her family kindly invited me to move in with them in their small council house – I was always being adopted by other people's families! – but I soon realised it wasn't going to be a long-term solution. Being with someone else's family rather than mine just reminded me of what I'd left behind. I needed to find a place of my own.

Dionne said that if I found a place she'd be my flatmate, so I got a job at a place called The Candy Bar in Westbourne at weekends to make some extra cash and charmed a local landlord into taking us in. Unfortunately, it turned out being independent wasn't all it was cracked up to be. My new 'home' was a mangy old bedsit full of dark furniture with a shared bathroom and kitchen – it was horrible. An old nun lived there too, so we'd try and eat during the day, huddled together on the bed eating our sandwiches so we didn't have to bump into her in the kitchen. I was doing my college course and working every night after college and at weekends, to support myself. I was trying to throw myself into college life and do everything everyone else was, but not managing to have as much fun because I had to work to earn money. Most of all, I missed my family. After about six months, when Dionne and I had a row, I ran home.

When I was there, back in that familiar environment and with my family, the previous months took their toll. I began to cry and I couldn't stop. I realised I wasn't coping as well as I thought. I was heartbroken and exhausted by everything that had happened in such a short time. I'd left home, started a new course, taken on jobs in the evening and at weekends and it had emotionally and physically drained me. I was tired of playing it tough. My mum took me back in and I stayed for a couple of weeks so we could sort out our differences. Whilst I was there I turned eighteen and for my birthday Mum bought me a china plate from a special offer in a Sunday magazine. It featured a painting of a young woman with shoulder-length hair carrying two suitcases, standing on the platform of a railway station. The title of the plate was 'An Actress Awaits'.

Mum told me, 'That'll be you one day, Amanda.'

I loved that plate and hung it on the wall of my bedroom. I used to stare at it and imagine myself waiting at a railway station about to travel to the West End or to take part in repertory theatre in a city. I so desperately wanted to be the girl on that plate. (There were moments I wondered if I ever would, of course – lots of them!)

A fortnight or so later, Dionne came to tell me she'd found a fantastic new-build house for us and our friends Alethea and Claire on a posh new estate on the Bournemouth Road near the Chase Manhattan Bank. That place was amazing: beautifully decorated and fully furnished with en suite bathrooms. With things resolved between Mum and me, I felt like this time I could move out for all the right reasons, with my family physically and emotionally close.

In our new house, we worked very hard and played very hard. We were notorious for our wild parties (though, ever the hostess, I would always lay out a buffet just like my mum. I would make quiche! I was known for my quiche). At the same time, though, we kept our little house beautifully – when my parents first came to visit they couldn't believe how clean and tidy everything was, with fresh washing hanging on the line and the fridge filled with food. No student squalor for us! I was all grown up at last, on my way with the career I had dreamed of, and I felt fabulous.

Within a few weeks of college I had met SD and started going out with him. I was very fond of him and we were very happy together for a full year, but his family saw me as something more permanent in his life and even at seventeen I knew it wasn't for me. Poor SD. I was totally freaked out when one evening his lovely mum got her wedding dress out and gave it to me to try on, saying, 'It fits you perfectly!' It was beautiful, but I got a sinking feeling deep in my gut and could feel the pressure of her expectations. I knew that SD wasn't The One, so I had to cut and run. On our first anniversary I chucked him in a letter. I couldn't say the words, 'It's over.' I just didn't have the guts. (Plus, I think there was something about putting my sentiments in black and white that appealed to my inner Jane Austen.)

It was then that GB came into my world and my life tipped topsy-turvy all over again. GB was a couple of years older than me and in the year above mine at college. He wasn't what you'd call traditionally handsome – he had auburn hair and a mole (he looked a bit like Michael Ball when he first started out) – but he was so funny, very bright, a brilliant writer and great at impressions. He's what my friend Jason calls 'a honey'.

My original plan had been to fix him up with Dionne, so I grabbed him in the corridor at college one day and pushed him into the girls' toilets to tell him to ask her out. Once he was pinned up against the wall, though, I looked into his eyes and thought, 'Oh no! What am I doing? I always liked you!' I've never been good at playing the waiting game or playing hard to get. I just don't like wasting time. To this day, I've never been asked out – I've always done it myself! I am a huge flirt but I can still count on both hands (and one foot) the number of people I have slept with. (I would have been hopeless in another era. No Mr Darcy fannying around for me – if I'd been Elizabeth Bennet I would have chased him on my horse and just told him how I felt!) So, I asked GB out. A bit later, I found out he hadn't wanted to go out with Dionne at all because he had a thing for me too. We had our first kiss walking out down the university drive, on one of the speed ramps. (Nice!)

The first week we started going out, we spent the whole time in bed, like Bournemouth's answer to John and Yoko. GB was my first true love – I'd never been in love before and I fell hard. My feelings were proper and massive.

He was very thoughtful and would cycle all the way from where he lived with his dad in Boscombe to put roses through my letter-box. (I'd wake up to find them half-dead on my doormat, but I guess it's the thought that counts!) At college he'd break into my locker and leave me a bowl of cereal and a little jug of milk for my breakfast; he wrote me poems and introduced me to experimental music like David Sylvian and Virginia Astley – the kind of stuff I wouldn't have discovered on my own. (And to be honest have never listened to since!) GB used to wear Kouros, which was very fashionable back then, and if I ever get a whiff of it now I think of him – sadly Chris's dad wears it so these days I smell it more often than not. I also adored GB's mother, who was older than my mum and seemed very worldly-wise. I called her 'Muesli' – I don't know why! She was separated from GB's dad and lived in a large Edwardian house in Roundhay, just outside Leeds. Visiting her with GB involved a nine-hour coach ride to Leeds but it was always well worth it. She ran a children's nursery in part of her house, so there were always children there, which was sweet. She'd have olive tapenade on toast and fennel tea, which I thought was terribly posh, and she knew all about opera and theatre and ballet. In fact, she had excellent taste and I still think of her when I'm looking for interior design inspiration. She was the first grown-up outside my family who seemed to really love me for who I was.

The love that GB and I shared was an intense, deep love – we were lovers, but we were best friends too. We talked about everything and never stopped laughing. Mum said I should have been 'sowing my oats', but I've always been a relationship girl. I don't remember it was particularly about sex, though obviously we had sex because we spent an awful lot of time in bed. There's a funny story attached to this. Very early on in the relationship, after doing the deed, I came downstairs in agony. GB was cooking tea – I specifically remember it was boil-in-the-bag cod fillets in parsley sauce (we knew how to live!) – but before we ate, I started to complain of chronic tummy pain. Within minutes I was doubled up and we called an ambulance. When they arrived, they took one look at me and said it was suspected peritonitis, a potentially fatal inflammation of the abdomen. Terrified, GB and I were whizzed to hospital, sirens blazing. They rushed me into A&E, after which a doctor examined me and gave me peppermint water. Then I farted, which must have lasted five minutes. I've never felt so embarrassed in my life, with GB by my bedside mopping my brow while I stank the ward out. After that episode, we both knew it was true love, and never tried that particular position again!

Of course, we shared a joint passion for acting and we were both very focused on doing well at college. Charles Lamb and Terry Clark ran a tight ship at the Jellicoe Theatre in Bournemouth and it was an excellent course. Our curriculum didn't just include performing – we learned every aspect of theatre such as lighting and sound. We put on our own productions and took turns to manage rehearsals and do sound checks, or to be stage managers. I enjoyed it all and I knew it would be great experience for my future career, but it never even crossed my mind to stay behind the scenes! In the event it was GB, not me, who made the first move towards a professional career in the theatre. Just before he graduated, he auditioned for the famous Webber Douglas Academy of Dramatic Art in London – one of the leading drama schools in the country – and was accepted. I couldn't have been happier for him: it was a tough school to get into and I was so proud.

It meant a huge change for us, as I still had a year to go at Bournemouth, but we vowed to see each other as many weekends as budget and National Express coach timetables allowed. For the next year, I'd either go to see GB or send him the money from my job to come home and see me. Our days together were so important. I lived for the weekends, and whenever GB came back, I came back to life. One day one of the girls in my house double-dared me to ride around the block naked on the back of her motorbike, which was like a red rag to a bull. No one turns down a double dare! Laughing, GB agreed to take me but insisted I at least wear a crash helmet. I pressed myself up against his back and squealed with excitement as he raced me naked around the block – I even waved to the doorman at the Chase Manhattan Bank and shouted, 'Say no to crack!' It was the easiest twenty quid I've ever earned.

With GB gone, it was now my turn to see if I could get into drama school. I applied to LAMDA, the Central School of Speech and Drama and Mountview Academy of Theatre Arts in Wood Green, north London. Mountview was much more commercial than GB's school but it had a great reputation. I had to save up the £50 for the audition from my weekend job. Thousands of people apply every year, so it was a massive deal.

The end of my course approached and as I waited to hear if my applications had been successful, I moved back home for a while. Every day, I'd wait for the post with mounting anticipation. One day, I was upstairs being chambermaid, changing beds in the attic bedroom, when I heard my mum coming up the stairs. As I peered out of the bedroom door, I could see she was ceremoniously carrying a letter on a cushion. It was THE letter from Mountview. We looked at each other nervously.

'This is it. This is the big moment,' she said, and we sat down on the bed together. Fingers fumbling a little, I opened the envelope and skim-read the letter, heart pounding. Finally, I read the words I'd dreamed of seeing. I was in! I'd been accepted at Mountview theatre school. That was such a special moment – a life-changer. The next important stage in realising my dreams.

It wasn't long before my euphoric bubble was burst. One weekend shortly afterwards, a friend had a party and GB came home for it. We all ventured down to the beach that night and went skinny-dipping. I was late going down and the others had all gone ahead. I'll never forget, I followed in my dressing gown, with a cup of tea in a china cup and saucer! As I walked down the street, I heard rustling in the bushes in the next-door neighbour's garden. I turned to look and a South African girl I was friendly with at college appeared, adjusting her dress. Close behind her was GB – *my* GB. They walked down to the party, hand in hand, without seeing me. It felt so surreal standing there in that dark street, in only a dressing gown, naked underneath, holding a cup of tea. You couldn't make it up. I could almost see myself and how ridiculous I must look.

To say I was heartbroken would be an understatement. I was wrecked beyond belief. I confronted them both and went absolutely nuts, screaming and fighting with GB. He denied it all, of course, but later my friend Andy was brave enough to tell me that GB had been having an affair with her for weeks. Every time I had paid for GB's coach fare home, he'd been visiting her as well.

After I'd got over the initial shock, I asked Andy to drive me to the coach station and I went to London, to GB's bedsit, and wreaked havoc. I tore up photographs and ripped up tapes and totally trashed the place. When I was finished, I found his flatmate Matthew in the Drama Centre's canteen and he confessed that he too knew all about the affair, which came as a double blow. I felt bereaved and betrayed. All our friends were there, trying to find out what was wrong, but I was inconsolable.

GB arrived home later that night and thought he'd been burgled, but then he looked around at what had been damaged and it dawned on him what must have happened. When Matthew and I got back to the flat, we could just hear this animalistic howling. It was GB. He took me for a long walk on Primrose Hill to apologise and he promised that it would never happen again. I was young and so much in love that I desperately wanted to believe him. Girls now know all about self-respect and how you should deal with that kind of situation, but I didn't know any of that. I was so naïve, and just desperately in love with him, and so I forgave him. We kissed and made up and, in a much happier frame of mind, I returned to Bournemouth.

A few days later, GB proposed to me over the phone by saying, 'Maybe we should get married.' I had no doubts whatsoever. When we next saw each other, he took me to the jeweller H. Samuel and we chose a Ceylon sapphire ring surrounded by tiny diamonds, and he proposed again, properly, on Primrose Hill.

Even though I was still only nineteen, my family weren't at all surprised – they liked GB and knew how much I loved him. His family embraced the news just as warmly as mine and his mum threw us a small party at her house in Leeds, with champagne and a cake. I had never felt happier. When I went to cut the cake, though, I accidentally sliced through the top of my finger. There was blood everywhere but I didn't really feel the pain – I was busy trying not to see it as a bad omen. GB's brother was a doctor at Leeds General Infirmary, so on what should have been a celebratory night he whisked me into hospital, stitched up the wound and went to get me some painkillers.

All of a sudden, the curtain to my cubicle drew back and Jimmy Savile was standing in front of me! At that point, he was still regarded as a legendary fundraiser and philanthropist. He looked at my bandaged hand and made a lame joke about me attempting suicide. I was completely taken aback. Then he asked me, 'Have you got any gynaecological problems?'

'No,' I said, thinking it was a bit bizarre.

He gave me a weird smile. 'Then I can give you one!'

Knowing what we know now, it was a seedy thing to say to me, but I dined out on that 'Jimmy Savile is a perv' story for years. (The rumours even when I was nineteen were that he'd slept with a fourteen-year-old – why no one did anything about it, I have no idea.)

Every morning on the bus to drama school I travelled past a bridal shop called Mirror Mirror in Crouch End. As the bus pulled to a stop outside, I'd peer into the window, imagining myself in the fairy-tale outfit I'd always dreamed of. It was early summer of 1990, Madonna was dominating the charts with 'Vogue' and I was starting out at drama school. GB, Matthew and I moved into a basement flat in Primrose Hill. (Although my drama school was in Wood Green and all my friends lived in Turnpike Lane, there was absolutely no way that I wasn't going to live in the nicest location I could, so I decided to work Saturdays and Sundays to live the dream!) I barely gave Bournemouth a backwards glance.

Living with my boyfriend on Gloucester Avenue turned me into a right little homemaker. I cooked and filled the place with candles and Laura Ashley cushions. I was so happy, and determined to make it work. Financially, it was tough, though – way tougher than I could have imagined. Mum and Dad were doing a bit better and could help me out with extra money and things – they always said we never had any toilet paper in the house! – but I was still skint. I remember I would have £5 for a week, which would do for my packed lunch every day and my bus fare, but I was always borrowing the odd pound for a jacket potato. I had a pair of navy blue canvas wedge shoes that I wore every day – they would be sodden in the winter and all crusty and dried up in the summer, but they saw me through a year of my course! I had a job at Hobbs for a while (when I got lots of shoes half price!) but it got to a point where it was affecting what I was doing – when I was meant to be learning lines and going out and contacting agents, I was working and trying to keep my life together instead. (I did treat myself to a bottle of Lambrusco every now and again, though. I'd make up some tagliatelle and packet béchamel sauce, sit on the floor, drink two glasses of Lambrusco and watch *thirtysomething*. I loved that show. GB used to sit in the back yard because he couldn't bear me crying at it every week!)

School itself was even more demanding than my last. At Mountview I felt like a minnow in a sea of sharks, surrounded by naked ambition, and it made me bashful and self-conscious. Once again I found myself fighting to be the loudest and became a total lovey. (Mum recently found a postcard I sent them from there that reads: 'Dear Mummy and Daddy, sorry I haven't written for ages but I have been working and have met a smashing group of people!' That kind of sums it up . . .)

My two best friends from this era are Jason Maddocks and Jane Wall. Jane reminded me when I was writing this book of how she first saw me standing on a table in the canteen wearing a white dress and singing ('either a show tune or an Abba song' – I do love an Abba song!), like something out of *Fame*. She took one look at me and thought, 'I could never be friends with someone like that.'

I think she just wanted to slap me. Thankfully we became very close and we are still best friends twenty-three years later.

Jason, however, says he heard me before he saw me, because of my 'outrageous raucous laugh' and liked my filthy sense of humour. He was often picked as my love interest in the plays we did together, which was hilarious as he came out to me as gay even before he told his parents. (We only found out later that it was Jason's place I'd taken at Bournemouth and Poole College, when he'd dropped out at the last minute to remain in the sixth form, and for that I owe him.) Jason became my flatmate, and knows me better than almost anyone. He says back then I came across as confident, ambitious and driven, but he knew how self-conscious I was inside and he constantly tried to instil confidence in me. On the opening night of *Thoroughly Modern Millie* in 2003, he said, 'If there was one person at drama school who was going to make it, we all thought it'd be you.' That meant the world to me.

The ethos at Mountview was tough love. The teachers liked to break their students and put them back together again. We had to be strictly disciplined, but most of all we had to learn to believe in ourselves. I usually avoided conflict but sometimes I fought back, particularly against a teacher who had no structure to his classes and was especially difficult. He had us doing free-form dancing, including what he called 'riding the tiger' which basically involved him watching us dry-hump the floor! He picked on people and singled out one girl who'd just lost her father, beating a drum and making her cry. He was a bully, and I couldn't stand it.

One day, me and the girls had had enough. At my house, we drank a litre of water each and every time we had a sip we cursed him. We then all pissed into a jug and added this to an Evian bottle. (I even added some Bloo to make it look less green.) The morning of his class my girlfriends distracted him and I swapped his water bottle for the piss bottle, my heart thumping. We sat in the circle, talking the usual drama school bollocks about finding yourself and your 'centre', while me and the girls never took our eyes off his bag. Sadly he never drank it on our watch, but I live in hope that all that drum beating built up some thirst in his next class.

Whatever happened with the curse, his bullying got worse, and I drew up a petition demanding that he be kicked out of the school. Everyone in the school signed it, but then panicked and wanted their names scrubbed out when he found out what was going on. I refused and instead handed the petition in to the principal. Eventually, he left and we found out that he had been sacked from several other schools for bullying. Rumour had it he was part of some weird cult, but we never did find out which one . . .

Like all the other students, my chief ambition at Mountview was to earn my Equity card – it was the be-all and end-all of our lives at that point. The fuller your CV, the better it looked, so I tried all aspects of performance art. I even put a group together in which my friend Sally Walker played the piano and I sang. (I wanted to call it Salamander – get it? – but she wasn't so keen.) Instead, it was called B Sharp. We used to say, 'B Sharp – book now!' We did gigs all over the UK (including all the hotels in my mum's street) and a couple of weddings to earn points for our cards.

During the summer holidays, I went back to Bournemouth and worked at my parents' guest house. Chase Lodge was doing really well. By this time, Debbie had also moved out and the main house was full of guests – all eleven bedrooms. I loved waitressing, and I didn't mind the cleaning either – Mum would leave all the bathrooms and toilets for me because I loved doing them! GB came back with me too that year, so Mum put a double bed in the shed for us to sleep in. It was comfier than it sounds, and warm (I only seem to remember gorgeous sunny summers in Bournemouth then!).

In September, I changed courses. I'd originally enrolled in Musical Theatre. Most of the girls had danced their whole lives, wore full make-up and dressed in unitards most of the time (I didn't even have a pair of leg warmers!). I wanted to dance and do musicals, but first and foremost I wanted to be an actor. I wrote to the college principal and said I don't think it's for me. Can I go on to the acting course please? I switched, and Jason followed suit.

It was much more my scene and for two years I was really happy. A few of my friends were into smoking spliffs, but that was never my thing. I hated the taste so much that a friend bought me some honey-roasted tobacco which she claimed would be gentler on my throat. She even blew the smoke in my face, but I always ended up coughing and wheezing like an old tramp. I hated it and didn't see the point – I never inhaled enough to get high! Increasingly, though, GB was never home. I used to wander out into the street and walk up to Chalk Farm tube station in my pyjamas, worrying about where he was. (This was before mobile phones, remember, so I couldn't just send him a text to find out.) I must have looked pretty tragic standing in Primrose Hill in my PJs. I knew it was ridiculous waiting for him like that but I couldn't help myself; I loved him so much.

There was another boy at college who I was very fond of. He was handsome and fun, and could tell that things weren't right between me and GB. One weekend, back in Bournemouth, he invited me for a walk along the seafront and asked me if I'd consider going out with him instead. He kissed me and was so sweet. I was flattered and grateful. In other circumstances I might have been tempted but I thanked him and told him no. He smiled and told me, 'GB's a lucky man.' I knew in my heart GB didn't think that at all.

Trying not to worry about my fiancé, I threw myself into my studies and was given some amazing parts in my final year, including the best yet – the role of Roxie in *Chicago*. I was also in an Anthony Minghella play called *A Little Like Drowning*. Mr Minghella lived in Crouch End, not far from the college, and came to see the play in person. Afterwards, he came backstage and told us what a good job we'd done. He said it was moving and subtle. I was awestruck. He made me believe I really did have a future in the business.

Alongside all the acting, I had my first brush with light entertainment. GB's best friend Ian had just been chucked by his girlfriend. During the summer, in August, we saw a sign for auditions for *Blind Date*, and as a laugh I went with him. Of course, I ended up auditioning and was the stupid loud one who got through, and he didn't. I had a boyfriend, GB – which I stated on the application form – but was still called to be on the reserve list. In the end, somebody's granny died and I was called to London to take part in a show. (It's still available to see on YouTube, should you wish!) Funnily enough, this has become the 'before I was famous' clip that has come back to haunt me over and over again. It was good fun and I loved the show, but it's not, as so many people think, the moment that I was 'discovered'. Afterwards, I went back to drama school and continued to train. (Before I was rejected I'd told Cilla that my dream date was Jack Nicholson because I preferred 'mature, experienced men'. In truth, I loved Jack because he was such a great actor. I'd seen him in *Terms of Endearment* on my thirteenth birthday and he made me laugh and cry. But instead that night I announced to some 17 million *Blind*

Date viewers that I preferred 'mature men'. I had no idea how that would come back to haunt me too ...)

In my final year we put on a production of a play by Sharman Macdonald (Keira Knightley's mum), *When I Was a Girl, I Used to Scream and Shout*. I played Fiona, and I had to simulate sex with Jason on a beach and go topless. As my former flatmate, he's certainly seen my boobs more than most. My friend Jane, who is thin and mixed race, was cast as the fat white Scottish girl Vari. It was hysterical – she had to wear padding. We had a girl of that description in our year whose nose was most put out of joint, as she wasn't cast in the role which was so perfect for her! The fourth part was played by our friend Diane Brunsden. Just before the play opened, I persuaded our director that to help our characters bond we needed to go to a seaside resort and work on our lines together. So we all piled down to Mum and Dad's and had a fantastic weekend eating real food instead of our drama school diet of pasta with packet sauce. We did far too much drinking and not nearly enough rehearsing, but the play was still a success.

I loved the work I was doing at drama school but, surrounded by so much fierce competition, I knew I had to be realistic. I gave myself until the age of thirty to make it – if I hadn't become a successful actress by then, I'd do something else. I love what I do, but coming from a humble background I was determined never just to 'make do'. So, I wrote to about thirty agents. I couldn't believe it when I not only got one, but a great one: Patrick Hambleton from Jane Lehrer Associates. He saw me in *Scream and Shout* and then appeared for my end of year 'showcase' on a West End stage. It was awful. I wore what he calls now an 'ill-fitting mauve dress with a dreadful hem' and sang a song which wasn't right for my range. It's a good job he wasn't there for the show where I was supposed to be a background performer but upstaged my peers by wearing a turban, smoking a pipe, blacking out my teeth and carrying a cat-o'-nine-tails! (I sourced this myself.) That night I was marked down by my principal for upstaging.

There were only a few of us who got agents that year, and I was so lucky that Patrick believed in me. Patrick championed me to everyone – and still does, even though he's no longer my agent. He always said he loved my 'bawdy' sense of humour and how I was always quite open about being ambitious. (I've never seen anything wrong in being ambitious and he doesn't, either.) With Patrick behind me and GB at my side, I felt that anything was possible.

Then one day Debbie dropped something off at my flat when I was away. She knocked and GB opened the door. There was a long corridor and she could see straight down to the bedroom. 'There was a girl in your bed, Amanda,' she broke it to me later.

I didn't want to believe her to begin with, but in my heart I knew it was true. When I confronted GB he immediately confessed and, as he broke my heart again, I had a flashback to a fortune teller I'd seen in Bournemouth who'd told me, 'You will never wear his ring.' The trouble was, I still worshipped the ground GB walked on. I couldn't imagine being able to even breathe without him and so, once again, I chose to forgive him. I knew there were other affairs, too – I think he was probably bonking everything that moved – but I chose to ignore it.

Just as I graduated from drama school in 1992, GB was picked for a theatrical job in Germany and he accepted without a moment's hesitation. As my friend Jason always says, 'GB was lovely, but useless boyfriend material.' I helped my fiancé pack his bags and we promised to keep in touch, both of us hoping that it might still work, but we knew it would never be the same. When I look back, I can't hate GB at all. He was young, with so many women after him. Why wouldn't he be tempted? I should have been single myself, and enjoying being a student properly, instead of being such a good girl ... GB taught me so much and gave me some of the happiest years of my life. Relationships have big impacts, and ours helped shape me. It took a piece of me for ever and I made choices about my future relationships because of it. I still think about him from time to time. (He is 'Advert Man', so I have no choice! Lego, gas repairs, pet insurance – he's on in every ad break. It's hilarious.) But the last time I saw GB it was face to face and I was with Lexi, coming out of the loos in M&S. He had a pram, and I just blurted out, 'Oh my God, is that yours?'

'Yes,' he said, pointing at Lexi. 'Is that yours?!'

We laughed and I had a little coo over his son. So I guess we both got our happy ending – just not with each other.

Chapter 6

Being Frank

'Hello, dahling. Is that Gabrielle Anwar?' (I always told Patrick he looked like the *Scent of a Woman* actress – he still does!)

Patrick and I quickly became great friends but I still couldn't believe how lucky I was to have an agent. I called him every few days to see if he had anything for me but I was always so aware that all his clients would be doing the same thing that I'd camp it up whenever I rang and try to make him laugh. (Because no one had mobiles, I remember legging it home every day to check the answerphone. If it was flashing, I'd think, 'Oh my God, this is my agent with a job!' Of course, it was usually Mum saying, 'I haven't spoken to you in two weeks!')

One of the first auditions Patrick arranged for me was the part of Alice Meadows in an episode of a TV series called *In Suspicious Circumstances* introduced by Edward Woodward. Philip Glenister was to be in it and his father John was directing. I travelled up by train, and as I walked down the road towards the studios a leaf floated down from a tree and fell straight into my hand. I took it as an omen that I'd get the part – and I was right. I walked in and they pretty much gave it to me there and then. It was set in London's Bloomsbury in the early 1900s, and I loved all the vintage clothes.

Then late November 1992 Patrick told me that they were looking for someone to play Liesl in a Sadler's Wells Theatre touring production of *The Sound of Music*. 'If that's not for you, then there may be some other parts available . . .,' he began. He had me at Liesl. Having watched the film every Christmas of my life at my grandparents' house, I knew that role inside out and upside down. I knew I could play Liesl. I *was* Liesl, I told myself.

By then I was living in a Georgian garden flat in Muswell Hill, north London, with Jason and Muffy the cat, that I had somehow found and rented from its owner for an absolute song. We had such a laugh living there. (Jason always says I can sniff out a bargain anywhere and we certainly lived a life of luxury on a pittance there.) He and I even had a flirtation with religion for a while and went to a beautiful church nearby every Sunday morning. (I think I just enjoyed a good old sing-song.) We'd go home via Threshers off-licence for a bottle of Harvey's Bristol Cream, which we drank while I made the Sunday roast, before falling asleep on the sofa in front of the telly watching *Antiques Roadshow*.

Not long after we moved in, Jason went down with a virus. When he didn't get better, he panicked – this was the era when AIDS was very prevalent – so I made him go to a hospital for a blood test. The results took a long, anxious week to come through. Suddenly it seemed that every headline was about AIDS and the effect it was having on people all over the world and on their relationships, friends and families, and the realisation that he could possibly have something so life-threatening suddenly felt very grown up and serious. When Jason went back to the doctors, though, it was nothing serious at all – but he could read his notes upside down on the desk and the doctor had written: 'Description of patient: Tired Homosexual.' When he came back and told me I thought it was hilarious. Can you imagine anyone diagnosing that now?!

Thanks to Jason's special eye for fashion, I turned up for the *Sound of Music* audition at the theatre near Leicester Square dressed in a pinafore dress with puff sleeves, my hair swept back from my face and decorated with a bow. The waiting room was packed with hopeful Liesls, many of them wearing similar costume. Among them were most of the girls from my Musical Theatre class at Mountview.

When it was my turn, I smoothed down my dress and took my place on that big West End stage. Looking out into a darkened auditorium I was very aware of the people out there watching me in the half-light who I needed to impress. Taking a deep breath, I nodded to the pianist who was to accompany me and began to sing. The song I had chosen was 'Time Heals Everything' from *Mack & Mabel*. That day, I sang it about GB and felt every word of the lyrics: 'Time heals everything but loving you . . .' I poured my heart out, and nearly burst into tears.

As the day went on the numbers went down to forty, and then to a handful of girls. I was still a contender! (And all of my Musical Theatre class had been rejected.) Finally the production team told me that it was down to one other girl and me. They asked us to take a break and come back to do our auditions again in a play-off. I had £1 in my pocket so I hurried to the nearest McDonald's, bought myself a coffee and found a phone box. When I told Mum the news, she shrieked down the phone at me, 'Oh my God, 'Manda!' She could hardly believe it.

Fired by her enthusiasm, I returned to the theatre and sang again, feeling all the emotion once more. I didn't know how my rival's audition had gone, but I felt I'd sung mine just right. I was on a high and felt like I'd done my best.

'We'll let your agent know in the next week.'

It was close to Christmas, so two days later I got the train to my grandparents' house. I'd given my co-agent Jane their telephone number and, sitting in that carriage heading west, I fantasised about my grandfather meeting me off the train and telling me that I'd got the part. If that happened, I'd be standing on the railway platform with my suitcase in my hand just like the girl on the plate. 'An Actress Awaits.'

The train pulled into the station and Papa was waiting, just as he'd promised.

'Hello, my lover,' he said, his eyes bright. 'We've had a phone call from your agent!'

I stopped dead in my tracks. 'How did he sound?'

'You got the job!'

OMG! I couldn't believe it and fell into his arms – I had never been so happy. We went home and celebrated with a glass of Harvey's Bristol Cream (which I still have every Sunday in honour of that day) instead of our usual milky coffee for elevenses. My nan and Papa loved that they were the first to know and dined out on that story for years. 'Oh yes, we were there when Amanda got her first big break!' It was such a big deal – for me, for them, for Mum and Dad, for everyone. Finally, I was on my way.

I wrote to GB in Germany telling him that I'd got the part and was about to go on tour for a year. I compiled a break-up tape for him. It included Abba's 'The Winner Takes It All' and Madonna's 'I Fucked Up' and I cried my heart out whilst I recorded it for him. GB told me later that he listened to that tape whilst going for a long walk around a lake and that he'd bawled his eyes out too because he knew that it was finally over between us.

Rehearsals for *The Sound of Music* began in January 1993. As of March we would take our production to just about every major theatre in the UK. Christopher Cazenove was to play my father, Captain von Trapp, Liz Robertson played Maria and the lovely Robin Nedwell (from *Robin's Nest*) played Uncle Max. Rolf, Liesl's love interest, was played by 'George'. He was young, good-looking and had given up a future in a successful family business to follow his theatrical dreams. One of the nuns was played by Emma Robinson, who became my best friend on that tour. We used to be so wicked, and we had so much fun together. There was lots of staying up late and drinking.

The show opened in Hull and we did a run of two or three weeks in each town. Bournemouth, Birmingham and Belfast – at each new venue the production company hired children from local drama groups to play the younger von Trapp family, so they had to rehearse afresh every time. And of course we had to be there early to help train them. Being part of that production was probably the hardest I ever worked in my life but I loved every minute of it. Everything from the glare of the stage lights to the sounds of applause connected with something deep inside me – something that I had craved since I was small. Despite all the turmoil I was still going through after my split from GB, I was living my dream. I was the girl on the plate, moving from city to city with my suitcase. Instead of dealing with my heartbreak, I tried to push it to one side and focus on the amazing opportunity in front of me.

Christopher Cazenove, who was married to the actress Angharad Rees with two children at the time, toured in his own motorhome so that he didn't have to stay in guesthouses. The rest of us, though, were allotted rooms. There was a Digs List put up on the noticeboard in each town and you took your pick. Most of them were very depressing and some were positively disgusting. I shared with Christopher's dresser Davina Elliot, known as 'Divs'. We had a right old laugh and I had a standing joke, 'When I'm a star in the West End dahhhling, I'll only have you as my dresser!' Neither of us thought for one minute that I'd be able to keep my promise, but when it did happen, I was true to my word.

We stayed with my understudy in one stinky house owned by a man we loathed. I look back on that tour and it's like seeing someone I don't know – I think I went a bit nuts. I'd been with GB for so long – five years in total – and losing him wrecked me. I was absolutely heartbroken and went totally off the rails. I tried to turn everything into a positive, and told myself it was good that I was free at the ripe old age of twenty-one thanks to GB. That I could now meet new people, experience different things. But I have always been a relationship person and have never really dated. So when George asked me out, we pretty much straight away became a couple. (Not only did everybody adore George, but he was a total sweetheart and very kind to me.) We had some lovely times together, and I was very fond of him, but I wasn't mature enough to know this was a time I should probably be spending working through my bruised emotions on my own, not in a rebound relationship looking to another man to heal my heartache! It didn't help my vulnerable state of mind when GB returned from Germany and got back in touch with me, trying to reignite our relationship. As we toured the UK over the following months, I was in a constant state of confusion and didn't know whether I was coming or going. Eventually, George and I finished. We were both gutted that it hadn't worked out, but deep down I knew he wasn't the one for me. It was all the more difficult as we had to face us playing boyfriend and girlfriend every night.

Early that summer, the tour took us to Plymouth, where there was a surprise in store. When I arrived at the Theatre Royal there was a letter waiting for me at the stage door. It was from Frank. He wrote that he'd seen I was in the musical and wanted to say hello as he lived near by. He added that he'd love to meet me and sent me his address with the final words, 'The ball's in your court.'

I rang Dad and asked his advice – I didn't want to upset him or Mum and I needed a voice of reason. 'If you want to see him then you should,' he said simply. Mum agreed and was mostly curious to know what Frank looked like. 'Take some photos!' she instructed. Then I called my sister who said she'd like to come along as well.

Waiting for that reunion was one of the strangest experiences of my life. The Theatre Royal has a huge glass frontage and stone steps and Debbie and I sat there for what seemed like an age, our backs to the flow of people, watching every man who approached in the reflection of the glass so our faces couldn't be seen. She was really nervous and kept saying, 'Oh my God, that's him! I can feel it!' 'Oh my God, that's him! I can feel it!' She did that half a dozen times until I had to tell her to stop. The only time I'd seen Frank since he walked out on us was the day Debbie and I saw him on our bikes. He'd sent a pair of fake pearl earrings for my sixteenth birthday and a Nintendo game called Oil Panic (where a man runs underneath an oil slick catching drips with his bucket) that a boy at school called Period Panic, which had made me go red with embarrassment. As I sat waiting for him outside that theatre I wondered what on earth we'd have to say to each other.

Eventually a silver-haired man appeared. It was Frank. The first thing I noticed was that he had exactly the same hands as Debbie, he had a shock of grey hair and the high Holden forehead. (Or, to quote some of the nicknames I've had, 'Spam Head' or 'Merrick', as in Joseph Merrick, the Elephant Man.) My mother used to claim that I walked 'with a swagger' like him, which I was always a bit offended by. A swagger sounds arrogant – one thing I am not.

Frank was with a woman he introduced as his girlfriend Pauline. Politely, I asked her to leave so that we could meet him on our own and we talked for a while, but it was all pretty strained and one-sided as he tried to explain his behaviour to us by saying Mum didn't let him visit. I didn't believe half of it – he was just trying to make himself look whiter than white. I'd have had more respect for him if he'd just told me he'd made a mistake and was sorry. We went for a pub lunch before he and Pauline came to see me perform in the matinee, and it was strange to think my biological father was out there somewhere in the audience, watching. I felt really self-conscious and probably tried too hard that day.

He came backstage after the show and we took a few photographs, then we politely hugged goodbye and I drove my sister back home to my parents' home in Bournemouth. Debbie sobbed all the way home, which I couldn't understand and had little sympathy for. At this point, I still hadn't realised that she felt the absence of Frank in our lives much more deeply than I'd imagined. I felt nothing – he was a stranger to me.

I found out later that Frank had been calling my agent, introducing himself as 'Amanda's dad' and asking questions about me. My agent thought they were talking to Dad, so they told him everything. When I heard this I contacted Frank and told him that I was happy to keep him posted, but asked him not to tell people he was my dad. He's not! With hindsight, Frank did me a favour. Missing out on the love he should have given us made me into the person that I am today. I am not bitter or sad, just disappointed that he only chose to come back into my life when I started to become 'famous' and not when I'd actually needed him. He has become the cliché celebrity dad.

Luckily for me, I have a dad who I love dearly. He and my mum decided that they couldn't afford any more children, so he sacrificed having children so that he could raise us as his own. I have no room in my life for another father but I've decided I'll keep in touch with Frank on a basic level. It will always be on my terms though.

Chapter 7

I Need Someone,
Older and Wiser . . .

The Sound of Music was booked for the summer season in my hometown of Bournemouth and so I arranged to move back in with my parents for a few weeks as a paying guest. It was here that I first discovered what it was to have a fan base – my mum. She was a very proud parent. All her guests were sent to see *The Sound of Music*, whether they wanted to or not. My friend and dresser Davina even had a T-shirt made for her which said, 'I am Liesl's Mum', which she wore to the show so that everyone she hadn't already told would know her connection to what she considered to be the biggest show in town.

As the summer season opened we – along with the casts and crews of all the other shows – were invited to an opening-night party in the Pavillion Theatre Bar. There was to be a huge welcome party for all the artists and there was a big buzz backstage as my fellow nuns swapped their habits for party frocks. I exchanged Liesl's prim little sailor suit for a white mini skirt Captain von Trapp would have blown his whistle at. (Lionel Blair, who was doing summer season there, still loves to tell me how young I was when he first met me. 'I remember, darling, you were a child.' (I was twenty-one.) 'And I said, "Amanda, darling, what would you like to drink?" And you said, "Gin and ice, darling." And I said, "Gin and ice, darling? Gin and ice, darling? You don't even want the tonic, darling?" And you said, "No, darling!"')

We began spending our nights off with the rest of the casts. This was when I was first introduced to Les Dennis. Les told me later that at first he thought I was loud, overconfident and a bit brash, which was probably true. I thought he was a bit of a miserable sod.

The more I got to know him, though, the more he surprised me. I always seemed to be on his team when we went bowling, and we used to have such a laugh. He wasn't the cheesy comic I'd expected him to be at all. He was good fun. He may not have been the youngest of the crowd in Bournemouth that year, and at thirty-nine he was almost sixteen years older than me. Even so, I felt like he needed mothering. He seemed sad, quiet and troubled and I instinctively wanted to help. He'd come up the hard way, via Butlin's and the northern club circuit. At twenty (in the year I turned three!), he'd won *New Faces* and married his childhood sweetheart Lynne. Then he'd worked a double act on *The Laughter Show* with comedian Dustin Gee but Dustin died of a heart attack in 1986 aged forty, leaving Les alone in the spotlight.

On our nights out, Les would confide in me. He told me how he'd lost both his parents young, moved to London from Liverpool, got married and had numerous affairs, as well as about his marriage break-up two years earlier and the guilt he felt at leaving his son Philip – who was just nine years younger than me.

He was pretty deep. He was having an on-off relationship with his girlfriend Sophie Aldred, who played Dr Who's assistant (it was currently off). I don't think I consciously fancied him at this stage. But he was charming, sweet, and very bright, and I was intrigued. We became increasingly close. Looking back, things were definitely building up. We had a karaoke evening for my friend's birthday and there was a lingering hug at the end, but at the time I think we were both just enjoying having found such a close friendship.

One night he had a party at the flat he was renting near the cliffs, not far from my mum's place at Alum Chine. It was a great party – Les is a brilliant host. Then all of a sudden he told everyone to carry on having fun but that he was going to bed. It hit me that he hadn't been enjoying himself at all, and I felt a lurch of pity for him, swiftly followed by disappointment that he was calling it a night.

I was on my way to the loo as he said his goodbyes and climbed the stairs to bed. We crossed on the landing and he came over to say goodnight. We were chatting happily and I jokingly asked him if he'd like me to tuck him in (I often speak without engaging my brain). But I am quite flirty by nature, and have always been very tactile, so I don't think Les thought he was any different from anyone else he had seen me with. I genuinely wanted to make sure he was okay and didn't want to think of him leaving his own party feeling sad and lonely. I found myself leaning over and kissing him goodnight. It was a strange thing to do, but yet it felt very right and natural. He was completely surprised. He kissed me back and then asked me out for dinner.

I left and went home to Mum's straight after. I remember walking home, a bit shocked at myself but thinking, 'Oh, that was nice, he's really nice.'

He and I dated the whole of that summer and it was so lovely and special. He properly wooed me – it was old-fashioned court-ing – and he was very romantic. My friend Emma Cooper – the singing nun – was the only one who knew, and she became our 'beard'. We called her the Red Herring. We spent days on the beach and on our nights off we'd all go to a gay nightclub called The Triangle that used to play a lot of Abba, as we both had a love of kitsch and this place appealed to us. Every time I walked in they'd play a disco version of *The Sound of Music*.

They were really fun times. And the more time I spent with Les, the more I liked him. Best of all, he seemed to *get* me. He had spoken so openly to me about his own problems that I felt able to talk to him about how much the split with GB still hurt me. Les had spent three years in therapy and could have been an analyst. He knew exactly what to say. He was older and wiser, just like the song I sang every night as Liesl in the show.

He said we were each other's teachers, and I loved that. I still do. Listening to his advice made me want the security of a relationship again and he made me feel safe. Before he came along I thought, 'I'm not going out there again because I just cause havoc, and my heart's bashed, and I can't take any more,' but something hap-pened with Les. I made a conscious decision that he was the right person for me to be with.

Falling for him was very different from anything I'd ever expe-rienced before. It was a slow burn, and felt very mature and important. We were friends first, who had deep and meaningful talks about proper subjects. He had lovely bluey-green eyes and was a true gent. He was very sweet and caring, and he was a grown-up. When I was with him, I felt like he could take care of anything. His experience meant our relationship worked on every level. And he made me laugh.

To try to prove to myself (and Les) that I was over my ex, I fixed Emma up with GB, telling her she'd be good for him. When they did end up together, she fell for GB hook, line and sinker and then he broke her heart too. I can't believe I did that to her or to myself. Looking back, it's bonkers but at the time it was just very painful.

Les helped me through that as well and taught me to accept that the memory of GB would torture me for years. The truth was that as I was letting go of GB I was slowly and surely falling in love with Les and I knew this was much more than a summer romance, that it was meaningful. From day one, though, I felt as if no one else understood us and that all eyes were on me for being with him. Les was a successful family entertainer and well liked by the public. As well as appearing in prime-time TV shows and end-of-the-pier farces, he'd been on the Christmas pantomime circuit for years. Everyone seemed to love him and he was often recognised in the street. I'd never experienced fame before.

As the summer ended, it was crunch time. Both our shows had finished their run and we didn't know what we were going to do about us. He kept telling me that it wouldn't work between us because of the age difference. He seemed fixated, even at the start, on the idea that he was too old for me, but as far as I was concerned I never really thought about it.

I felt as if we were in a strange kind of limbo, and so, with a heavy heart, I moved back to my flat in London. The bubble of our perfect summer had been burst and our relationship was left totally unresolved as Les flew off to Los Angeles for meetings. (Les had always wanted to make it in America, either as a comic or serious actor.) Meanwhile, I got a job in Boots the chemist, spraying perfume, auditioning for my next part and living off my earnings from *The Sound of Music*.

We missed each other madly and spoke every day on the phone but it was tough. I had no idea what the future held for either of us, and whether it would be together or apart, but all I knew was that what we had was special and that I missed him. A lot. I tried to focus on work, but all I could think about was when we would see each other again and for how long.

The time Les was away felt interminable, but in reality it was only a matter of weeks – long enough, however, for Les to decide that we were going to be together.

In November 1994, Les suggested I move in with him, to his converted railway workshop down a cobbled street in Archway, north London. Although I was sure about us, and knew this was what I wanted, it seemed like a big step so soon, and I asked for time to think about it. I wanted this to be right and wanted to be mature about it, but there was no doubt we were both committed.

Instead, we picked up where our summer romance had left off, but this time with a new depth of feeling and certainty about where we were headed. We spent every moment we could together, and it felt like such a huge wrench to be parted again a few months later. I saw Les off at King's Cross station on his train to Scotland, where he was booked to do panto in Edinburgh, and he wept (his emotions were always quite close to the surface!) and said, 'Please never leave me. I love you. This is it for me. Whatever happens with us we'll face it and we'll deal with it.' I felt the same, and once he was settled in Edinburgh, I visited whenever I could. His cast were a lot of fun and, best of all (from my point of view!), they liked and accepted me.

Les being away gave me time and space to think about his suggestion that I move in and I decided we were ready, so after his stint in Edinburgh that's exactly what I did. We bought a Cairn Terrier puppy and called him Nobbie. Andy Grainger had spotted him in a pet shop, so I rushed out and brought Nobbie home. We were now a little family, and it felt great.

Even so, I was careful from the start not to take advantage. I've always been fiercely independent, and I always paid my way and was often the one to treat Les. When Les left his wife Lynne after sixteen years, he was incredibly generous to her and to their son Philip and at that point financially, as well as emotionally, had to start again from scratch. He even lived in his car for a while. I'm all for child support but as a woman and a mother, I've never wanted to be the sort of woman to take advantage of a man and I never have. Despite his lucrative job hosting *Family Fortunes*, doing pantomime wasn't just a bit of fun for Les: it paid his maintenance and other bills.

I got to know Les better than I knew myself over the next few months. When he was at his best, he was great – usually after a glass or two of wine. Those first few months together were our happiest times. We were in love and I was so happy and relieved to be in what I regarded as my first adult relationship. We shared the same musical tastes, my friends and family got along well with him and most of the time he was good company.

But I was equally focused on our family life, and early on in our relationship I entertained Les's estranged family. He was from a working-class Liverpool background and had drifted away from them over the years – especially during his marriage to Lynne. I persuaded him to reconnect with them at a red-brick hotel in Liverpool one day, where I met his sisters Margaret and Mandy, his brother Ken and his Auntie Pat for the first time. 'Our Marg' was always very grateful and I was happy that Les had them back in his life.

Les never stopped working and business began to pick up for me too. My agent Patrick got me an audition for the role of

Carmen, a stallholder, in *EastEnders*. I appeared in five episodes, mainly as a sidekick to Ian Beale. It meant horribly early starts, but I loved it. At the time, I'd have killed to have my character developed further. (Against Patrick's advice, I would repeatedly fax slightly desperate suggestions to the director about what Carmen's surname might be, including 'Carmen Get Me' or 'Carmen Make Eyes at Me'.)

Whatever it was, Les always encouraged me, even if it meant I might be away from him for weeks at a time. He'd been in the business a lot longer than me and he understood that an actor has to go where the work is. So when I was offered a season at the English Theatre in Hamburg, Germany, playing Cecily Cardew in *The Importance of Being Earnest* (where my deportment lessons from Estelle Westcomb came in v. handy), he was genuinely happy for me.

He took me to the airport and held me close, and off I went, suitcase in hand, to a country where I didn't speak a word of the language. It didn't get much better, it was exciting but daunting. The theatre had been described as bijou in an art deco building, but was actually depressing and smelly, right next to two tandoori restaurants and a dentist. Added to this, the show was strange – not least because Lady Bracknell was played by a man. (Note this was meant to be serious theatre, not panto.) His name was Ginger Halstead and he was skinny as a whippet. He'd walk around backstage in his wig and padded knickers, with no top on, fag on the go. 'Do you think they know I'm a man, darling?' It was an eye-opener to me.

I was thrown into digs with the actress who played Gwendolen and became close friends with a lovely actor named Philip Goodhew. He and I clung to each other for mutual support and spent all our time together. To top it all off, we got burgled.

Les would fly to Germany for a few days whenever he could and

I lived for those visits. He and Philip got on really well, and we always had a ball. Then Les took a short break with Andy Grainger. Les would call me every now and again but, in the days before mobiles, we were never able to chat for long. It was so hard as I missed him terribly. He felt so far away.

My play hadn't even started and we were still in the middle of rehearsals one day in June when we were interrupted by the company manager, telling me I had a phone call from Les. We were rehearsing the first scene of the second act – a big scene for me, full of double entendres and mistaken identity, where my character is proposed to by someone she believes is someone else.

'Oh, sorry about that,' I said, embarrassed to have been the cause of the stop mid-scene. 'Can you ask him to call back later?'

'But he insisted I put him through!' the manager told me rather crossly in front of everyone. 'He said it was urgent.'

Red-faced, and by now a bit worried (overseas calls were expensive and I wondered what on earth could be so important that he would interrupt his break and mine to make one), I asked for some time out and hurried to take the call. But far from a man frantically trying to deal with an emergency, I was greeted, on the other end of the line, by a man who'd clearly had a long (and very boozy) lunch. The ship-to-shore connection wasn't great as it was, and then he started rambling on about dates and proposals. I thought he was suggesting some social event for when he got back.

'Can we talk about this some other time?'

There was a time delay and the line crackled back at me. This time I could only make out the word 'proposal'.

'Yes, Les!' I said, getting annoyed now. 'That's the bit I'm rehearsing now!'

The line crackled more indignantly this time and suddenly his voice was crystal clear. 'I'm proposing to you!'

I was stunned. We were on a £12 a minute ship line complete with satellite delay and interference – hardly the most romantic way for Les to ask me to be his wife.

In the end, I laughed. 'Les, are you asking me to marry you?'

'Yes! I mean, I'm in a phone box on a ship!'

'Are you serious? You've been drinking . . .'

'Absolutely.'

There was a long pause as I held my breath and tried to take in what this meant. I felt giddy with happiness.

'Amanda?'

'Yes, I mean, yes!'

I went back into the rehearsals in a daze and announced to the rest of the cast that I was engaged. Everyone was happy for me, especially Philip Goodhew. I couldn't quite believe it – we were getting married.

It was amazing. I was so excited. Les flew out to join me as soon as he could and we went on a ring-shopping trip. I chose a modest, understated gold band with a pretty little diamond. (I deliberately didn't pick a blinger. Even at that happy moment I was second-guessing what others would think and how everything would be judged.) We went for a romantic stroll along the banks of the River Alster so that he could find the perfect spot to give it to me.

After a few minutes a swan paddled past us. I thought that was lovely, and it made us both smile. Then a second, dead, swan floated past. Swans mate for life, and this poor specimen was obviously its other half. It kind of took the shine off the moment.

I thought, 'Don't see that as symbolic.'

Chapter 8

Our Survey Said . . .

I've always loved an empty theatre. It's something about the discarded props and scenery. You can almost smell the history. During a run, I like to get there in time to stand on the stage and soak up the atmosphere. I played Elaine Harper in a national touring production of *Arsenic and Old Lace*, with Tom Baker, Josephine Tewson, Steven Pacey and Patsy Byrne, including a stint at the Theatre Royal, Bath, one of the most beautiful in Britain. Theatres are superstitious places and actors are notoriously superstitious too. Bath theatre has a legend that if an actor sees a butterfly inside, either your show will be a success or you'll make it in the business. (There is some logic to this – in the old days shows were lit by candles and that warmed the butterfly pupae to life. The candles were only lit if an audience was in, so a butterfly came to represent good luck.)

One day in Bath I arrived early as normal and, backstage, I came across an old chest that I hadn't noticed before. Without thinking

I lifted the lid and a butterfly flew out – a big, brightly coloured butterfly which fluttered around my head for a while before flying up into the gods. I was gobsmacked and my heart was pumping with adrenaline. It felt like a real movie moment for me – I was excited and utterly amazed, but thought no-one would believe me.

After this, Les and I bought a new house in Highgate and once we'd revamped it, we filled it with people. Les was welcoming and generous to my friends – Jason, Jane, my sister Debbie – and my friend Emma 'the nun' even moved in with us for a while. After her relationship with GB ended I'd fixed her up with Andy Grainger, so the four of us had even more laughs together.

I was quite domesticated back then and cooked all the time (which Chris finds hard to believe now), but Les was the real gourmet. He knows so much about food and fine wine and to my twenty-three-year-old self he seemed so cultured, sophisticated and worldly-wise.

When my tour ended, Les took me to Norfolk, a place he loved. I fell in love with it too – it's so flat and wild, with vast open skies. I had never seen anywhere like that in my life before and I felt instantly at home, and able to breathe and relax. We stayed at The Hoste Arms in Burnham Market. The owner, Paul Whittome, was a good friend of Les's, and was always so welcoming. Paul was a larger-than-life character who was very theatrical, funny and devoted to his wife Jeanne. He called our dog 'Snobby' because he claimed he had delusions of grandeur. (It's true! He had a real air about him. He would never dream of rolling in poo or anything like that!) Paul never judged Les and me – he treated us as equals and I loved him for that.

That Christmas Les and I worked together for the first time, in *Aladdin* in Glasgow. I played Princess So Shy (big stretch!).

We set the date for our wedding – 4 June 1995 – which gave us

Me being fitted for my first sheepskin

My first Pedi

Me with my sister Debbie. 'Mum, what am I supposed to do with this?'

Me practising my *Saturday Night Fever* moves

Debbie's christening on Frank's Naval Ship. Mum actually left her on-board by mistake! (L–R: Me and Mum, Vicar, Nanny with Debs, Papa and Frank)

My first *FHM* shoot

Mum, Debbie, Nanny and Me in my Grandad's (Papa) pants!

Using my Portaloo

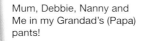

Waiting for a free kick! (L–R: Maternal Great Grandmother, Nanny, Mum, Debbie and me)

Me and Debs . . . Sherlock and Watson

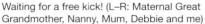

There wasn't a day when I didn't hurt my knees on that pole!

Football fans. With our dog Elsa in our Brian Clough green polo necks – my Dad took his look too far!

Christmas Day, too cold to ride them outside!

My first puppet show (I'm behind the expensive blanket), with a captive audience . . . I locked the back gate!

Putting on a brave face with scary Chucky Doll!

Me and Debs on the way to Devon for holiday, our modesty protected!

Rare pic of first wedding! (L–R: Debbie, Me, Eric Austin and Jamie)

Looking slightly bewildered from a fresh bump on head in the playground

The human slot machine!

Mum's Wedding to Les.
L–R back row: Cousin Bridgett,
Uncle Winston (sporting an aerial),
Auntie Vivienne, Nanny, Mum, Les.
Front row: Debbie and Me

My Mum's attempt at being a Mafia Boss!

Me and Debs outside Papa's shed, the 'Daisy Chain Café' (or cruise liner – weather dependent!)

Always first to the bar! Me with Mr Sawyer at Bishop's Waltham Gym Club, Elite Squad

Said, very enthusiastic looking, Gym Club!

Me and school BF Amanda Loveday. My t-shirt reads 'Neil is a really amazing guy right?' How prophetic!

Papa, Me and Nanny hanging out in . . . STROUD!

Me on keys with a Wham inspired haircut!

Bishops Waltham Little Theatre members –
Me showing Ye Olde Right Leg in authentic
Victorian towelling sock wear

Me and my puss, Silvester

Very last day of school
(L–R: Vik, Wendy Hopkins,
Me, Lucy Abraham, Clare
Buckler, Kirsty Rollinson,
Luci Matthews)

Dracula spectacular in a dress Mum had specially made me – I'm clearly questioning the authenticity of my leading man's moustache

Typical Saturday night, live from our lounge

Maybe I was considering jumping off? Sporting yet another astounding haircut

Me singing for my supper at my parents 'Chase Lodge' guest house

Having a family dinner before I left Bournemouth to attend Mountview Theatre School

six months to plan. We couldn't wait for the big day. All of our friends and family could see we were in love. Even Jane, who years later admitted that she was initially baffled as to why I, straight out of drama school and with so much ambition, wanted to get embroiled not only in the institution of marriage (she considered herself a feminist!) but also to a much older man. She got to know the homely, family-orientated side of me and understood that I had always wanted those things from a very early age. Les and I provided those things for each other and, at the time we married, I had no doubts we were in love and we knew we were doing the right thing. Our wedding day was one of the happiest of my life.

I recently unwrapped my wedding dress again, nearly twenty years on, and when I pulled it out of the chest, wrapped in tissue paper with bags of lavender, I felt quite emotional. I'd been so full of hope the day I wore it. I bought it from Mirror Mirror in Crouch End just as I'd always planned, only my bridegroom turned out to be Les, not GB. It was sleeveless white satin, beaded, with a square neckline and pleats and the back had a full cathedral train. I wore a pearl tiara and long white satin gloves, and carried a bouquet of yellow roses. I was also wafer thin and looked so young. I had four bridesmaids: Jane, Emma Cooper, Tamsin Mallinder (a friend from Mountview) and my sister Debbie.

The ceremony was at the United Reform Church in Bournemouth – the only church we could find that would perform the marriage because of Les's divorce. It was also big enough for our 120 guests, mostly family and friends. It was very camp. Les's son Philip was his best man. Nobbie, our dog, was an honoured guest and wore a ribbon for my 'something blue'. My dad gave me away – it never even occurred to me to invite Frank. Of course, the newspapers found him anyway and he gave them the predictable 'I can't believe I'm not invited to my own daughter's wedding' story. On the day I was warned to keep a lookout in case Frank was lurking in the background somewhere. It made me really anxious – I was terrified it would upset Mum and my nan. Thankfully none of us ever saw him and if he was somewhere watching, we weren't aware and there were no unpleasant scenes.

As Dad and I were getting ready to leave Chase Lodge for the church, he surprised me with a horse and carriage. I was thrilled. As we were about to step up into it, he asked me the traditional question, 'Do you need to talk about anything before we go, lover?'

'No,' I told him honestly. 'I want this, Dad.'

He nodded and said, 'Let's do it then!'

Thanks to the combination of the photographer's demands and the slower pace of the horse and carriage, I ended up being forty minutes late to my own wedding. (In the event, it was just as well because Jason got stuck on a broken-down train and almost didn't make it.) At the church, whilst Les fretted that I'd changed my mind, Lionel Blair stood up in front of the guests and hosted a riotous game of *Give Us a Clue*. It's probably the first time a wedding congregation has been sad to see the bride arrive.

At the reception, at Rhinefield House Hotel in the New Forest, Dad gave a really funny speech and, rather than the usual bawdy best man's affair, my new stepson Philip gave a sweet speech which my mum typed out for him. Taking on a teenager had turned out to be easier than I'd thought it would be – Philip and I got on from the start and were good friends with an easy relationship. Since the divorce, Philip's mother had been quite overprotective and his relationship with Les had been strained, mainly revolving around Sunday visits to the movies where they couldn't communicate or talk things through, but I wanted us to be part of his life and encouraged Les to talk to him more and do more interactive things with him.

Two days after the wedding, Les and I flew off to Jumby Bay in Antigua for our honeymoon. It was so romantic. On holiday I love to lie on a sun lounger or beach, read a book. I don't like drinking at lunchtime because it makes me sleepy, but Les enjoyed wine with lunch, followed by a power nap. This habit carried on through our married life. My mum used to say to me, 'If you have children, Amanda, Les can't disappear off for the afternoon and sleep.' But at the time I never complained (he'd always be much more cheerful afterwards!). Our holidays together were our happiest times and, over the next few years, we had some great ones. I took him to the George V in Paris and on a three-day cycling and wine-tasting tour of the Chambertin region of France. We spent the whole time drunkenly riding bikes around the vineyards! But my best memories of my marriage to Les are all in Tuscany, where we rented fabulous places near Montepulciano and had great holidays with and without friends. Florence is my favourite city and we'd stay up in the hills near by, sampling fine wines in between trips into the city. It all felt very grown up.

I looked grown up, too. When I flick back through photos of me then I look so much older than my years – dressed in suits and blouses with scarves and matching accessories. When I was with GB I'd worn quirky outfits. With Les, I looked like an air hostess. I think I did it to make myself seem older than I was – to make myself fit in. I looked so much like my mother, but I was trying to match Les.

That summer, Les was booked for a 16-week season at the end of Blackpool North Pier in a show also starring Su Pollard and Roy Walker. Despite working hard at auditions, I had no work on and so, eager to be a good wife, I went too, with Nobbie. We stayed in a big old house that I nicknamed The Pink Palace and I invited Jason and his partner Taro up to stay. The four of us went to some of the famous drag clubs there, including The Flying Handbag and Funny Girls. We took Les on the Big One rollercoaster but he was not a happy bunny. Jason has a photo of us on that which he vows never to destroy as it still makes him laugh.

Determined to be the perfect wife, I threw myself into supporting Les and spent a lot of time backstage, soaking up the atmosphere.

During one show, Les farted next to Roy Walker. Roy went mental, stormed off stage and came into the Green Room where I was sat peacefully enjoying a cup of tea. Les came in, Roy picked up the coffee table (which was big) and charged round after him with it, shouting, 'I can't believe you're so unprofessional! You farted, you farted!' Su ran in, topless and bottomless save for a pair of American Tan tights pulled up to her breasts, shouting, 'Stop! Stop, Roy!' She stood next to me and I came face to face with her beaver – she'd obviously forgotten to put her knickers on in her panic trying to break up the fight. It's moments like this I wish I had my camera! Roy refused to talk to Les for a week and avoided eye contact with him on stage, before finally buying him a book to say sorry.

I loved being able to throw myself into my new role as Les's wife, but the flip side was that the more time I spent fixing his life, the more I began to feel consumed by it. I was so happy that I didn't notice it to begin with, but after a while I realised I was not only having to fight against other talent to get the roles I wanted – I was also having to battle the blonde bimbo persona the business had created for me after my marriage. As a result I had to prove myself more and had to fight even harder for all the roles I got auditions for. The irony is that being with Les didn't give me the leg-up that people thought it did. It actually made it harder for me during the early days of our marriage. There was so much snobbery in the TV industry, I wanted to prove to myself and others who I really was and what I was really capable of.

Then, out of the blue, my Hamburg friend Philip Goodhew offered me a small part in a feature film – a black comedy – he'd written called *Intimate Relations*. He'd sent it to Julie Walters and, to his amazement, she had agreed to do it with him as director. I played a single girl named Pamela. I suggested Philip offer Les a part too. (Les wanted to do straight acting, and Patrick says I was always looking for opportunities and suggesting jobs for him.) He played Rupert Graves' brother in a few scenes. We filmed it in Abergavenny, Wales, and Les was so keen not to miss out on his first feature film that he hired a helicopter to fly him to the location between his Blackpool shows.

Around then, Les suggested we buy our own little retreat in Norfolk. My reply was obviously 'Yes!', but with the stipulation we got something 'really small and cosy'. I wanted us to have something homely, not overly grand. Finding the right place turned out to be less straightforward than I'd thought, but after some hopeless searching we were sent the details of a house near Burnham Market. Debbie and I went to see it at Easter, and as soon as we started driving down the track, past a big white farm, I knew it was the one. We rounded the bend to see a semi-detached red-brick workers' cottage. 'This is perfect!' I took one look at the place and offered the asking price.

Our new next-door neighbours Bob and Pat were Norfolk born and bred and we loved them. They had cats and a coal fire and kept chickens (Pat even sounded a bit like a chicken when she talked). She was often stuck in a chair in their little kitchen with a bad hip but enjoyed making up rude songs about 'bums and tits' while Bob died of embarrassment. They treated us like royalty because they were huge fans of *Family Fortunes* and if she could, Pat would have virtually stood to attention every time she saw Les.

The cottage wasn't at all fancy. It had three bedrooms with a downstairs bathroom and the tiniest kitchen with an old-fashioned oven and a butler's sink. There was an outhouse complete with a toilet, sink and cobwebs. We loved that house so much that we drove up from London at least twice a month to stay there and always had breaks in it at Christmas and Easter. We'd take great long hikes across the fields and have picnics in the countryside or on the beach, and we'd even collect eggs from under the bushes in the garden laid by next-door's chickens. My nan and Papa came to stay, and my parents and my sister. On our first New Year's Eve we crammed fourteen people in. Les made lamb stew and we drunkenly let off fireworks at midnight. Sometimes I'd go on my own just to be alone. Other times I might take a girlfriend. Mostly, I'd go with Les. We were at that little cottage through good times and bad.

My career in theatre was now going strong, but I was desperate to do more TV so I changed agent after five years. I picked Amanda Howard, who got me five auditions in my first week (although to be fair Patrick had nominated me for two of them). After months of tumbleweed, it seemed suddenly every one I went for I seemed to get. I was on the phone to my mum constantly telling her, 'I'm going to be in *The Bill*!' or, 'I landed a part in a show called *Thief Takers*!' She was thrilled, as was I!

Les was encouraging, but I was conscious his own acting ambitions weren't being fulfilled in the same way. As my job offers started to come in, he began to joke about the Judy Garland movie *A Star is Born* in which the young wife becomes famous while her husband's star wanes. Again, his morbid obsession with the age difference between us surfaced and his mood became very black. 'That'll be us one day,' he said glumly.

I was torn between wanting to make him feel better and realising my long-held ambitions. A fulfilled wife would be better placed to help him fight his demons, I reasoned. As always, I found a one-liner to diffuse his mood. 'Well, please don't run into the sea the way James Mason did in the end, okay? Apart from anything else, I'll freeze my bloody tits off trying to save you!'

Chapter 9

Les Misérables

I'm not sure why buzzers have played such a huge part in my life. Now, of course, there are the *Britain's Got Talent* buzzers which I love but one of the things that started off making me laugh but then really got on my nerves the whole time I was married to Les was that, wherever we went, we were followed round by the *Family Fortunes* buzzer noise. People would make that noise whenever they saw Les – it's actually quite a negative noise and it made him depressed. Throughout our relationship the spectre of the life he had before we met – his wife Lynne, his son, his career – loomed large, and it always seemed that our relationship was of less importance to outsiders, as well as to Les himself. He'd been very under the thumb during his first marriage and this dynamic continued through the divorce and into our marriage, too.

At a celebration dinner for Russ Abbot's *This is Your Life* show, for example, which many of our close friends were invited to, Les was placed on the 'top table' with his ex-wife Lynne whilst I was shoved on a table at the back with the kids, even though they had been divorced for nearly six years and we'd been together for three! It felt very pointed and deliberate, and made me feel very small, like I had been sidelined in favour of Lynne – especially when Les failed to stick up for me. If that happened now, Chris would make a point of saying, 'Amanda should be with me', but Les said nothing. In fact, if that happened now I would say something, but back then I was so young and gauche. I didn't want to make a fuss, or upset Les. Instead, I made up a story that I had to leave early because my mole was hurting! (It was true – I had just had a mole removed – but mostly I was too humiliated to stay.)

As an isolated incident this might not have rankled so much, but right from the start Lynne's presence infiltrated nearly every area of our marriage. She was a huge defining force and all too often my existence came a poor second to her wants and needs. Every week, Les and I would go to pick Phillip up from Lynne's house. I wasn't allowed in, so I stayed in the car. (I can see that it might have felt odd for her to begin with and I tried to be understanding, but I wasn't the first woman Les had been with since they'd split and when Les and I met they had been divorced for two years. However the ban continued way into our marriage! I used to say to Les, 'One day, she'll come out and she'll say I'm allowed in, and I hope I have the balls to say, "Bugger off, I'm quite happy sitting here, thanks."' Eventually, after about five years, I was finally allowed in – and no, I didn't say it: I didn't have the balls!)

Even after their divorce, Les felt he had to get her a lavish Christmas present. Everything had to be jewellery. As it had been this way throughout our relationship, I never questioned it, until one year, sick of seeing him stress out over it, I said to him,

'Remember, it only has to be a token, Les,' so he found her an attractive but unassuming watch. That was immediately sent back; it wasn't good enough. But buoyed by feeling a little more in control of her, and determined to stick with it, the next time he bought her a book or something. Not wanting to see him upset or make relations any worse between them, I naively tried to help out and for her birthday I found this pretty vanity mirror with two little drawers under it. Again, that came back. She said, 'It's very feminine, Les. I can tell that Amanda's picked it, and it's not for me.' That time, Les himself said, 'Okay, don't have it then.' And so he put it in our own house in Norfolk instead!

I managed to keep my next experience of *This is Your Life* fairly Lynne-free as I helped secretly organise Les's show. We arranged for Michael Aspel to surprise Les during a *Family Fortunes* show. All of Les's friends, family and colleagues, past and present, were there.

It was while I was organising this that I got my first big TV break (in a Channel 5 launch comedy sketch show *We Know Where You Live*). I was so excited, not only about the project but the people I'd be working with – Simon Pegg, Fiona Allen and Sanjeev Bhaskar. Simon Pegg and I became really close, partly because he came from Gloucester and his mum lived just up the road from my nan, but mainly because we had the same sense of humour.

This led to more auditions – like the part of Mel, Caroline Quentin's receptionist in a new sitcom *Kiss Me Kate*, but they told my agent they were looking for someone who was more quirky than me. However they called me back, and after the initial disappointment of thinking that I wasn't in the running, I started to think I might have a chance.

I went for about four different auditions in total. With each one I was feeling a little bit more positive, but trying so hard not to get my hopes up. I didn't tell anyone, either – I didn't want to jinx it! After each one, I'd come home and wait for a phone call from a guy called Nick Simmonds. The suspense was almost unbearable! In the end, fate worked in my favour in the shape of Darren Boyd. He changed the role that he had auditioned for so much that our characters worked better with him, as he was younger than the role was initially written for, and I got the part! I'll never forget the day I got the phone call. We were at home in Highgate with Andy Grainger and his new wife Ruby. It was a huge thing, and we had a champagne barbecue to celebrate. It was major – absolutely a dream come true.

All of the three series were filmed at Carlton Studios in Nottingham. We rehearsed all week, had the dress rehearsal on a Thursday and filmed on the Friday in front of a live audience before driving back to our hotel. Caroline had a posh suite, so I'd go round to hers in my PJs for pasta nights, to drink wine and watch telly. It was fun, but also reassuring to know I had someone like her as a friend and support.

Caroline wasn't just a good friend, she became a huge inspiration for me. She's so professional: she's never late, knows everybody's names on set and always chats with all the crew. She showed me how empowering women could be without being intimidating – when she was working on *Men Behaving Badly,* she refused point-blank to carry on unless they paid her and Leslie Ash the same as her male co-stars. When I first met her she was reeling from her divorce from comedian Paul Merton but still seemed like she wasn't frightened of anything. (On the first day she told me to shut up when I was chatting away to someone in the background. I didn't do that again!)

By the second series of *Kiss Me Kate,* Caroline was seeing Sam, a runner on another show she was in called *Jonathan Creek,* and one day she swore me to secrecy and told me she thought she was pregnant. Conspiratorially, we got her a test and I was the first to know when it came up positive. It was a very special moment – she was so happy. She couldn't stop telling everyone, but then wondered how everyone knew. It was all her and her excitement!

Things were looking up for Les workwise too, when he got his first dramatic stage role in the David Hare play *Skylight* at The Watermill Theatre in Newbury. No one was more delighted than me, and he was brilliant in it. He'd never been taken seriously as an actor before and I was thrilled someone had finally given him a chance. When our schedules didn't clash, he and I began to be invited out to events and photographed as a 'showbiz couple'.

We loved our Highgate home but we decided it was time to upgrade and we found a property in a tree-lined square in my old stomping ground of Primrose Hill. It had six floors and took what seemed like forever to renovate. We had a great offer on our previous house, so we sold and rented a little furnished one-bedroom basement flat while the work was being done. It turned out to be one of the nicest things we ever did. We put all our furniture in storage and lived really simply again, with throws on the rented sofas, TV dinners and students living above us. It was a complete contrast to what was going on in our careers, and those were some of the happiest months of our whole marriage.

When the house was finished, though, the tempo went up again and our home became the central party destination for our family and friends. Les really got into cooking in his brand-new kitchen and I was feeling more confident and loved my role as his party co-host. We threw dinners around our massive Victorian dining table (until one night when Vic Reeves danced on it and broke it . . .!) and had all-night parties almost every week. It was always an eclectic crowd – at any one time we might have TV execs sharing pudding with a make-up artist, colleagues from my latest productions or friends from my drama school days plus random neighbours and relatives. Andy Grainger and his new wife Ruby came round for their tea most nights and we had daft, lovely times with them both. We were incredibly sociable and suddenly were hardly ever on our own.

Les had always been prone to mood swings and moments of intense introspection, but I'd been able to gently coax him out of them, or find a way to cheer him up. Now, these moments seemed more frequent – or maybe I was just noticing them more – and I was shocked not only by how often he had them, but by the depth of the dark side of Les's personality that was starting to appear. In the mornings, I would wake up before him and watch him sleeping. Seeing him so peaceful, I'd wonder where these lows came from, and what kind of day we'd have. It all depended on his frame of mind, and although I'm not confrontational and will do anything to avoid an argument, I became less inclined to put up with his anger management issues. Anyway, he was a master of making something out of nothing to pick a fight.

So we began to row, until it seemed he felt more comfortable being in an argument than when everything was normal. Whenever we fell out, he'd get very melodramatic and tell me to leave. He'd say I was 'too good' for him, or 'too young'. He was like a stuck record. He'd flare up over something insignificant and then bait me with, 'Go on, leave me! You will anyway!' For me, this was more than unsettling. I was just finding my feet in one area of my life and the rug was being pulled from under them in another. It seemed that he was trying to wear me down and giving me a licence to go.

When the rows got out of hand, though, I would take on the role of pacifier again and try to diffuse the situation by making him laugh, which wasn't easy – when Les lost his temper, his blood pressure would rise and he'd get pinker and pinker in the face until he looked like Piglet from *Winnie the Pooh*, which became his nickname. One day he lost his temper over nothing and hurled his cup of coffee at the ceiling. We both sat in stunned silence, watching it drip down. As usual, I tried a one-liner. 'I think I can see the face of Jesus appearing up there.'

It takes a lot for me to snap and generally I would keep calm, but one evening I really lost it. It must have been summer, as Les had shorts on. During dinner, he tipped a full bowl of soup upside down on the table, then picked up an umbrella and smashed a beautiful dried-flower arrangement that framed an archway in one of the doors. I went into the kitchen to calm down, picked up a saucepan lid and said, 'I have had enough!' I got the lid, chased him out of the room and panned him all the way up the stairs. With every step, I'd whack him on the leg. By the time he got to the top he was laughing, but later that night when he was cleaning his teeth he had half moons all the way up his leg!

I'd passed my driving test the week before our wedding and after a lot of our rows (as soon as I could escape) I would drive up the A1 to Scratchwood services to have a cup of tea and calm down before I went back. I always did go back, though – I really wanted our marriage to work. I'd have put up with any amount of crap to make that happen (and I did!). He'd always make it up to me the next day – usually with a meal out or a huge bunch of flowers – but the self-pity that had first made me want to mother him now sometimes threatened to overwhelm us both.

If Les wanted a row, he'd have it, no matter where we were, or who we were with. Mum and Dad came to stay with us during the summer and Mum and I went out shopping. We were only about ten minutes late coming home, but Les just lost it. He started taking all the pictures off the wall and hurling them across the room. I was confused, and embarrassed. This wasn't how wedded bliss was meant to be and I would never have wanted Mum to see that.

But as it turned out, it was not the only occasion. Les and I spent a lot of time with Mum and Dad – he was a real family man – and so they got to know this side of him very well. Mum and Dad moved to Devon and during our first visit Les, predictably, started a row. Mum, as she always would do, must have taken my side over what-ever it was about, and as she and Nan walked off down the lane on their way to church, Les opened a window and shouted, 'Fuck off! Fuck off, then!' (Mum was devastated – she'd really wanted to make a good impression on the neighbours, and there was TV's Les Dennis screaming obscenities out the window.)

Whereas our marriage had always been full of happy times with close friends, these occasions now became the source of even more upset, and Les would often take offence at something and go off in a big huff. Like the time Andy and Ruby joined us at the beach and we were all playing cricket. It was lovely weather and a fun game, and just when we were all having a brilliant time, Andy out-bat Les, which Les took to heart, and he stomped off up the cliff like a six year-old. All we could do was stand and watch him march sulkily over the horizon.

The worst row, though, was in a restaurant in Soho with friends one night when he kicked me under the table and called me a 'cunt'. I told him I was leaving him and went outside, where he tried to stop me. A group of men on the other side of the road came rushing over to rescue me because they thought I was in danger. Then I got in the car anyway and drove all the way back to Bournemouth with my mum and my nan. He turned up at their house the next day, crying in my mum's lap and saying he was sorry and had no idea why he'd lost it.

I can honestly say I found it heartbreaking. I was bereft, it was killing me. When I look back, it seems clear to me that Les – consciously or subconsciously – was intent on sabotaging our marriage through his volatile behaviour. By his own admission, Les has now said he has struggled with depression. During our relationship I was blissfully unaware of this. It was only as time went on that I began to realise just now hard that is – both for the person suffering and the people around them. But at the time I was very much in love with the 'normal' side of him (as my mum says, 'He was a good chap really'), and it all happened so gradually that it took a long time to see how this other side was making our lives together a misery. We had so much going for us, after all, that in my role as marriage peacemaker and Les-'fixer', it was easier to focus on the positives – I threw myself into my work.

And there was so much else going on to keep me positive. I was offered one of my best ever parts – Miss Titley the teacher in the new sitcom *The Grimleys*. It was set in Dudley in the Seventies and shot in a real school, during the summer holidays.

It was in Manchester that I first met make-up artist Jess Taylor – she's become one of my closest friends and I've taken her with me to almost every job since. I call her 'Spirit Level' because she's the most grounded person I know. Before the first script readthrough, she had no idea who I was (one of the crew told her I was 'that bird who's married to Les Dennis'), but she said I was so vulgar that she knew we'd be friends straight away. When Les came to visit me on set with Nobbie, she was surprised by how quiet and shy he was – she says now he was 'always on the back foot'.

On and off, I had three years up there in Manchester staying at the Victoria & Albert Hotel opposite Granada TV studios and partying with the *Grimleys* crew. *Cracker, Coronation Street* and *Loose Women* were all filming at the studios at the same time and every night the bar would be full of people I knew. If you weren't in your room learning your lines for the next day, there'd always be someone to have a drink with.

Scripts were sent direct to the hotel by producer Spencer Campbell and one night I read to the end of the script and saw that my character got hit and killed by an ambulance. I couldn't believe it. In fact, I think I actually cried! No one had warned me that was going to happen, and I was totally gutted. I was straight on the phone – I rang my agent, the producers, the writer, everyone! – saying, 'What's going on, I am contracted until blah, they can't do this to me!' Several calls later, there was, it turned out, no need to panic. It was their sick idea of a joke! (But I got my own back via a newspaper column I was writing at the time, standing in for someone in the holidays, and put a 'before' and 'after' picture of Spencer in the paper. His 'before' pic was from the Seventies and his hair inspiration I can only assume came from Brian May. He opened a national newspaper and his embarrassing photo was there for all the world to see. Ha!)

Things were going better than I could have hoped in my career, but I couldn't let myself relax about it. Nor did I lose my drive to do more, be better, go further. I kept plugging away for new parts and pushing for more work. I was asked to be a guest on *Goodness Gracious Me* and I appeared in early episodes of cult show *Smack the Pony* for Channel 4. I helped write some of it too and they wanted me to do the whole series, but it wasn't really me. (I'm a traditionalist. I like a punchline!) Of course, it then went on to win an Emmy – what did I know.

The only downside of all this work was all the travelling it involved. In fact, I was away so much that coming home started to feel odd. It began to dawn on me that maybe it wasn't the place that was wrong, but the person. Home is where the heart is, after all – and although I was still very much in love with Les, home wasn't the nurturing, calm, loving place I wanted it to be.

Les would come and visit me between his own gigs, often with Andy and Ruby. In fact, Ruby and Les were both in an episode of *The Grimleys*! Ruby then appeared in several more as Miss Thing. The most time that Les and I spent alone together were on holidays abroad or weekends in Norfolk, and I was finding new ways to handle Les's tantrums – or avoid them altogether. One way to cheer him up was to take him shopping for the house – he was never happier than when he was buying things for it. But where I tried to manage his moods, Mum had no such patience and he and she still clashed frequently because she didn't like his 'petulance'. Whenever the two of them were in the same room they'd both vie for my attention – it was exhausting. I constantly had to tell him to not be so clingy with me when Mum was around.

Not only that, but the age difference was actually beginning to affect our relationship for the first time, rather than just in Les's head. Where he'd once been really spirited and full of fun, now he became a miserable old heavyweight. No amount of joy, money, friends or even me seemed to be able to pull him out of it. He was still hosting *Family Fortunes*, doing the odd play and filling his summers with end-of-the-pier shows as well as pantos, but when he saw the variety of the work that I was getting, he became obsessed about his own acting career to the point that it was all he ever talked about.

Les's agent Mike was the only person other than me who could snap Les out of the darkness, usually by telling him how much money he was earning and reminding him he had nothing to worry about. He used to jokingly call Les and me 'Burton and Taylor', because he thought Les was deluded in wanting to become a serious actor. When Les was in one of his black moods, I'd call Mike up and plead with him to get him out of the house and give him a pep talk.

Noddy Holder, who played music teacher Neville Holder, was another amazing sounding board for me. He was so kind and sweet – he frequently gave me a shoulder to moan on, although he eventually told me I should leave Les if neither of us was happy. That was the last thing I wanted to hear right then. I couldn't – I loved him, and I knew a part of me always would. We were good together; we were a team. And anyway, I am a fighter!

After seven years together, Les was a good husband and we still had some great times, even if I felt as if I was walking on eggshells much of the time. We had our beloved Nobbie dog. We had beautiful homes and great friends with whom we'd have hilarious times if Les was happy.

So, I tried even harder to fix things. We added a second dog, Fudge, to our little pack. He was mixed race, part Jack Russell and part Yorkshire Terrier. Les spotted him tied up in the basement of a house and rescued him, and little Fudge arrived to terrorise Nobbie, to destroy my sunglasses and bite the noses off my teddy bears. In my head I was determined to work at my marriage like I'd worked at my career. That had paid off, after all. Luck had undoubtedly played a part in my success, but it was more down to my sheer bloody-minded determination. I resolved to apply the same approach to my marriage.

What could possibly go wrong?

Chapter 10

Me Behaving Badly

When the first episode of *Kiss Me Kate* went out on the telly, Caroline Quentin told me that she had held a party in her Soho flat for her friends and invited her *Men Behaving Badly* co-star Neil Morrissey over to see it. She told me afterwards that when I came on the screen he said, 'Who's that?' She replied, 'That's married.'

A few months later, I was asked to audition for a two-part comedy drama for the BBC called *Happy Birthday Shakespeare*. Produced by Gareth Neame, who went on to win numerous Emmys and Golden Globes (and to produce *Downton Abbey*), it was a bittersweet story about unhappily married coach driver Will Green. Over the course of a coach tour around Britain, Will gradually fell for his tour guide Alice. It was a black comedy, so I was thrilled when I got the part of Alice. The part of Will went to Neil Morrissey, which didn't really mean an awful lot to me. Neil and I had never met, and Caroline's story was the only thing I knew about him other than his previous roles.

We got on very well from the start. During filming, I was just one of the lads. During lunch breaks, rather than sit in the van with the other actors, I'd go down to the pub with the sparks, the crew and Neil. Neil was ten years older than me and was dating Rachel Weisz. He was funny and incredibly easy to talk to – very charming, lovely and not initially flirtatious. But there was a dark side to him, too: he thinks he's an intellectual with quite a militant streak and could be a bit chippy. (He never did anything a minute before his union-regulated break was over!) He had a very unsettling upbringing which makes him vulnerable and childlike. A new set of problems to solve . . .

One of my earliest scenes with Neil involved some filming at Stonehenge. We were allowed to get close to the stones, so it felt very special, if cold! It was a bitter November day and I was wearing really flimsy clothes. I was bloody freezing! While I stood there, teeth chattering, Neil was to one side waiting for his cue, all wrapped up in a big Puffa jacket. When he saw me shivering he shouted my name and opened up his coat, as if to invite me in. It was totally innocent – or so I thought. He was almost a foot taller than me and it was toasty in there! But it was undoubtedly then that things changed. That's when a spark happened. Suddenly there was a tension. (I remember saying to Neil, 'There's something between us' – and it wasn't his loose change!) After that, I didn't stand a chance, and he totally went after me.

All filming took place around Somerset in some really romantic locations. With each day that passed on set with Neil, I felt a knot of anticipation tightening inside me because I knew where the script was heading. Before too long our characters were due to share a passionate kiss. Further into the filming, we'd be taking a bath together.

The day of our first kiss I was nervous but ready. What I didn't legislate for was how great a kisser Neil would be. I think that's what finally did it for me – especially as I was feeling so vulnerable. I absolutely fell for him (or at least, the idea of him). I just couldn't help myself, I found him attractive – he was the catalyst for the change I'd longed for. I don't think women have sex with someone without feeling something – at least, I don't. One thing inevitably led to another and before too long Neil and I ended up sleeping with each other.

We were insane, lost in our own little world. Whenever we could have a moment together, we did. Instead of going home to Les (and Jane, who was house- and dog-sitting while we were both away working and she saved up for a deposit on a flat) or to Norfolk at the weekends, I'd pretend I was working and sneak to Neil's flat in Crouch End. I didn't even feel that I could confide in Jane because I didn't want to put her in a difficult position at home with Les. (She still says now she is grateful she didn't know.)

I agonised over what we were doing. My behaviour reminded me of what GB had done to me, and I would think back to when I was nineteen, waiting on the street corner for him to come home, and how wretched I'd felt. Yet here I was, doing the same thing to my husband. I knew in my heart that my marriage was on the rocks but the guilt was unbearable and I hated myself for being so deceitful. I knew Les had been unfaithful to his wife (and lover) in the past and that Neil was being unfaithful to Rachel, but I'd never done this kind of thing before. I'd lie awake at night, feeling how wrong this was, and wanting to stop it. I absolutely hated myself.

Eventually, of course, filming finally ended and I went home to Les, Jane and Primrose Hill. I was still seeing Neil whenever I could but it wasn't easy, and we communicated mainly through texts. I had no idea where Neil and I were heading but I became jealous when he went back to Rachel. She didn't live far from me and I'd walk Nobbie along her street and feel gutted every time I saw his car parked outside her flat. He always had the perfect excuse about how she'd needed to see him or how their relationship was 'mostly intellectual'. (To this day I have no idea what that means, probably because I'm not intellectual enough!)

Les undoubtedly had his suspicions. He asked me outright if anything was going on between us. I was completely wrong-footed and went bright red and hot. I was shocked – at the directness of his question, and at myself, because a lie just came straight out of my mouth – I'm not normally very good at lying. I hated myself, because I was being everything my mum said Frank had been. I could imagine her telling me, 'You're just like your father!' That thought alone put me in a state of depression with a lurching sense in my stomach. I lost my appetite (very unlike me) and then I lost almost a stone in weight.

My anxiety not only wore me down, it affected Les too. On Christmas Day that year, at my parents' house in Devon, it all came to a head. Les flared up when I announced that some presents I handed out from the tree were from me, not from 'us'. We had a huge row in front of everyone and he got in the car and drove off. I burst into tears, told Mum I wanted to leave Les and then ran upstairs and hid in the wardrobe. I hadn't done that since I was little. As I sat there sobbing, two decades later, I didn't feel different to when I was a little girl. I was utterly miserable, and had no idea what would become of my marriage. But once again I picked myself up and got back into work.

The new millennium brought good news for both Les and me. I was offered two new jobs – a part in a BBC drama series called *Hearts and Bones* and a major role in a two-part drama for ITV called *The Hunt*. Ironically, Les was picked to play the cuckolded husband

Amos Hart in the West End production of *Chicago*. It wasn't just good for our careers, I reasoned, it would be good for my head, too – the new projects enforced distance between Neil and I.

Hearts and Bones was a really well-written series exploring the loves and lives of a group of mates living in Coventry. It was a proper drama, and one of those special career moments – it was an amazing collaboration of actors (Sarah Parish, Dervla Kirwan, Rose Keegan, Andrew Scarborough, Damian Lewis and Michael Fassbender), and a tough part, but it is still the acting job of which I am most proud. My friend Jason says it is the best thing I have ever done. (That's what friends are for, after all!)

Aside from what was happening in my personal life, it was a fun and thrilling time. It was the first chance I'd had to form my own circle of friends and contemporaries – other up-and-coming actors and actresses – and much as I loved our joint friends, I was enjoying making new ones too.

Before my next project started filming, Jane and I went on a much-needed break to Cuba. Jane had recently split up with her boyfriend, I was in a total state about Neil, and there we were in the most romantic place we had ever been. As we got off the plane in the airport lounge there were musicians playing music from the Buena Vista Social Club. Couples were everywhere – old, young, holding hands, smooching, dancing ... We stayed at the Nacionale, and people thought Jane was a Cuban prostitute (her words)! She had to show her passport to get back into the hotel after one evening out.

While we were there, we hired a car to see the rest of Cuba. I drove, and we couldn't work out how to get out of the one-way system. The car's brakes weren't working and Jane thought we were going to die, so we ditched the car and stayed at the hotel for the whole time. We talked and talked. I needed time to think and she has always been such a wise influence on me.

My next project, *The Hunt* starred the actor I had started my career with, Philip Glenister, as my grouchy husband. I played a married woman named Sarah who had everything but who risked it all to have an affair (the irony!). There was one small problem. I'd written on my CV that I could ride a horse, as all actors do, but I couldn't so I had to take a crash course in horseriding.

I was cantering in the middle of nowhere with my instructor one day when I felt my mobile phone vibrate. My tummy flipped when I saw it was from Neil, and then again when I read, 'I love you.' I was stunned, and hesitated a moment before texting back, 'I love you too.' I looked around me at the surrounding countryside but for a moment I couldn't focus on a thing. This was huge. Neither of us had ever expected to say that to each other, and all I could think to myself was, 'Oh God, Amanda, you're really buggered now!'

My friend Jess had been in India and I called her when she got back and told her everything. She was incredibly understanding and full of common-sense advice (as ever!). She, of all people, knew how hard it was to love Les sometimes and she was adamant. 'We knew it was never going to last.'

Despite our relationship deepening, it was really difficult for Neil and I to see each other and one spring weekend he suggested we hire a cottage near Yeovil, close to where I was filming. Les was busy doing eight shows a week in *Chicago* and, in spite of my gnawing guilt, I couldn't wait to be reunited with Neil.

We had the most blissful few days. We didn't just hole up in our hideaway as we'd planned. The weather was beautiful, so we went for long walks and to the local pub for lunch together – in public! We visited stately homes like an ordinary couple. The woods near our cottage were beautiful, and carpeted with bluebells. We found wild garlic nearby and took some back to our cottage where Neil prepared us scallops with a garlic and butter sauce and we drank champagne. It was all so ridiculously romantic – we even came across an old boat on a pond and took it out for a row, just like the scene we had filmed together in *Happy Birthday Shakespeare*. Everything seemed to have a movie-like quality to it. We thought it was our little secret, but it was so stupid.

I returned to the set of *The Hunt* in Somerset the following week still glowing from my time with Neil. I'd become close friends with my other co-star Samantha Bond during the course of filming, and to make things even cosier, I'd got Mum and Dad some work as extras in a funeral scene and they were on set too. Nobody had any idea what was happening in my life. Not yet, anyway.

I was immersed in a dramatic scene one sunny Saturday in May in which I'd packed my bags and had to leave my on-screen husband. During a short break, I switched on my phone to check for texts from Neil but instead took a call from my PR agent.

'Hi, darling!' I said. 'What's up?'

'We've just had a reporter on the phone,' she said. 'Are you having an affair with Neil Morrissey?'

My stomach fell through my arse – it was like dropping twenty floors in a lift. I stood there speechless; frozen in time, aware that somewhere in the distance the director was calling my name. 'One more time please, Amanda?' Somehow, I managed a shaky smile and waved back at him. 'I'll be right with you!'

'Yes,' I said, 'I have been seeing Neil.'

'Does Les know?'

'Not yet. Oh God, what am I going to tell him?'

'Ready when you are, Amanda!' the director called.

I looked up and saw the entire cast and crew waiting for me. I told my PR that I'd call her back, plastered a smile on my face, turned myself around, and shot the scene all over again.

Standing over Philip Glenister as Rob Campbell as he sat slumped dejectedly on a sofa, I walked myself through my lines and, as per the script, asked him if he'd be alright. 'Yeah, fine,' he replied glumly (as per the script). 'New house, new life, new women . . .' Then he looked up at me and said, 'We had some good times didn't we, Sarah?' I was almost unable to speak. I nodded and said, 'Loads.' I ran out of the house crying and jumped into a car to be driven away. My tears weren't fake, though, and when the director shouted 'Cut!' I felt like I was dying inside.

I had to confide in my make-up artist, and she was so good to me – she was like a therapist. She cleared everyone out of her trailer, made me peppermint tea and radioed the director to say, 'Amanda's had some horrible news. Can you go to the next scene?' As I sat blubbing into my mug, the first thing she asked me was if Les knew yet (cue more tears!).

When I could finally catch my breath enough to speak, I rang my PR, Alison back and she told me the *Sunday Mirror* planned to run the story the following day, that they claimed it had been going on for months, that we had been in a cottage together last weekend, and – the worst bit – that they had photographs. All I could say was, 'What am I going to tell Les?' At that moment, it was the only thing I could think about. 'So it's true, then?' she asked. I said nothing so she sighed and added, 'Okay. Tell me everything.'

For the next hour, as I sat in my trailer or wandered around the car park in the middle of nowhere, she and I tried to work out a plan of damage limitation. (My parents were still around but at that point I couldn't even talk to them about it.) Les was in London and I knew I had to speak to him before somebody else did. Suddenly it was all so real – what I'd done, how much it was going to hurt him – and I felt wretched.

My make-up artist sat with me for moral support as I made the call. I dialled his number with trembling fingers and listened to it ring. When Les finally picked up I said hello and then blurted out, 'You know when you asked me before about Neil Morrissey? Well, I lied, Les. I'm sorry, but I lied to you. It's going to be all over the newspapers.'

I can't remember exactly what he said to me but I do know he slammed the phone down, which I couldn't blame him for at all. I called back, of course, and after our initial row, I was amazed when he took my call. All I could do was cry. He listened to me sobbing and eventually he asked me if I was alright. 'No!' I wailed. He said, 'I'm coming to you now.' He sounded unbelievably calm! I, however, was anything but. I put down the phone and called my friend Jess, who promised to come too. I went back to the hotel to wait for Les, who was being driven from London because he'd had too many drinks to drive himself. I was nervous, but so badly wanted to see him. He was the only person in the world who could truly comfort me. He was also the only one who could forgive me. I must have called Neil but I don't remember it. Maybe we just texted.

When he finally arrived, Les and I fell into each other's arms. I was apologetic and full of self-loathing, and both of us wept. Once we'd stopped crying, we had an incredibly normal, rational conversation about it. He didn't want to know the whys and wherefores; he only wanted to know one thing: 'Do you love him?' That was my next betrayal, as I told him 'no'. I didn't want to hurt him any more, but inside I felt that I did love Neil. How else would I have justified the whole situation to myself all along?

In response, Les was heroic – there's no other word for it. He stayed with me, and when the newspaper article about Neil and me was published (headline: 'Amanda and Neil's Romantic Weekend Trip'), Les and I read it together. I can't bear to think how that must have felt. I stared red-eyed at the photographs of me and Neil on one of our weekend walks and emerging from the local pub. I felt so ashamed.

When Les left for London to return to his role in *Chicago* (after missing just one night's performance) we were both wrung out, but it was time to go back to work. Jess came back to work with me, and Philip Glenister greeted me at my door with a bottle. Samantha Bond was so reassuring, telling me that Les and I could survive if we worked hard enough at it. The problem was, I didn't even know if that was what I wanted.

By the Monday morning, I was back filming scenes in front of a director and crew who now knew every sordid detail of my personal life. To their credit, they didn't treat me any differently. The plot line I was acting out was – once again – the story of my life. I was so embarrassed but I somehow held it together. No one judged me and they were all very kind.

As soon as the news of the affair leaked out, the press swarmed around everything in our lives. There seemed to be photographers lurking everywhere. I had at least one more week of filming but the media attention almost got in the way of that. I had to hide in cars to get on and off set – it was like nothing any of us had ever experienced before. No one had been particularly interested in Les and me before that; we just didn't get that kind of attention. But suddenly my hotel, the set and our home were surrounded.

Les had ten cars lined up outside our house around the clock and one newspaper spotted my slim, beautiful, mixed-race friend Jane leaving and reported that Les was being 'comforted' by Diana Ross! His sister Margaret stayed with him for extra moral support and Andy Grainger kept an eye on him too. Neil was under siege as well, and had to ask a neighbour to buy him bread and milk – he needed a police escort just to get to his own car.

But that wasn't all. Stories kept appearing about us that were so intensely private that even close friends came under suspicion. I had a phone call from a friend in the press who tipped me off that a tabloid newspaper was tapping my phone. She advised me to put a security code on my phone. I was devastated at the idea of hacking but did as I was told. I never thought to go to the police. I never even thought, 'How bloody dare they!' At that point, I think most people in the public eye just accepted that phone-tapping was an inherent risk of the job.

Piers Morgan was the editor of the *Mirror* at the time and was one of the chief protagonists chasing me. I wanted to kneecap him – I felt he was cruel and showed complete lack of understanding about my situation and that of Les. He persecuted me for five years from the day Neil and I were caught, which is something I never thought I'd be able to forgive him for. (One night, much later, Chris and I were having dinner at The Ivy and I spotted Piers Morgan sitting across the room, stuffing his face. I didn't even want to breathe the same air as him. 'Look at that bloated fat shitbag!' I said, but Chris stopped me going over and saying something.)

When *The Hunt* finally wrapped, sick with tiredness, I fled back to London where reporters and photographers were practically camped outside our house. I was never able to watch that show when it was eventually broadcast. I couldn't – it would have been a reminder of the worst time of my life.

I moved out of the home I shared with Les and into a new-build one-bedroom flat I rented. It hurt to leave my home and my marriage, but it felt like the only solution. I spent a lot of time soul-searching and, now I could talk to her about it, confiding in Jane. Jane loved Les, but she felt the balance had been tipped from the start, and she made me feel less of a cow when she reminded me how maudlin and full of self-loathing a sober Les could be, let

alone when he was drunk, and how tricky he was to be married to.
'You seem to spend your life chivvying him along,' she said, 'and
you can only do that for so long.' She also reminded me how not
long before, she'd seen me at home after a major shopping spree
at Harvey Nichols and Selfridges. I had bags and bags of stuff all
wrapped up in tissue paper. Jane asked me what I had bought and
I said that I didn't really care as the thrill had already gone. I didn't
even unwrap the bags, no fashion shows like when I was a little
girl, nothing. She said she'd had a sense on that day that I was
really low – sad and trapped.

But despite all that had happened, and all the hurt I'd caused,
Neil and I couldn't give each other up – not yet. Even though I had
left Les, and was living in my flat, the press followed Neil and me
everywhere for months, desperate for pictures of us together, so if
I wanted to see Neil I had to creep out in the dead of night. He had
an even worse media backlash than I did and really got it in the
neck for having an affair with a married woman (he was perfect
headline material – 'man behaving badly' and all the rest). As if
he'd had to twist my arm! I had made one attempt early on to push
him away when I told him, 'No, I'm not doing this!' – but I clearly
didn't try hard enough. I felt it was me who should shoulder the
blame, because I was the one who was married.

But Neil ignored all the fuss, and continued to support me any
way he could – which mainly meant feeding me. He was so worried about how much weight I'd lost that he even baked scones and
always had a glass of red wine waiting for me. Looking back, Neil
and I were never really sober during our time together – there was
always a bottle of wine open.

Right in the middle of it all, I was having dinner with Andy
Harries, executive producer of *The Grimleys*, when I got a text from
Neil. It said, 'Will you run away with me?' I was so surprised that

I told Andy, who said, 'Why don't you just ask him to join us?' So Neil came over, and Andy told me afterwards he had never seen two people so in love, which shocked me – and it was then I started to question exactly how Neil and I really did feel about each other. Without the excitement and the secrecy, without having to justify our actions, I wondered just how in love we were. I think we wanted to think that we were in love because it made it a cleaner, nicer situation. And now that we were finally facing the consequences of our actions, I think we both knew that there was only one possible outcome.

In all the time we were holed up in his flat in Crouch End until I'd sneak away at dawn, we never discussed our future together, simply because we both knew there wasn't one. We rarely spoke about my marriage and Neil never asked. We knew it could only end badly, but we didn't seem to be able to consider that then or even stop what we were doing in any kind of rational, normal way. 'Normal' for us didn't exist, and once the initial passion had subsided, we were so worn down by everything that had happened that it got to a point where we hardly knew what to say to each other any more!

We were the only two people in the world who knew what we were feeling but that wasn't enough. Until one of us had the courage to end it, we were just drifting along. By that point, I think we were clasping on to each other because there was no other person in the world that could possibly understand the hype and all the uproar we'd been through. We had become caught in a situation of our own making, and were both shy about splitting from one another because we had been so thrown together by the press. By saying we loved each other I think it made it better for us.

After dinner with Andy that night, we drove all the way to Brighton and stayed with an old friend of Neil's. It was meant to be a romantic hideaway, and he was so welcoming to us both, but honestly, I have never felt more lonely in my life. Every night I'd go to bed while they were downstairs drinking heavily. One night we went to Zoë Ball and Norman Cook's house and had a nice evening, but again I felt really out of place. I had never felt like that with Les, and I began to question why I had ever left him.

That weekend another article appeared in the papers, this time featuring Frank. He came out of the woodwork to call Neil a 'home-wrecker' who'd 'ripped his family apart'. 'His bloody family?' I thought. The whole feature really annoyed me, especially coming from someone who had wrecked *our* home and didn't know me.

Not surprisingly, back in London Les was becoming increasingly wound up by the never-ending media attention. His general depression only got worse, which crucified me. I honestly never meant to hurt him so badly. From the day we met, I'd wanted to sort out his problems. Now, I *was* his problem.

A few weeks later, totally by coincidence, Les and I ended up filming in adjacent studios in Nottingham. He was making *Family Fortunes* and I was filming *Kiss Me Kate*. I felt awful. Les obviously felt the same way, and during a break in filming, we decided to drive to Norfolk to spend some time together and have a massive heart-to-heart.

It was wonderful to be back in our little cottage where we'd had so many special times together. During a long walk in that bleak wilderness I loved so much I told Les that I really wanted us to try again. And on that day, in that place, I really did.

During our first tentative weeks at trying again, we went to an event together and halfway through the evening I went to the ladies' loos. On my way back I was cornered by a famous comedian, who grabbed me, tried to kiss me and put his hands in places they shouldn't have been. I was scared and I tried to push him away, making light of it so he would leave without causing a fuss, but he wasn't put off. As I tried to fight him off, I looked over his shoulder and caught sight of our reflection in a large mirror on the opposite wall. My body went limp, and I just stood there as he groped and nuzzled me, observing myself from afar. I felt so cheap and utterly worthless. I didn't dare tell Les – he would only have made a scene. Only when I confided in a family member did I realise it was sexual assault. Part of me felt like I deserved it.

Shortly afterwards, Neil got a role in a play by David Mamet, *Speed-the-Plow*. I took my friend Rose Keegan to see the play, and after the show we went backstage to see him in his dressing room. We drank some champagne and then we hugged. Before I left, I secretly put a letter for him on the sink explaining that I'd decided to go back to Les. It was over – and I was relieved.

Chapter 11

Double or Quits

Several months into our reconciliation Les and I were invited to attend two events to present awards, our first appearances in public since we'd got back together. However, our appearance at the National Television Awards made headlines in a way that none of us could have expected.

Les was nominated as the host of *Family Fortunes* and we were asked to present the award for the best Daytime programme at the NTAs. All eyes were on us as we announced the winner as *This Morning,* presented by Richard Madeley and Judy Finnigan. But not for long! God bless her, Judy took all focus away from us that night. As she leaned in to accept her award from Les and then kiss me, her black dress fell open to reveal a ginormous, gleaming white bra.

As her double-D cup was exposed to the nation there was a roar of appreciation from the crowd, but Richard, who was bliss-fully unaware of what was going on, thought it was a shout for him to do his Ali G impersonation. Laughing, he refused 'because the real one's here!' The cheers continued. Les and I had stepped back to allow them to make their acceptance speech so we had no idea what was going on, and it was only when we looked up at the monitors on the side of the stage that we realised. 'Oh my God!' I whispered to Les, 'Her tits are out!' Before I could leap in to help, TV presenter John Leslie ran up on to the stage from the front row and gallantly covered Judy up. The clip went viral and our first public appearance together was completely forgotten in the fuss.

Our schedules meant that Les and I wouldn't be spending very much time together in the foreseeable future. *The Grimleys* was recommissioned for a third series, and Les was in his fourteenth year as host of *Family Fortunes*. The space gave us chance to gently try to find our way back to each other, and for the next year we really did try to make it work. We holidayed on the French Riviera and in Italy, and attended premieres and opening nights, holding hands and smiling into the cameras so that everyone knew we were making a go of it. But we still filled our lives with other people. We always had friends on holiday, rarely had dinner on our own and most nights our house was full. (Looking back, though, I don't think this was why our relationship ended – I think it's what made it last as long as it did.)

It had got to the point where it seemed pictures of me could suddenly appear on the front page for any reason at all (and frequently did). That summer, when we were on holiday at a private villa in Tuscany, the *Daily Star* ran topless photos of me and promised more the following day, but our lawyers managed to injunct them and later reached an out-of-court settlement for gross invasion of our privacy.

My holiday reading that trip was a script I'd been sent for a new

TV drama about rival hairdressers called *Cutting It,* by the producer of *Hearts and Bones*. At first I wanted the part of Allie, the down-to-earth northern girl whose salon was across the street, which Sarah Parish had already auditioned for. I couldn't see how I was going to make 'my' part – Mia, a bitchy blonde with a posh hair salon called Blade Runners in direct competition with Allie – likeable. But the writing was brilliant, and once I'd seen the character's huge potential it was a no-brainer. We both accepted, and before filming started in Manchester later that year, I worked for a week at Daniel Galvin Senior's London salon, training under the lovely Lino. I was meant to be shadowing Lino and watching him sashay around the salon ('It's all in the pelvis, darling!') but I seem to remember sweeping up a lot of hair, too.

Overall, I was feeling more optimistic than I had for months, and as a surprise for my nan's eightieth birthday we stole her passport and took her to New York (she didn't have a clue!). I flew my sister from Vietnam to Manhattan, and she was waiting for us at the airport behind a big name board as we landed. It was a very emotional reunion – not least because we were missing Papa. He was in the first throes of Alzheimer's and not in the best of health. In fact, we'd only been able to leave him because Les offered to take care of him at our house all week. It was an act of huge generosity and kindness – looking after Papa was hard work and Les was amazingly patient with him.

He took Papa everywhere with him, even to the BBC for the Jonathan Ross show (although he did admit Papa went missing in the radio station for a while!). Papa put his wallet down somewhere that day and thought he'd lost it, so when Les gave it back to him Papa thought Les was wonderful for 'finding' it. Another night, they ordered a Chinese takeaway. Papa chose his meal from the menu, but when it arrived he kept complimenting Les on his cooking. No matter how many times Les reminded him it was a takeaway, Papa would forget again and give him another compliment. (I think Les secretly enjoyed that week even more than Papa did!)

We had a fantastic time dashing around New York and Nan walked so fast around Manhattan that we could hear her hip clicking! We were real tourists – we took photos of Nan at the Empire State Building, on Fifth Avenue, at Ellis Island and at breakfast at the Twin Towers. We went to show after show, stayed at the Plaza and had tea every day in the foyer. You'd never believe Nan was eighty. She was amazing – but then, she always has been.

Before long, Les and I were back in the States – in LA, for pilot season. It's a huge part of the Hollywood calendar, when shows are commissioned and parts are offered. Les had been before and found the whole experience disheartening but my agent thought I should go and do some auditions. We stayed out there for ten weeks in a beautiful house on Mulholland Drive in LA, near to where Billy Connolly lived. Jess and her mum came with us and later Andy Grainger and my mum joined us too. It was fabulous – we went to all kinds of Hollywood parties and met so many people. My then US agent, Melanie Greene, lived next door to Jodie Foster and her girlfriend Cydney, and we all had dinner one night. Jodie was pregnant with their first child, and they were both lovely – so positive and encouraging.

Melanie also set up a 'meeting' (LA-speak for audition) with Quentin Tarantino, who wanted a girl for a part in *Kill Bill*. The experience was completely bizarre. I knew it was supposed to be a dark-haired role, so I bought a wig. It was hideous – I had a big headband and I looked like Sophia Loren gone wrong! But I was recalled, and recalled, until there were only a few of us in there, including Naomi Campbell, who was marching up and down the corridor, learning her lines. I was also sent for meetings with the people from *Ally McBeal, Friends* and *Joey*, as well as being recalled twice for a part in *Anchorman* and *The Mexican* with Brad Pitt. I was recalled for some but mostly, it was just an amazing experience. I loved the way Melanie spun each 'meeting' – she was always so positive.

Les studied each day's itinerary, plotted the route between studios and drove me to every audition. One morning, I'd changed umpteen times and finally settled on a pink suit but couldn't find the matching belt. 'I can't find my pink belt! Have you seen my pink belt? I can't go without my pink belt!' I repeated, walking around and around the house. I must have asked everyone a dozen times if they'd seen it, whilst Les went pinker and pinker with frustration and annoyance. Jess, who was lying by the pool with Andy (both desperate for us to go out so they could have some peace and quiet) finally said to me, 'Amanda, if you don't find that fucking pink belt then Les will and he'll bloody strangle you with it!' (Once we'd gone, she, her mum and Andy came up with a script for a TV murder plot called *Amanda's Pink Belt*, in which Les did exactly that.)

By then Les's agent Mike was semi-retired and spending a lot of time in LA, so we saw him every now and again. His son Chris was out there for a while, too. I'd met him twice before – most recently when I took my stepson Philip to the premiere of *Lord of the Rings*. Chris was also at the premiere with his friend Lady Victoria Hervey and he'd come up to say hello. (I'd said it back but had no idea who he was!) When he told me, I remember being struck by how good-looking he was.

The only man on my mind at that point, however, was Les. Once pilot season was over we travelled to Palm Springs and Venice Beach. Then I took him to Las Vegas for a couple of days with my mum and Jess, Andy Grainger and our friends Jules and

Andy, where I planned to give him the surprise of his life. I told him I'd reserved a table for a quiet dinner one night, when really I'd booked to take us to the Little White Wedding Chapel, where we were going to renew our marriage vows. (I can't now imagine what I was thinking except that I wanted to reassure Les that we were going to be alright.)

It was all perfectly planned. However, about an hour before we were due to leave (Les still none the wiser), he kicked off and we had a huge row. I went to see Mum and Andy and said, 'Right, that's it, I'm not going to do it.' I called up the woman at the chapel and said I was so sorry, but I needed to cancel. She said, 'Okay, ma'am, if you wanna change your mind just call back.' So I did! I must have changed my mind three or four times. It was like a Ray Cooney farce, going in and out of my mum's room. At one point Mum and I went for a walk to clear my head and I said, 'I've probably got to do it, Mum, haven't I?' and she said, 'You've got to make up your mind,' but suggested I shouldn't do it as everyone could see I wasn't happy and should stop over-compensating. As we both looked up we saw Les on a bridge – the fake Ponte Vecchio – picking his nose! (As usual.)

This had become an increasingly bad habit. So much so a lyricist friend of ours had written a poem which included this verse:

He picked his teeth
He picked his toes
There isn't a square in London where
He hasn't picked his nose.

Eventually, I decided to hell with it, we should go ahead with it and renew our vows. It was a bizarre night. Les was gobsmacked. Jess was my bridesmaid and Mum stood stage right the whole time, saying in a voice just loud enough for us to hear, 'Oh, he's a miserable old fart! I don't know why she's marrying him AGAIN.' Afterwards, we all had dinner together in a private room that the Brat Pack used to sing in.

Our 'honeymoon' was short-lived. Les started drinking a lot and we had some major alcohol-fuelled rows. Jess and Andy sat on the sidelines, watching our marriage unravel. It must have been more depressing than *EastEnders*!

Philip, Les' son, then flew out for a week, and I hoped his visit would cheer Les up. One day during his stay, we decided to drive to San Diego for the day with Philip, Jess and her mum, who wanted to see SeaWorld. Les was driving, and not long after we set off he took a call from his ex-wife Lynne, who wanted 'to check that he'd paid for Philip's insurance' while he was in the US. The call put Les in a foul mood, and he started driving erratically and throwing the car around. When Jess's mum asked him to drive more carefully, Les completely lost it. He started shouting at her and when I told him to calm down he yelled, 'That's it! I'm going home!' He then swerved across three lanes of the highway to reach an exit. We were lucky we weren't all killed, and everyone was very shaken up. That day became known as 'The Day We Never Went to San Diego' and cast a shadow over the rest of the trip.

We kept trying back in the UK, and on Christmas Day we went for a walk on Primrose Hill (on our own for once!) with a bottle of champagne and some panettone for an impromptu picnic. We passed a woman sitting on a bench, and I smiled at her but in return she pulled a face and told me under her breath, 'I'm a reporter. They're taking pictures of you right now and they want me to ask you questions about your marriage.' (It was Christmas Day! Had they got no shame?) I told her to go home to her family, and we went straight back home, the moment ruined.

Amongst our guests for New Year's Eve was an Australian actress, who I'd become friends with at the Victoria & Albert Hotel when I was filming the latest series of *The Grimleys* and she was doing *Loose Women*. Since they were on the other side of the world to the rest of their family, I invited her and her mother and brother to spend time with us over Christmas and then to see the New Year in with friends in Norfolk.

I had noticed her flirting with Les in London, but thought nothing of it until in Norfolk Jess saw them actually kissing by the bins (how romantic!). I was hurt, of course, but mostly angry – at both of them. I'd invited her as part of our celebrations and yet she'd repaid me by coming on to Les. I confronted Les directly and asked if he'd kissed her and he admitted that he had and on more than one occasion. After a night sleeping on the sofa, I left Norfolk to get a wig fitting for a new show for Sky called *Now You See Her* by Red Productions with Jess, my relationship with Les in tatters yet again.

Les continued to pursue his dreams of becoming an actor and was offered the lead in the play *Misery* at the Oldham Coliseum. At this point the papers were already calling him 'Les Miserables', and they had a field day with this. Back in London, I went to the Comedy Awards with a group of friends. It was a lovely night – until the next day, when the *Mirror* ran exclusive pictures and suggested that there was something going on between the producer and me. We were all furious. Les and I were both good friends with him, and it was pure fabrication. (Les even wrote to Piers Morgan demanding that he stop printing 'salacious and vicious' gossip. Piers, of course, published his letter . . .) The press went crazy, and once again Les and I became prisoners in our own homes. I escaped to Majorca with Jess and photographers followed our every move.

One day, Harry Enfield, who lived nearby in Primrose Hill with his wife and kids, shoved a script through my door for his new show *Celeb*, featuring ageing rocker 'Gary Bloke' (Harry) and a WAG type (me!). Of course, I said yes. I was over the moon to be asked – I adored and admired Harry. I based my character on a cross between Posh Spice and Jordan, and Harry based his on Mick Jagger. The reviews were great, but not so good for Harry. It was recommissioned and we were even nominated for a Rose d'Or comedy award, but after that Harry retreated back into himself. He lost confidence and so cancelled the second series.

Les and I went to Norfolk on our own to see if we could patch things up again, and – in a slightly desperate attempt to convince ourselves that we were still going to make it – we ended up making an offer on another house overlooking lavender fields. We promised we'd always keep our little cottage but convinced ourselves that this new property would give us another fresh start. (I don't know who we were trying to kid!)

Around this time, Mike called Les to tell him that there were plans to move *Family Fortunes* to a daytime slot. Les saw it as an insult and it sent him spinning into one of his mammoth depressions. After much soul-searching, he decided to find himself a new agent. Mike had been brilliant for him and had set him up for life in terms of work, investments and pensions for when he reached a certain age. (Almost everyone who was managed by Mike had not only enjoyed a fantastic career but seemed to be well off in retirement.) Les was sorry to be finally parting company with the man who'd done so much for him over twenty-five years, but I think Mike was just relieved in the end.

Les entered into discussions with Carlton about *Family Fortunes*. As well as moving his show to a daytime slot without a live audience, the production team were insisting he take a big pay cut.

Having considered all his options, and taken advice from his new agent, Les decided to walk. After that, he became convinced that his career was in a downward spiral. He still hankered after some real acting. He desperately needed to feel wanted.

Meanwhile, I was working almost non-stop. I auditioned for a role in *Die Another Day* opposite Pierce Brosnan as a Bond girl at Pinewood Studios. I spent all day in my underwear learning how to fence, with Colin Salmon playing my 'Bond'. (Instead of looking sexy and empowered, most of the time I was red-faced and sweaty!) I was up against Saffron Burrows and Rosamund Pike, and I couldn't believe I was there – I never believed for a moment I would get it, and I didn't. I'd have loved to have done it and it would have taken me down a path I ultimately wanted. The role went to Rosamund, and she did a fantastic job in the film.

Also, most of the time I was based in Manchester filming *Cutting It*. I had my own flat up there in a block shared by my co-stars (Sarah, Angela Griffin, Lucy Gaskell and Siân Reeves, plus 'honorary girl' Ben Daniels). It was hilarious. We got to know each other so well – it was a bit like being students again, but with a bit more cash. (Sarah had a running machine so that she could get fit, but she hung her washing on it instead!)

We held *Sex and the City* nights on Wednesdays, curled up in our underwear with a bowl of crisps or a curry (and a lot of white wine!). Each of us had an alter ego in the show, and we decided I was a cross between naughty Samantha and homebody Charlotte (because I was up for most things but always liked to do it in 100 per cent Egyptian cotton sheets!).

The *Cutting It* schedule was brutal – long, cold days and nights. What no one realises about dramas is how cold they are! You always film in the winter, you do sixteen- or seventeen-hour days, and you're normally filming in buildings that aren't heated because they're empty. In what is supposed to be your home! You can often see your own breath, it's that cold. In *Cutting It* we were always saying, 'Can't you see our breath?' to the cameraman!

Our enforced separation wasn't helping Les and I get our marriage back on track, and when he was invited to take part in *Celebrity Big Brother* I have to admit that I didn't discourage him. Les was told by the production team that *CBB* was only for ten days, would raise a lot of money for charity and that there would be just five other contestants. He decided to accept after telling anyone who'd listen that he wanted to be seen as something other than 'telly wallpaper' and someone other than 'Mr Amanda Holden'. (I think he hoped a bit of reality TV would give him a chance to reinvent himself.)

Just before Les was due to go into the *CBB* house, we were both invited to Norfolk to celebrate our dear friend Jeanne Whittome's 40th birthday. Jeanne and Paul were so important to me, I desperately wanted to get there – I even looked into hiring a helicopter from Manchester! – but in the end I couldn't make it. It was a few weeks before I returned to Norfolk when in, of all places, a car park in Fakenham, Les suddenly confessed that he'd slept with someone I knew at the party. This new revelation was different to when he'd snogged my Australian actress friend the previous year, though. It was more than a quick snog. I remember consciously wondering how I should be feeling. Angry? Hurt? Betrayed? The truth is, I felt none of them. Sadly, I just felt relieved. His infidelity was to become my passport out. It was over two years since my affair with Neil Morrissey had first been exposed and we'd done everything we could to try to fix our marriage, including marriage counselling.

I was with Les the day he went in to the *Big Brother* house and I wished him all the best. I genuinely hoped the show would work for him. I wanted him to have something new and exciting to build on for his future away from *Family Fortunes*. However, I didn't watch it at the start. I couldn't – we were on a night shoot and I had no time to watch it. After a few days, though, the crew started talking about Les's behaviour – about how he talked about me all the time, moaned about the press, and sang show tunes with fellow contestant Anne Diamond. And then there were the chickens ... I was told how he chatted to them, imitated them, and danced with them. (I think he originally did it to be funny, but it apparently just came across as mental.)

Everyone became obsessed with finding a TV so they could watch it. I was kept informed by my PR Alison Griffin and it seemed he was having what I can only describe as some sort of breakdown. The footage was carefully edited and manipulated, of course, but even the most skilled production team couldn't fake him singing to himself, agonising over voting other people out – or his tears in the diary room. He came across like a man on the brink, which is what he was. I was the only one who knew it was really about our relationship, but for once I was powerless to help. The best thing that happened to him in there was Mark Owen from Take That befriending him (at least he had someone to talk to other than the chickens!).

The whole experience backfired badly. Piers Morgan labelled Les 'the most pathetic man in Britain'. I was genuinely mortified on his behalf and prayed he'd get voted out. Of course, the public voted for him to stay in – they wanted to see more of his craziness – and he ended up coming second to winner Mark. The *CBB* production team asked me to the live evictions and – just as with the Norfolk birthday party – I did try, but it wasn't possible because of my schedule. In the end, they filmed me sending him a message in some really cheesy piece to camera. I was petrified, and begged

Sarah and Ben, my co-stars in *Cutting It*, to come along for moral support. I thought it would come across as fun, but instead I was told it looked insincere and mean. I never dreamed it would come across that way and looking back I know it must also have hurt Les that I wasn't there in person, but my producers wouldn't allow it, and rightly so.

In the week or so after his eviction, we hardly saw each other – I was still in Manchester and he was invited on to one TV sofa after another to talk about the show. As the media speculated on how long it would be before we were reunited, we both knew our marriage was crumbling around us. Most of our conversations were over the phone. They were still very loving conversations, but sad and short. Eventually, back in London, we admitted to each other we needed to part for good.

I knew that was the right thing to do, but I wanted us to save face and have one last Christmas together. I didn't want to ruin it for our family. Les, however, couldn't pretend any more. He said, 'No, Amanda. I'm going to my family this Christmas.' I was gutted but, true to his word, he packed his bags and went to stay with his sister. Before he left, he told me we should get divorce lawyers early in the new year. I appointed Fiona Shackleton, she was brilliant and we remain friends to this day.

Even though I knew that it was inevitable, the word 'divorce' shattered me. Les and I had spent nearly ten years together, travelling the world, making some wonderful friends, and enjoying some of the best times of our lives. We had our two dogs, Nobbie and Fudge. We had a decade of memories at our adorable cottage in Norfolk and in the London house we'd chosen and lovingly furnished together. We still had that elephant of a place in Norfolk on which we'd recently exchanged, but never lived in. (Les sold it within days of completion.)

Without doubt, Christmas 2002 was the worst of my life. But, as always, I plastered a smile on my face and pretended everything was okay. Mum and Dad, Nan and Papa were coming and I'd begged Debbie to come too. However, she had a new boyfriend and left for Germany. But nevertheless, I did the works: champagne and smoked salmon, a huge turkey and presents under the tree. And everyone had a stocking from Santa. But when I woke up alone in my bed on Christmas morning I just felt lonely and depressed. (I texted Les 'Happy Christmas', which just made me feel worse!)

Halfway through the morning, I was feeling so down that I told everyone I was going for a bath. After forty minutes or so – definitely no more – Mum burst in to complain that I'd been too long. 'Your grandparents are waiting downstairs. You're being selfish!' I couldn't believe it. I'd been gone just over half an hour. Dinner was on. Did my family really need me to entertain them? I explained that I was feeling a bit sad and needed some time to myself. But instead, she told me to pull myself together. 'Don't be silly – you're not sad! You've needed this for a long time. Now get out and get dressed!'

Three days later, Les and I issued a statement announcing that we'd separated for good. It sparked headlines such as 'Showbiz Amanda Ditches Sad Les' and claimed Les's friends and family were on 'suicide watch' with him. It was finally over. He flew off on holiday to Shaker's Rock (how relevant), South Africa with Andy Grainger and Paul Whittome while I gathered my *Cutting It* girlfriends and my childhood friend Fig and decamped to the Hotel Arts in Barcelona for New Year.

The press made us out to be the UK's answer to *Sex and the City*. None of us were in the party mood, but we cheered ourselves up by doing a bit of shopping and, all things considered, we did have a brilliant time. All of us had recently split up from our partners and we decided to make the most of it. There were at least twenty photographers following our every move.

On New Year's Eve we sneaked through the kitchens and used the laundry lift rather than the main entrance (it was like something out of *GoodFellas!*). The hotel asked all guests at the gala dinner not to take any photographs, so we relaxed, drank far too much, and had an amazing time. The girls and I still say that, even though it was the direst of circumstances, no New Year has ever topped that one for us. Unfortunately, though, the camera ban didn't extend to tape recorders, and someone sitting near by recorded everything about our night and someone got a picture of me on their phone. The next day the *Daily Mail* published a full transcript, alongside a photo of me in a Groucho Marx nose and moustache from my New Years Eve goodie bag, with the headline, 'Amanda Holden: Leave me alone. I'm grieving.' When I read it, I found it very funny. But what the press didn't know was that shortly after the clock struck midnight I crept away and quietly called Les to wish him all the best for 2003. I told him I hoped it was a better year for both of us, and I meant every word.

There had to have been something seriously wrong with my marriage for me to have started an affair with Neil, and Les later admitted some responsibility for it. It's no defence, but the bottom line is, if you're happily married you don't seek comfort elsewhere. Women don't seek sex, but love and affirmation, as I have said before.

I know I could have handled things better. I should have left Les first or figured out a better way of saving what we had. I could never have anticipated the viciousness of the fallout from the tabloid media! It's such an awful punishment for having an affair in this country as a woman. I had always been such a good girl, but the press turned me into this utter vixen, and I was never forgiven for it. I never would have thought I'd end up being a girl the tabloids would be interested in. If you'd told me as a young drama student I would be all over *The Sun* or the *Mirror* because of my love life, I would have absolutely died. It all made me lose sight of who I was.

I ruined my reputation – professionally and with the press – but most importantly with the public who had always been so supportive. My family knew the full story and loved me no matter what, but it was embarrassing for them to face it all so relentlessly and publically. Even when, much later, Chris met me, he said I was constantly justifying myself, apologising, telling people I wasn't the person they thought I was. I felt like I couldn't hold my head up, like everyone I met was judging me. I was fast approaching my 32nd birthday and had more than achieved all my teenage ambitions to be working full-time as an actress. I wouldn't have to fall back on my Plan B. But I felt like a slut. I was portrayed as a minx and Les as a middle-aged game-show host, a helpless national treasure. I had done what every journalist was waiting for me to do. I had fallen right into their hands, and I had to fight for twelve years to get that perception of me changed.

Chapter 12

Hughes a Lucky Girl

I suppose there are less public ways of announcing a new chapter in your life than an interview with Michael Parkinson on prime-time TV in front of several million viewers ... But for me it seemed the right way to mark my new status as a single girl. When Parky asked me outright if there was a man in my life, I shot back cheekily, 'Are you asking?' (He wasn't.)

'No, there isn't,' I said, more seriously. 'I absolutely don't have anybody in my life. It's going to take a very brave man to love me.'

I was, of course, fibbing. What Parky – and even my close friends – didn't know was that I'd already found that man! Unusually for me, I hadn't told anyone that I was dating Chris Hughes. He'd stressed to me how he was wary of getting involved with someone whose life had been splashed over the tabloids for years. I was determined that nothing – and no one – was going to get in the way of our fledgling love affair.

Les and I now only spoke through lawyers, even though, as we had no children and I didn't think Les owed me anything, I had asked to take very little away from my marriage. All I wanted were Nobbie, Fudge and our Norfolk cottage. Les gave me the dogs readily, and I bought him out of the cottage. It was my 'heart' place, and I was determined to hang on to the happy memories we'd had there.

Before I moved out, and whilst the divorce was being finalised, I flew to Thailand with my nan to visit my sister Debbie. We had both been looking forward to being on the other side of the planet and out of contact for two weeks. Thailand felt like a world away, and that was exactly where I wanted to be for a while. And in more ways than one, Thailand *was* worlds away. My sister was working in the middle of nowhere as a diving instructor. She looked fantastic: tall, slim and brown, relaxed in a sarong and a bikini top, and fully immersed in the laid-back Thai culture. I, on the other hand, turned up in killer heels and a designer dress, and needed six locals to pull my suitcases off the boat (Joan Collins had nothing on me!).

Debbie just laughed at me – until I embarrassed her by over-tipping. She joked that I was screwing up the whole economy and laughingly said I was also responsible for an upturn on sparkly flip-flops. Suddenly everyone seemed to be wearing them, and she put it down to me! My Nan, aged 83, went scuba diving! I finally had some space and time to get my head around the huge changes that were happening in my life. For the first time since I was sixteen, I was truly on my own. It was huge, and it was frightening. When I got home I resolved to enjoy some time with my girlfriends and my family, and to focus on my career. It was going to be *my* time.

And so, when I got back, I moved into the Philip Stark St John's Wood flat I'd bought as an investment. It was in a really cool apartment building, and was home to other people in the public eye, so it was also very secure. I decorated my new home in purple, with movie posters, books and a chaise longue. My girlfriends called it my 'boudoir'. It was dark and cosy and safe, and it was my refuge.

Then, out of the blue, during London Fashion Week, my press agent Alison Griffin told me that Chris Hughes was involved in an event and had asked her if I would go. It was on the same day as the *Elle* Style Awards that I was already going to with Jane and a gang of girlfriends, but there was plenty of time to attend both. Chris offered to send a car and so it seemed like a no-brainer to go to his event first.

When Jane and I arrived, we were really well looked after and felt very special. The whole place looked amazing and it was the first time I'd ever been to fashion week. Jane and I were given seats on the front row and were like giggly schoolgirls. We couldn't believe our luck. Then Chris turned to me and sweetly said, 'I think you are the prettiest girl in this room!'

I blushed and replied jokily, 'Oh, bog off! This place is full of models!'

I already knew a bit about Chris through Les. As well as being Les's agent, Chris's father Mike Hughes was one of the biggest light entertainment manager/agents and concert promoters during the Seventies and Eighties. Mike had many other clients, including Russ Abbot, Freddie Starr, Joe Longthorne, Tom O'Connor and the late Dustin Gee.

Chris's parents had divorced when he was very young and he was sent to boarding school when he was ten (he says now he was way too young to be sent away from home). He also said that boarding school was like a long prison sentence and that time of his life wasn't easy for him. Chris went to live with his father Mike in Kensington, London, at the age of twelve. At seventeen, and against Mike's wishes, Chris said he wanted to leave school mid-A levels and work in the entertainment business. Mike let Chris leave school but made it very clear that going into his business wasn't an option and that Chris would have to make his own way.

Within five weeks of leaving school Chris landed a job with a sports insurance broker, and was handling the insurance interests of the Premier League, the Football League and The Football Association. He did this for six years before he and another colleague helped move all the business to another broking firm. During this time Chris's company was sponsoring a young racing driver called David Coulthard and they became close friends – they still are today.

Chris then branched out into the music business, managing recording artists, producers and songwriters. He also had a production company and made records for Simply Red and Fleetwood Mac, to name a few. (He has never, I hasten to add, been the drummer with Adam and The Ants, despite numerous incorrect press reports linking me with that Chris Hughes, fifty-eight.) Our paths had barely crossed and I'd never thought of him as anything other than Mike's son.

I already had an outfit lined up for the *Elle* Style Awards but that afternoon, as Jodie Kidd walked down the catwalk in a designer dress, I fell in love with it immediately. The problem was, it wasn't even available to buy at that point – but Chris very sweetly offered to talk to the designer and ask if I could borrow it for the evening. He promised to have it waiting for me at his hotel and we agreed that I'd pick it up before the awards.

On the way home I said casually to Jane, 'Chris Hughes is lovely, isn't he? So easy to get on with.' (She wasn't fooled. She told me later that, even though I was playing it cool, she could tell 'all those hot and bothered chemicals were having a PARTY'. She knew I was interested in him. We instantly clicked.)

She was right. I couldn't wait to see him again, and at home I quickly got ready, put on a little pink tracksuit and got a taxi to his hotel. He'd got the dress ready and waiting for me, as promised, and I asked if I could change in his bathroom. On Jodie Kidd the dress had been knee length, but on an Oompa Loompa me it practically came down to my ankles. I didn't care – I came out of the bathroom feeling like a million dollars. I felt brave, so I told Chris I had a spare ticket and asked if he wanted to come to the awards with me. He quickly freshened up and changed into a crisp white shirt. He looked great – and smelled *divine*.

He was the perfect date, and sat down at the table chatting easily with my girlfriends. Halfway through the evening, I leaned over and told him quietly, 'I think you're incredible.' He was fairly taken aback. Even I was shocked I actually said it out loud! I found him breathtakingly handsome and had honestly never fancied anyone so much in my life, Even though I can be a loud cow, I never thought I'd be able to speak to him properly because he was so good-looking. But there was this connection, and I actually found I could string a sentence together.

I cherished my new secret. Right from the start, it all seemed so romantic and exciting. We saw each other secretly whenever we could – at the Royal Garden Hotel in Kensington, his flat in Chelsea or in my apartment. Sometimes we escaped to a place in the Cotswolds. We texted constantly.

We did have secret, snatched conversations of course, and even Jess didn't know who I was talking to, despite our spending so much time together at work and in our spare time. It drove her crazy as she loves a gossip. After discussing it with the cast and crew of *Cutting It*, it was decided that I was DEFINITELY seeing someone new, and it must have been an actor in *Cutting It*. An unofficial investigation was launched, and when I wasn't looking DCI Jess Taylor lifted my mobile phone out of my handbag, pressed last number redial and watched across the room to see if an actor answered his phone. Apparently her face was a picture when one didn't ring!

My feelings for Chris ran very deep from early on. I decided he was The One, and I told him so (although I was too scared to say it outright, in case it frightened him away. So I said, 'I could fall in love with someone like you.') Children hadn't even come into my head until then, but I knew I wanted them with him. Chris sparked something primitive in me – I had to be with him. That was the challenge. But he was still so wary of the publicity that went with being involved with someone in the public eye. He had seen some of what that was like with his best friend David Coulthard, and he despised that kind of media attention. The indecision and uncertainty was killing me, and I threw myself into work with *Cutting It*.

Bizarrely, the one person I did tell about Chris was Les. He needed to know I'd found someone new, and I wanted him to hear it from me first. 'It's Chris Hughes – Mike's son,' I said finally. He was really sweet about it on the phone to me, but I found out later that he rang Mike about it – in Les's autobiography he talks about driving past Mike's house and seeing Mike playing in the window with his young son, and how he never would have imagined that one day that young boy would be married to his ex-wife (me). Chris says this could never have happened – for a start, their house had no windows that could have been seen from the road, and besides, his dad never played with him when he was younger!)

In the middle of all this, I was offered a six-episode show for the BBC called *Mad About Alice*. It was a show written for me, in which I played a mother of two, divorced from a man I couldn't get out of my system. I was involved in casting and we saw some brilliant people, but when Jamie Theakston appeared I knew he'd be perfect. He was like a Labrador, all bouncy and daft and full of energy.

He never seemed to get used to his height. I became very fond of Jamie and still am – he's really intelligent and well-travelled, and a brilliant photographer. The tabloids were all over us, claiming Jamie and I were an item. It would have made the perfect showbiz story, but there was nothing in it.

One night during filming, Chris rang me– there had been a van parked outside his house for three days. He can be a bit of a worrier but I knew straight away that it would be a press photographer. I felt helpless. All I could do was apologise, but I knew the writing was on the wall for us. He had made it perfectly clear that he'd always been an intensely private man who cherished his personal life, and the last thing he wanted was to be linked to a celebrity. Once he realised he was being followed, I sensed him begin to back away from me.

A few weeks later, Vodafone called Chris to tell him that his 'wife' had been asking for his telephone bills. He told them that he didn't have a wife and that somebody must be trying to access his calls, in order to see if he was dialling my number – therefore proving our relationship. The media interest didn't end, of course. Like me, he was followed and his every move was scrutinised; he even had empty packages delivered to him just to see if he was in. I was used to constantly being in the camera lens as the press waited to see who I'd date next, but Chris wasn't, and he felt under siege. He said it made him feel like he'd done something wrong, and gave him a permanent guilty conscience.

At this critical point of trying to convince him that we could have a private life, I was invited to a Formula 1 ball at Stowe School. It was a glittering gala of a night, so I got my mum and dad tickets too. I borrowed a dress from a designer and had my hair and make-up done specially. Chris snuck over to see me as I got ready in the hotel. Then Sarah Parish rang and said that Neil Morrissey had been invited to the ball too. This would be the first time we'd been seen together in public since our weekend away in Somerset three years earlier. There was no way round it – it would definitely hit the headlines.

Chris was concerned and kept asking me, 'Did you know Neil was going?' I felt sick for Chris and sick that the shadow of Neil and I still loomed over me. I would always be a marriage-wrecker when Neil's name was mentioned. Chris knew that and didn't want anyone reminded of it. He didn't want me to go to the ball and tried to convince me not to, and I would totally have cancelled if my mum and dad hadn't been so excited about it. I couldn't let them down.

One of the first people I saw at the ball was Simon Cowell, who came straight over and introduced himself. He chatted to my mum and was really lovely with her, telling her how close he was to his own mother after his father had died. Neil and I spotted each other across the room but stayed in opposite corners until the dinner, when he suddenly came over and said quietly, 'Shall we just get this out of the way?' He grabbed a chair and sat next to me as all the photographers crowded around and took their fill of photographs. Neil said hello to my parents and they were brilliant with him. We were remarkably relaxed, considering.

I looked at Neil and thought, 'I am so over you.' He was with someone new by then and I suspect he felt the same way. He and I were both in a very different place to where we'd been before. (He told me I was 'a changed woman' from the one he'd fallen for on *Happy Birthday Shakespeare*.) The photographs of us appeared on every tabloid front cover the next day, and my body language spoke volumes. I was sitting with my back turned away from Neil and my legs firmly crossed. Everybody picked up on the way I was sitting and could tell there was absolutely nothing between us. Chris was really upset that the whole thing had been dragged up again, though. That episode finally did it for Chris, and he ended it with me, saying, 'I love you but this is not what I want my life to be about.'

I was utterly heartbroken that my actions three years before were still affecting my life. No one was letting me move on. I certainly didn't want to let him go, but I didn't feel like I had a choice. Miserable, I went to visit my parents and had a heart-to-heart with my mum. I lay in bed in my pyjamas and she, of course, told me to fight for him.

So, a few days later, I wrote Chris a heartfelt letter about how he had to get the tabloid nonsense out of his head. 'You know who I am,' I wrote. 'You deserve to be loved and cherished properly – something you have never had in your life. I know you love me and for once you must let your heart rule your head. Let me love you.' I even used Julia Roberts' line from *Notting Hill*: 'I'm just a girl, standing before a boy, asking him to love her.' I was not Julia Roberts, of course. But equally, I was not the Amanda Holden who was in the newspapers. I was just me, and I knew that he loved me and I loved him.

I was convinced that really was the end, but *still* didn't give up! He texted that he still had my pink tracksuit and said we should fix a date for me to collect it. I sensed it was time to play it cool, so I told him to keep it. I even turned my phone off, but there was always a text waiting when I turned it back on again. Sometimes he would just send a kiss and I would analyse and analyse that single letter, wondering what it really meant. But eventually, he sent the tracksuit back to me, which I took as a sign it was over once and for all. Chris went on holiday to Ibiza with David Coulthard. I was devastated and went to Norfolk on my own, believing that I had lost him.

It was then that my agent Sue Latimer asked if I'd like to fly to New York to audition for the lead in a forthcoming British version of the musical *Thoroughly Modern Millie*. The show was already a Broadway hit and had won all sorts of awards. The producers planned to open it at the Shaftesbury Theatre in London with a new Millie, and someone had suggested me. My audition was to be in front of everyone who had anything to do with the show and I was the only Brit they were planning to see.

I could hardly believe my ears. It would be my West End dream come true! Papa had always said he wouldn't believe I had made it until he saw my name in lights. That hadn't happened yet, no matter how much I secretly wished for it – but now, I hoped it might while he was still aware enough to enjoy the moment. I flew across the Atlantic wanting that job almost as badly as I wanted Chris. I remember staring out of the plane window, hoping that both wishes might come true.

At the audition, all the other candidates turned up in sweatpants – it was like being back in my Musical Theatre class. (I, however, arrived all done in my false lashes!) When it came to my turn, I found my spot centre stage and sang the three songs they'd sent me from the score. Then I acted out a short scene, adapted from the original. I thought I did okay – not amazing, but okay.

I looked at the panel, headed up by Tony-award winning arranger and composer Jeanine Tesori, and tried to read their reaction. My heart was thumping. My mouth was dry. Finally, Jeanine spoke.

'Honey that's great. But tell me, where are your shoes from?' (They were Kurt Geigers, black, with big shiny bows on the front, since you ask.) A couple of weeks later, I was offered the part and my extensive shoe collection became a standing joke amongst them.

The hard work started straight away. I booked ballet lessons, tap lessons, I even had tennis lessons to get my general fitness levels up. I took it all very seriously and started to rearrange my schedule around it. I still had a major role in *Cutting It* but I usually only ever do three series of anything (apart from *Britain's Got Talent* – eight series in, I still love it!) and for me, the show was slightly running out of steam. Unless you're in America, where you have to sign up for about seven series, three series of one show always feels about right to me. It's at that point the writing often starts to take a dive, or the plotlines become less credible. I told the producers that I wanted to leave and they were very sweet about it. We agreed that I'd take time out of *Millie* rehearsals to film a few final scenes, and they even rewrote the script so that I could come back if I wanted to. In the storyline I went a bit mad and was put into a mental institution – which wasn't that far from the truth at that point!

Chris was one of the first people I told that I'd got the part of Millie Dillmount (of course he was – I was still crazy about him!) and he was genuinely pleased for me. I hoped the new show would keep me busy and help me forget my heartbreak. (Who was I kidding? I was gutted.) Then, just as I thought I couldn't be any more miserable about him, I received a text from him from Monaco. It said, 'I still love you. Is that wrong?' I was stunned.

A few minutes later, he called me and told me that he had just bought a penthouse on the river in Richmond, Surrey. 'I really want to make this work. I want to be with you, so we've got to be strong. Let's just move in together and do this!'

I couldn't believe it. He had gone from one extreme to the other. 'Are you sure?' I texted back. 'Are you sure you won't change your mind?'

'What's the worst that could happen?' he replied.

Poor Chris was still wary, though, because he knew he'd have to open up his entire life to public scrutiny. Up until that point he'd led the lifestyle without any of the negative consequences. Compared to him, I am chaste – but the difference to being male would have been if his life had been in the papers, he would have been applauded for it as a 'playboy'!

I understood his reluctance, and I was overwhelmed that he was prepared to risk all that for me. I didn't think he loved me enough to be with me but I was wrong. So, on 31 August 2003, I moved in with Chris P. Hughes, the day after he flew home from Ibiza. I have never left!

Chapter 13

Diamonds on the
Soles of My Shoes

A front-page tabloid headline 'Holden Onto Her Nipple', with a picture of my right nipple peeking out of a designer evening dress, maybe wasn't the ideal way for my relationship with Chris to go public. Nor was it the way I had imagined my long-awaited West End debut would be reported! The first show of *Thoroughly Modern Millie*, though, couldn't have gone better. Virtually the entire chorus were watching from the wings on the opening night, giving me the thumbs up or mouthing, 'Break a leg!' Out in the packed house of the Shaftesbury Theatre sat Chris, Mum and Dad, Nana and Papa, Jane, Jess, Jason, Debbie and almost all those nearest and dearest to me.

Before the show started that October night I took Papa to the front of the theatre and pointed up to the illuminated marquee. Alzheimer's had been held at bay by drugs but I was slowly losing my Papa by then, but he was aware enough to appreciate what I was showing him. 'Look, Papa! You always wanted to see my name in lights in the West End. Well, there it is!' He looked at me with watery eyes and smiled, and I hoped I'd made him proud.

In the opening scene, I stood with my back to the audience – a small-town girl with two battered suitcases, one gripped tightly in each hand – for the entire duration of the overture until the curtains swung open and the spotlight found me. Turning, wide-eyed, I'd stare incredulously at the skyscrapers of New York.

The overture came to an end and, on cue, I turned. Facing my first West End audience in the spotlight, suitcases in my hands, was one of the greatest moments of my life. I had finally made it to the place I had always dreamed that I would be and, even better, Chris was watching me. I was the girl on the plate!

The rest of that night went by in a blur, apart from remembering to blow a kiss to Chris from the stage as I took my final bows. For many people – including friends and family! – it was the first time they even knew that he and I were dating, let alone living together.

At the big old fuss of an after-show party, I was on a high. I was wearing a beautiful low-cut red dress by Valentino. I'd been taped within an inch of my life into the plunging neckline, and I felt like a million dollars. It was my night, and nothing was going to spoil it – or so I thought . . . As I leaned forward to shake hands with Iain Duncan Smith, MP, my boob sprang out of the tit tape. I was aware of it happening, of course, but to be honest it never occurred to me you'd be able to see anything (Mr Duncan Smith saw nothing from where he was standing, I hasten to add!) and nobody else noticed. It was only the next morning that I – along with the rest of the world – realised that from the photographers' angle my right nipple could clearly be seen. (I'm

Me and Sally Walker in our 'efforts to get an Equity card' – Be Sharp# Book Now duo

Me 'doing a Marilyn' at my birthday – Sally Walker clearly not impressed!

One of my first publicity headshots

Blind Date: 'what's your name and where do you come from?'

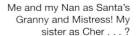

Me and my Nan as Santa's Granny and Mistress! My sister as Cher . . . ?

Me and G.B, my first love, graduating from Mountview Theatre School, 1992

Playing Roxy Hart in Mountview's production of *Chicago* – Jason Maddocks on my left

First job, *In Suspicious Circumstances* for ITV, with Phillip Glenister

Me in the National Tour of *The Sound of Music* as Liesel Von Trapp with Christopher Cazenove

Me and Les in Jersey

Me and my beloved boys: Nobbie and Fudge (all my pets *must* have slightly cheeky names)

Our lovely friends (L–R: Me, Ruby, Andy Grainger and Les)

Me and Les engaged

Me and Les on our Wedding Day, 4 June, 1995

Cast of *We Know Where You Live* (L–R: Jeremy Fowlds, Fiona Allen, Simon Pegg, Me and Sanjeev Bhaskar)

Me and 'CQ', Caroline Quentin, using me as her pillow

Cast of BBC1's *Kiss Me Kate* (L–R: Chris Langam, Me, Cliff Parisi, Caroline Quentin and Darren Boyd)

Cast of ITV's *The Grimleys* (L–R: Noddy Holder, James Bradshaw, Me, Brian Conley and Ryan Cartwright)

ITV's *The Hunt* (L–R: Adrian Lukis, Samantha Bond, Me and Philip Glenister

Me and Jessica Taylor.
Definitely 'radiator' people

Me and Rose Keegan:
'From Italy, with Mud'

Me and Sarah Parish, clearly
thinking we were in Nashville

Me and Jane Wall in Cuba

Me and Jason Maddocks
at his 40th birthday

Cast of *Hearts and Bones* (L–R: Back – Hugo Speer, Damian Lewis and Andrew Scarborough. Middle – Rose Keegan, Me, Dervla Kirwan and Sarah Parish. Bottom – Kieran O'Brian)

Cutting It billboard shot. Me and Sarah Parish with loaded hairdryers

Harry Enfield, his left testicle, and me in BBC's rock sitcom *Celeb*

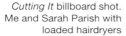

Cutting It cast (L–R: Sian Reeves, Me, Ben Daniels, Jason Merrells, Sarah Parish, Angela Griffin, James Midgely and Lucy Gaskill)

Ready when you are, Mr. McGill (L–R: Top – Paul Seed and Phil Davies. Middle – Jack Rosenthal, me and Bill Nighy. Front – Sir Tom Courtenay, Sally Phillips and Sam Kelly)

Me and Neil Morrissey finally meeting again at a Grand Prix Ball. Obviously I was distracted by those shoes

Me and my co-star in *Big Top*

ITV's *Miss Marple 4:50 from Paddington* (Geraldine McEwan, John Hannah and Me)

Me in one of three documentaries from ITV's *Amanda's Fantasy Lives*. In this one I was being country and western singer – I sang at the Broken Spoke in Texas baby!

Me as Millie Dilmount (looking like the girl on the plate my Mum bought)

Me and the girls performing 'Forget About the Boys' tap number in *Thoroughly Modern Millie*

Showing 'my boss', co-star Craig Urbani a bit of leg in *Thoroughly Modern Millie*

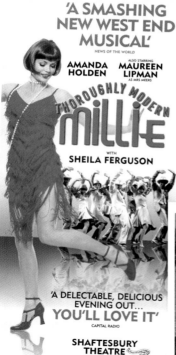

'A SMASHING NEW WEST END MUSICAL'
NEWS OF THE WORLD

AMANDA HOLDEN

ALSO STARRING
MAUREEN LIPMAN
AS MRS MEERS

THOROUGHLY MODERN
millie

WITH
SHEILA FERGUSON

'A DELECTABLE, DELICIOUS EVENING OUT...
YOU'LL LOVE IT'
CAPITAL RADIO

SHAFTESBURY THEATRE
210 Shaftesbury Avenue, London WC2

Millie Poster

ITV's *Wild at Heart* (L–R: Top – Lucy Jo Hudson, Stephen Thompkinson and Luke Ward-Wilkinson. Bottom: Me, Rafaella Hutchinson and Hayley Mills)

considering getting my nipples their own agent, since one appeared on *Britain's Got Talent* in 2013, as well as a bit of side boob at that year's wrap party!)

In the three months leading up to that opening night, my life had been a whirlwind of singing, dancing, and falling in love. I lived out of a bag of Lycra as I hurried back and forth to Waterloo for intensive rehearsals every day. I loved getting to know the cast and crew and I made some great friends – especially Vicky Hayward, a bubbly blonde in the chorus, and Pippa Jordan, a beautiful girl who ended up working with me later as a choreographer's assistant. And of course, Divs. I kept the promise I'd made what felt like a hundred years earlier and she couldn't wait to join me as my dresser.

Whereas in television these days everyone has stylists – or what used to be known as 'wardrobe', who help choose clothes and put 'looks' together – in the theatre it's customary for actors to have a dresser, kind of like an old-fashioned lady's maid. Your dresser is essentially your personal assistant – they are responsible for your costumes and other PA duties like running errands, getting your lunch, dressing you and small but very important details like making sure your tights aren't laddered. It's very old school, but then theatre is like that – they are so old-fashioned that actors are addressed by their surname – I get called 'Miss Holden', which I love. But being a good dresser is a really skilled job. You need to be nimble and quick, and have nerves of steel. During *Thoroughly Modern Millie* I would have to do an entire costume change (including wig!) on stage behind the chorus in just nine seconds whilst they sang a song. The costumes are usually made traditionally – there is no Velcro – so you have to be able to do a hook and eye really fast! Divs has done it for years, and she's the best.

Because Chris is self-employed, my punishing schedule didn't affect our time together too badly – in fact, we had a lot of fun with it. He'd pick me up after each show and take me out to dinner. Meeting me at the stage door took him straight back to the happiest days of his childhood when he used to go to shows with his father and stay up late. Every night we arrived home to our as-yet-unfurnished penthouse apartment where we'd stay up late, enjoying getting to know each other better.

To begin with I made him come everywhere with me, because I didn't want people to think our relationship was a flash in the pan or start speculating that we had split up. I still felt that people saw me as a marriage-wrecker and I desperately wanted to prove them wrong. I still cared so much about what people thought! What a waste of energy! But every time Chris came on the red carpet with me he broke out in a stress rash (he still does!). He also hated being my 'plus one' and I knew how demeaning that felt after my early years with Les. And after a while, I realised I didn't have to prove anything to anyone. Instead, I'd take one of my girlfriends or my lovely friend Ben Cooke, who is tall, gay and handsome – the perfect 'red carpet husband'.

From the start of *Millie*, I'd been getting lots of fan mail, and letters from one person in particular, saying 'I'm going to propose to you,' 'I love you' and 'I want you to be my wife.' Kind of nice, harmless stuff, that made me and Divs laugh. But then bouquets of flowers started arriving for me at the stage door, with notes letting me know that he'd been sitting in the front row. Then one day he sent me a teddy bear with a note saying how happy he was that I was going to marry him. That's when it started to feel more menacing, like I was being stalked, and I thought, 'This isn't right.'

I'd not responded to him at all, and as soon as it felt like it was something more sinister we reported it to the police. Almost immediately, it was leaked and appeared in the papers. I felt awful because it turned out he had mental health issues, and his family were absolutely mortified that it went public. I did release a statement saying I was glad he was getting help, but it was a scary time.

During the first few months of *Millie*, Frank wrote to me out of the blue to tell me that he and his partner Pauline were coming to a matinee. I invited them backstage, but the atmosphere was awkward and our conversation was stilted even though I did my usual and annoying thing of talking too much to make everyone feel less nervous – that time, it definitely didn't work.

But those were two blips in an otherwise magical time. *Millie* had some great reviews and I was later nominated for an Olivier Award, which was the icing on the cake. Being in that show and living with my new man felt like a fairy-tale ending to what had been such a horrible few years – I was unbelievably happy.

By February, however, five months of performing eight shows a week with hardly a day off had taken their toll and I was physically and mentally exhausted. Chris and I flew to Venice for a romantic break, but it didn't turn out to be quite the holiday we'd hoped for. From day one, I suffered with a painful back, so I assumed I must have pulled something from doing all those high kicks. I could only hobble, so we had to abandon all our plans for romantic strolls around Venice. I was in so much pain I had to sleep in a hot bath! Chris, meanwhile, was determined not to miss out on Venice, and went for a walk on his own – however, he got completely lost and it took him hours to find his way back to our hotel. I had made him watch the famous horror movie classic 'Don't Look Now' before we left, so he was shitting himself, endlessly walking up dark alleys and wondering if he would bump into a red-coated dwarf!

In our room, heat and rest hadn't improved my back, so we called the hotel doctor. He gave me a quick once-over, marked a cross on my arse with a pen and handed Chris some syringes full of cortisone with instructions to 'Stab this in the middle of the bottom!' (I'm not that kind of girl – honest!)

We flew home a few days later but the pain only got worse. I thought it must be a trapped nerve, but then I developed a fever. I was paralysed with pain. We called an ambulance and I was taken to hospital, where I was diagnosed with a serious kidney infection – something called pyelonephritis which, left to its own devices, could have killed me. I had never known pain like it, and it was clear to everyone that I wasn't going back on stage any time soon. I thought, 'I'm in so much pain why don't I just die now.'

I was in hospital for a week and had to take three weeks off the show, which I was in total panic about – I'd seen the repercussions after Martine McCutcheon had dropped out of *My Fair Lady* through illness in 2002 and everybody had called her unprofessional. Thankfully, that didn't happen to me, but before I went back I had to totally retrain – I even had a reopening night.

After my illness, *Millie* continued to do well until it finished – we had our Olivier nominations, had performed a medley of songs from the show in front of the Queen at a *Royal Variety Performance* and most importantly, we'd had a wonderful time doing it. It was time for the next adventure!

And it turned out 2004 had lots of other lovely surprises in store for me. I have always loved animals and had, in the past, done work for PETA and other animal charities. That year I was invited to become a patron for the Born Free Foundation. I was delighted – what an honour! My first job was to help Virginia McKenna release seven tigers rescued from circuses, pet shops and zoos. We made a documentary about it, and flew to a reserve near Bangalore in India. (The tigers flew first class – eye masks, glass of champagne, the lot!) We then travelled for twelve hours across India, drinking beer in huts and peeing in fields – it was an amazing experience.

To celebrate being free of my gruelling stage schedule, I took my friend Jane to Necker Island for a travel piece for the *Daily Mail*. We had an absolute ball with Richard Branson and the American actress Daryl Hannah. We all took a catamaran out together one day, then came back and played poker after dinner. Richard was unbeaten, apparently. But he hadn't bargained for my poker face. He couldn't believe it when he lost to me.

Daryl was a lot of fun, too, and we stayed in touch after the holiday. We had a few dinners in LA, and then one time she called me up at home out of the blue and said, 'Hey, honey, I'm in town – what are you doing?' We were going out to our local Indian, so we sent a car for her and took her for a curry! They were quite used to us bringing people off the telly – we'd recommended it to Trevor McDonald, and taken Brian May, Anita Dobson and David Coulthard on other occasions – but even for us, a bone fide Hollywood actress was quite random!

Chris and I were enjoying being a couple, having lots of nights out and weekends away – even going to football matches. Chris is a die-hard Everton fan and since I met him I have become an avid supporter too. My dad supported either Pompey (Portsmouth, where I was born) or Southampton, so I roughly followed them before I met Chris, but my heart wasn't in it. Now, I joke to Chris that if anything ever happened to us I would still be a blue through and through. We are lucky enough to always be in the boardroom whenever we go, which makes it extra special. There is no feeling in the world like walking down the steps to my seat, listening to the crowd going mental and singing the *Z Cars* theme tune. I even did a breast cancer campaign for them wearing one of only twenty pink Everton tops! It was billboarded all over the city – God knows what the Liverpool fans drew on my forehead. The shirt became so popular it ended up being their away kit the following season.

There was just one little niggle. Chris and I were in a wonderful place, and so very happy, but there had been no discussions about our long-term future. This worried me, and I'd creep up behind him when he was working or listening to music and make him jump by saying, 'Yes!' into his ear.

'Yes what?' he'd ask.

'Oh, nothing,' I'd say, innocently. 'Just practising . . .'

I sat him down and told him, 'I am thirty-four and I have to say I have to start thinking about kids.'

His face fell. 'I'm not sure about all that yet, Amanda,' he said. 'We're not even engaged.'

I had to respect his decision – there's nothing worse than forcing a man's hand, and I was crazy about him. So instead we carried on like that for several months, until one day he called me into the bedroom and said he wanted to talk to me. I wandered in and found him sitting on the bed. He looked so serious that I thought he was going to end it between us and I immediately felt sick.

Trying not to panic, I sat down in a chair and said, 'Okay then. Come on. What do you want to talk to me about?' I was terrified, until, still very serious, he said, 'I think we should take our relationship to the next level.'

I was gobsmacked.

'I think we should get engaged.'

I had no idea it would be so formal, and I was so not expecting it – Chris always keeps me on my toes! I couldn't have been more delighted. We talked about what kind of ring I might like (a square emerald-cut diamond – not that I'd thought about it a lot or anything . . .).

A few weeks later Chris drove me down to a jewellery shop to show me a ring he'd seen, but when he peered in the window he said, 'Oh, it's gone!' We went inside to ask and the manager told him, 'No, sir. We never had a ring like that.' It turned out he'd taken me to the wrong shop – there was another jeweller's next door! Eventually, we found the right store and there it was – beautiful, sparkly, simple, not too ostentatious and just perfect. After all that build-up, I had romantic visions of Chris putting it on my finger there and then but, to my disappointment, he said, 'I'm glad you love it. Let's have one made just like it.'

'Okay then,' I said brightly. 'Whatever you think!'

Weeks passed with no developments until one night when I was preparing dinner for our friends, the actor John Gordon Sinclair and his wife Shauna. I was stuffing a chicken – even though I'm a veggie I cook meat for other people – and my hands were covered in grease and garlic, when I heard Chris shriek from the bathroom, 'Mandy! There's a spider in the shower!' (Chris is such a girl when it comes to spiders.) I grabbed a glass and a piece of card with my oily, chicken-slick hands and rushed in, ready for combat, to find Chris standing there, looking petrified.

'In there!' he shrieked, pointing to the shower cubicle.

I opened the shower door, and instead of a big hairy spider, there on the tiled floor was a ring box. Again, I was so not expecting that! Once I'd washed my greasy hands, I opened the box to find the perfect ring. He'd bought it from the shop the next day. He placed it on my finger properly and then we kissed and it was wonderful. Chris told me not to tell our friends that night, because there were other people we needed to tell first. That was really hard for me – I wanted to share my happiness with everyone and show off my ring. Instead, I had to wait until the next day to call everyone.

Chris and I were now engaged after two years, and I really couldn't have felt happier that everyone now knew how serious and happy we were. I showed my ring off for the first time on *Children in Need*, after I had sung. It felt so special and such a buzz as I showed Terry Wogan (I have always been a huge fan!).

Over the last two years I had started to rebuild myself and my reputation, both personally and professionally. I felt I could hold my head up and be proud of who I was and was determined not to let any bad press or the odd stupid comment from the likes of Jonathan Ross hurt my feelings any more. I still have no excuses for my behaviour during my marriage but find it totally unacceptable that women like me can be victims of a witch-hunt for having an affair. Even thirteen years, three children and loads of other news-worthy stories later, it still gets brought up by the occasional comedian or newspaper. It is never the same for men in the public eye who have done far worse!

The arrival of the beautiful diamond meant the issue of babies came creeping up on me again. To be fair, until I met Chris I had no real maternal instincts. I adored kids but never felt that womb-ache that some women do, and I'm so glad Les and I didn't have them together. It clearly wasn't right. But now, approaching thirty-five, I realised I'd have to face it, and so I asked Chris if we could try. A life *without* children wasn't for me, I knew that much. When I brought the subject up, Chris asked if we could continue having a fab time for another year or so, but I knew that then age could become a problem. We had both already agreed we wouldn't be going down the whole IVF route if we couldn't con-ceive and I realised that to get pregnant we had to give it a fighting chance and start practising now. It was scary having the whole conversation – it's really grown-up stuff – and however much I loved him, I didn't know if I would be able to continue in our relationship if Chris had flatly said no. Luckily for me, he agreed!

Meanwhile, Jane – who had met The One, Joe, three years earlier – was planning her wedding. She had this beautiful pink-lace cocktail dress, which she thought she might wear on the day. It was very pretty but I was certain it wasn't what she really wanted for her big day. So I suggested that we should meet around the King's Road one morning. She knew I had some plans and I could tell she was intrigued but, to her credit, she didn't ask too much. We got in a cab to Catherine Walker, a super-stylish and posh boutique, where we were sat down, given a glass of champagne and Jane was asked what styles of dresses she liked. The assistant looked at her body type, led us upstairs to a carpeted dressing room and brought in this amazing, beautiful, sleek dress – I could tell from Jane's face that she loved it already. When she appeared out of the dressing room wearing it, though, I burst into tears. She looked so beautiful. Then she did too, and there we both were, crying in Catherine Walker's changing room. It was such a precious moment – I'll never forget it. On the big day itself, I was her bridesmaid, and as her surname was Wall, we all sang Oasis's 'Wonderwall' as we walked into the church.

Early in 2005 I got a call for a new TV show called *Wild at Heart*, with Stephen Tompkinson playing a vet named Danny who relocated with his family from Bristol to the African bush to help restore a game reserve. I was auditioning to play his wife Sarah, but the producers initially thought I was too young for the part. I took along the photographs of me releasing the Born Free lions and tigers into the wild, and that helped. That first contract tied me to three months of filming in South Africa, and they hoped the show would run for three years (it ended up running for much longer). It was a long time to be away from home, but this was a big prime-time show on ITV. It was an amazing opportunity. Chris told me, 'You have to do it!' So I said yes.

My African adventure was about to begin – and with it, one of the best experiences of my whole life.

Chapter 14

The Lex Files

Before leaving for Africa, I realised I could be pregnant. We did the test and it came up positive. Chris and I were stunned – we'd only been trying for a month, and I was leaving the UK to film for months! As I handed him the pregnancy test stick, the phone rang and without thinking, I answered it and said, 'Hello,' as if it was a perfectly normal thing to do when I'd just discovered I was pregnant with my first child.

Chris looked at me and said, 'God, Mandy!' He was in shock and he couldn't believe I had just picked up the phone at such a crucial moment, but I guess I was in shock too. He expected me to put it straight back down again, but he reckons I then went out of the room and was on the phone for about twenty minutes while he sat there, holding the stick and trying to read the test instructions, all the while dying to talk to me himself. But bless Chris, once we had confirmed it, it still took him a little while to get his head around it. When we started trying, he thought he had bought himself six months or so – not just one!

A few days later, I went up to Gloucester to say goodbye to my family. I was too superstitious to confide in them all about my pregnancy before the twelve-week scan, but I wasn't sure when I'd next see Debbie, and I wanted to tell my sister myself, so I swore her to secrecy. At the pub, I pretended to have a hangover as an excuse for not having any alcohol. My mum said, 'Oh, you can drink with your friends but not us!' Back at Nan's after lunch, Nan was searching for something under the kitchen sink and she jokingly tried to punch me in the stomach (tactile Nan strikes again!). I flinched, instinctively protecting my tummy, and she said, 'You're pregnant!'

'I'm not!' I lied.

She wasn't fooled. 'You are! I can tell. Look at the bags under your eyes! You're pregnant!' I said nothing, but did not confirm it, and walked away.

Back in London, I told Chris my nan thought I was pregnant but I wasn't going to tell them until after twelve weeks, and that was my right. I flew to South Africa, excited about our secret, nervous about being so far away from home with my first pregnancy, and with an uneasy feeling about the whole incident.

From the first week I spent in Africa I knew this was going to be a magical, life-changing but ultimately isolated experience. It was either incredibly hot or freezing cold and I missed Chris and my friends and family so much. What I hadn't bargained for was the even more life-changing event that I'd be going through while I was out there.

We were based in a secure complex on the outskirts of Johannesburg. I had a stunning five-bedroom house across from a lake, and a driver, but the city was an hour and a half away and so it was all a bit like living in an open prison. There was a Wimpy and a Spar in a little parade of shops and that was literally it! We filmed twenty miles out into the bush at a place called Glen Afric Country Lodge in Broederstroom. The hours were long – we'd be up at 5 a.m. and not finish until dark at around 4 p.m., but the scenery was gorgeous. The crew and local people were so accommodating and helpful, and it was such a privilege working so closely with the animals.

My co-star Stephen Tompkinson was lovely. It was a small cast but we did our best to have fun and entertain each other. It was Lucy Jo Hudson's first time away from her family and now husband Alan Halsall (Tyrone in Coronation Street), so she and I sometimes had a little cry together when we felt homesick. We'd all get together in the evening for a drink or to watch TV and I'd always have everyone round for big Sunday lunches. In that close-knit environment, though, finding excuses for not drinking without letting on I was pregnant got pretty hard.

Of course, living that close to the African bush and all its wildlife, there were amazing moments. Before I moved into my own place, I was staying in the main house and my room had a loo with a view. I was sitting there once when a giraffe stuck his head through the window – you don't get that every day! But after a few months, even that became normal. We all got a bit blasé and after a while would be like, 'Can we just move that zebra out of shot please? Anyone?'

But whilst I loved South Africa, I came to see there was still a lot of racism. I became good friends with my driver, Richard, who lived in one of the townships and had a new house built from the money he earned driving me. (He called it the Amanda Holden House and asked me to 'open' it. I went with Jess as she was visiting – I gave a little speech and lifted a ceremonial tea towel, which was all lovely!) When he ran me to the supermarket he'd help me with my shopping, and I'd get a few bits for him and his family. I thought nothing of it, until one day we were standing together in the queue and a white couple behind us started openly calling us names. They found it unacceptable that not only should there be a black man standing as an equal with a white woman, but that he should be ahead of them in the queue. I know this attitude is in the minority in South Africa, but I found this archaic and, in that area, pervasive.

Although to begin with I kept my pregnancy secret from the crew and fellow cast, I did tell Elliott Baulkham, the show's drama coordinator – I needed to let someone know! We were very well taken care of, and I grabbed the opportunity to eat as healthily as possible and give my baby the best possible start. But one morning, there was a terrible grating noise when I was making my breakfast fruit smoothie. I drank my smoothie regardless, but it wasn't until I swallowed a huge mouthful of plastic that I realised I'd accidentally left the plastic stopper inside the blender. Ditzy baby brain! I totally went into panic mode – I was so afraid I might have harmed the baby that I rushed out to find Elliott and tell him. As it turned out, everything was fine, but we still had the twelve-week Nuchal scan to get through. Chris flew out to be with me. Eventually the test results came back. The scan had looked normal, but my bloods were high and my hormones were double what they should have been. Put together, it meant we had a 1 in 20 chance that our baby had Down's syndrome. We were devastated. We tried to keep calm, but really didn't know which way to turn. I knew I had to have more tests done at this point, and I was grateful I hadn't told Mum that I was pregnant but I really wished my sister and my nan didn't know.

Then, in the middle of everything, my nan called me and said,

'You need to call your mother, you're breaking her heart, and I'm sorry but I've told her you're pregnant.' I had always thought my nan would be one to keep a confidence. Until now, she had always been fair, diplomatic and solid. I was deeply hurt. I was also angry. There were still conversations I had to have with Chris and I didn't want anybody else's opinion. I knew if the whole family were involved it would turn into a decision about everything other than us. It felt like emotional blackmail – it was a total nightmare.

Staying focused on filming and keeping my pregnancy secret was hard enough, as well as having tests on my days off. I couldn't process anything else. I was lucky that I didn't suffer from morning sickness, but I felt sick to my stomach about everything. It was a horrible, worrying time, and the only way I could cope was by avoiding talking to any of them.

There was a filming break, so we flew back to the UK for my CVS test. I literally had three days off – I was to have the test, wait the three days for the result, then fly back when it was safe to after the procedure. It was stressful, and I don't know if it was a maternal thing but I also had an overwhelming urge to see Nobbie and Fudge, who were being cared for by a friend of my sister's in Bournemouth.

I phoned Debbie and told her I was coming home, and said I was desperate to see our dogs. I asked her if she could bring them to London for me (she was coming into town anyway). Her response was, 'Can you come to me?' I was really taken aback, after a twelve hour flight a two hour drive wasn't what we needed, and she knew I was pregnant. Eventually, reluctantly, Debbie did as I asked, but at the train station she just handed the dogs to me and walked away. She didn't hug me or wish me well with the baby or say anything at all of comfort. I was so cross I sent her a text, pointing out that she was maybe being just a little unfair, which she immediately sent on to my mother. She totally took my sister's side, which I felt was misplaced and unjust.

But Chris and I had more important things to focus on as we waited anxiously for the CVS test results. To our great relief and happiness, the doctors told us we were having a little girl, who was healthy. Chris was over the moon that we were having a girl, too – he'd always wanted one. (He thinks they're kinder, apparently. His theory is that girls will look after you but boys will leave you alone in your old age!) But best of all, we could finally tell everybody who didn't know already.

I told my mum first, of course, but sadly there was no joy in it, because she already knew. All she did was bollock me for telling my nan first, even though I told her I hadn't, and that Nan had guessed. Then, of course, I was in the wrong for telling Debbie, who'd had to 'bear' the secret without being able to discuss it with either Mum or Nan. I couldn't win! Still, when I returned to South Africa and we could finally announce it, everybody on set made a huge fuss of me and it finally felt like the momentous, incredible event it really was. The cast and crew couldn't do enough for me. I had massages and they made me put my feet up, fetched me deckchairs whenever I was waiting for my cue, and cooed as my little bump swelled. Fortunately for continuity, my boobs grew to a not-so-impressive 34C; noticeably bigger than they had been when filming started, but not what Chris was expecting – or hoping for!

We weren't out of the woods yet, though. My next batch of tests showed that I had something called placenta previa (or placenta Prada as I liked to call it!). This is a low-lying placenta, which meant that I'd have to have the baby by Caesarean section. I felt very well and had a good feeling about it, so I promised Chris everything would be alright.

When I finished *Wild at Heart* I took Chris to Norfolk with the dogs for a few days. He now loved it as much as I did, although he did make me redecorate and extend it so that it became 'our' place and no longer the cottage I'd had with Les. We went to all my favourite beaches and had dinner with lovely Paul and Jeanne at The Hoste Arms. For more of an exotic treat we also flew to Necker Island in the Caribbean before I wasn't allowed to fly any more. Even though I was heavily pregnant, we had a wonderful time, and I randomly played the best tennis I'd ever played – my swing improved in order not to hit my bump!

When we returned to England, it was finally baby countdown time. Chris and I had a last lovely Christmas in London on our own together, when I had a little glass of bubbly, and just after Christmas my friend Sarah Parish threw me a baby shower in a London hotel. I was papped getting out of the car, looking like Mr Greedy from the Mr Men.

I'd been nesting and hormonal for weeks. The nursery was all painted pink and white. My dad had put up a crib and assembled the pram.

The baby was due on 2 February but because I could pick the date, we chose Monday 23 January. The Friday before we had booked *Brokeback Mountain* at the cinema but then I had the first indications that something might be about to happen. I rang my doctor and he said he thought my waters might be 'leaking', and suggested that I admit myself to the hospital later that day. Chris joked we might as well wait until after 6 p.m. to avoid paying the congestion charge! So instead I went home, straightened my hair, put some make-up on and had my nails done. (Priorities!)

As we made our way to the hospital, I felt totally prepared. Once there, Chris took a picture of me in my gown, posing in my support tights, and then he and my obstetrician, Professor Eric Jauniaux, sat scrubbed up on the floor talking about music and their favourite gigs. It reminded me of the Abba Gold CD I'd brought in my bag for the birth, but when Chris went to put it on, the CD case was empty. Disaster – this was, I might add, the first bit of panic I'd felt. 'We must have something, Chris!' I told him. He went out and reappeared shortly afterwards having bizarrely found a magazine with a free CD covermount of Burt Bacharach songs – one of my favourites.

It took them five attempts to get the epidural into my spine, which was hideous. Chris held my hand throughout and to the strains of Cole Porter *My Heart Belongs to Daddy* (how appropriate!) Alexa 'Lexi' Louise Florence was finally brought out by Caesarean section. It was 11.30 p.m. on 20 January 2006 – she just missed being an Aquarian like me. I felt fantastic – euphoric, even! – if a little tired. The nurse took a picture of the three of us. We look ecstatic and even my lip gloss stayed on!

Chris slept on a Z-bed next to me for two days and then he went home, to get the car seat and freshen up, leaving me on my own for the first time with my precious Lexi. I held her gently in my arms – she made sweet little mewing noises like a kitten and when she yawned I noticed she had inherited Chris's dimple. She was tiny and perfect and I could not have loved her more. I stayed in hospital for five days and had the most brilliant time. Chris was besotted with Lexi, but just really practical and caring of all of us – he even took one of her Babygros home so that Nobbie and Fudge could get used to her smell!

All my girlfriends came in to see me with champagne, and Mum bombed down within hours, all of our disagreements seemingly behind us. Fantastically, Lexi's birth brought the family back together. I told my mum, 'Whatever happens, whatever our differences, I want Lexi to know her family.' The trouble with my nan dissipated and I said, 'Let's start again for the sake of the baby.' Although she still wasn't talking to me, my sister sent a text to Chris which said, 'Congratulations on the birth of your daughter.' We took some lovely pictures of my mum and dad with her, and Chris's parents. I was gutted that I wasn't able to share the greatest day of my life so far with my little sister. This trivial argument lasted for several years. Debbie was living and teaching scubadiving in Thailand at the time, so I do believe that distance didn't help our relationship and perhaps that's why it went on so long. She only met Lexi once during that time.

As soon as Lexi was born, Chris admitted that having a baby was the best decision we'd ever made. He knew by then that when I made my mind up about something I'd seldom change it, or as he put it, 'Amanda doesn't bend easily.' If I want something badly enough I get it. He told everyone – and still does – that I was a great mum, which meant everything to me. Nothing prepared me for how much I would love my baby, or how important being a mum would be to me. It's the centre of everything I do.

Chapter 15

Simon Says

After five amazing months getting to know our little girl, and loving being her mummy, the following year I was back in South Africa with Lexi and a friend to help me. Chris flew out every three weeks for ten days, bonding with Lexi while I worked.

My real saving grace that year came from a surprising quarter. My 'mother', Caroline, had made an appearance in the script. One weekend, Chris and I went to Paris to stay with his friend Mick Hucknall. As we were getting on the Eurostar I spotted Hayley Mills boarding too. I was like, 'Oh my God, Chris. It's Hayley Mills. I adore her!' (Little did Hayley know it, but she and I had 'history'. Her father, the late, great Sir John Mills, had been the president at Mountview and he presented me with my certificate when I graduated. Another time, at an awards ceremony, it was my job to stand next to him and escort him to and from the stage. I was very cheeky to him and we got on really well.)

All of a sudden, boarding the train, it hit me. Hayley Mills *had* to play my mother! We even looked alike. It was almost tribal. Straight away, I was on the phone to executive producer Charlie Pattinson, telling him he had to try Hayley. They called her in and she got the part, and our connection was instant and total. She is a real character – a funny, down-to-earth woman – and I loved her. (She calls me 'Twink' and I call her 'Tumble'; don't ask me why!) Over the next couple of months, she totally bonded with Lexi and would read her stories for hours at a time. She also fell in love with Africa.

The rest of that year passed in a blur. We have some amazing photos of Lexi in Africa, and I sometimes wonder if she'll end up becoming a zoologist or something because of all those incredible experiences she'll have stored deep in her memory banks.

The climate played havoc with my skin, though. I was in South Africa and filming constantly in the bright light and I wasn't allowed to wear sunglasses in any of the shots. Before I knew it I had developed deep crease marks around my eyes and was look-ing horrendous from constantly squinting – and that's when I first had a little Botox. A journalist once asked me if I ever had it and I foolishly admitted that I had – I'm too honest! I never thought about it as a poison and it definitely worked, but that one careless comment has never left me! It's the only 'work' I've ever had done, and I hate it when the papers claim that I've had something else done – like my lips, for example. Every now and again the news-papers will claim I have no facial expressions, run a piece on me and interview a random plastic surgeon about what he or she thinks I've had done. Apart from anything, if you went to see a plastic surgeon and came out unable to move your face then you would sue them, surely!

There is more to this irritation than just vanity, though. I have a lot of younger followers these days (the Holdenites!) and it's important to me to be a good role model to them. I get loads of messages on Twitter from girls asking my advice about everything. I don't want to be seen as someone who is so unhappy that she's constantly having work done. All I did was to stop a few lines appearing. (As Lexi tells me, I look very much like my mother but 'without the cracks'.)

Once filming for the second series of *Wild at Heart* had finished, I threw myself back into being a full-time mum, relishing having so much time with my baby. I took Lexi swimming one Friday, and when we got home I put some soup on for tea. I was stirring it when I suddenly noticed I had five missed calls from my agent. I thought that was unusual – it was half six or something – so I called her back. She said, 'Amanda, something quite interesting has come up in the office. Simon Cowell . . .'

'Yes!' I said immediately. I didn't let her finish, even though I didn't know what it was they were offering me! All I knew was, I'd admired Simon for years and was definitely up for doing anything he was involved in. Our paths had only crossed twice since the Stowe ball. One was when I read in a magazine that he didn't generally like blondes but he liked Amanda Holden because 'she looks naughty' (he's right!). Then, before Chris and I got together, I was staying with Jane in LA for some meetings when Simon and I had dinner together.

Jane's friend is good friends with him, and it was her birthday, so Jane suggested she call Simon up and get him to take her out for dinner! She rang and said I was there too, and he said, 'In that case, definitely.' I was terrified as he was very flirty, so when he gestured to me to sit next to him, I said, 'Darling, I have a meeting in the morning and will need to leave around ten thirty.' (I had booked my cab in advance.) Simon, however, tells the story that HE booked my car and when it got to 10.30 p.m. he announced I had to leave. What we both agree on is that we were having such a good time that I was gutted and left, but absolutely didn't want to. Pride made me!

The next day, he texted me with the number 9. What did that mean? I agonised over it for days. Was that what I scored on the night? In the end I decided that it meant 'room for improvement' and left it at that.

When my agent got The Call for 'a new talent thing', it was all very last-minute, and they were in the middle of doing the deal, but my agent said that if they closed it successfully, I'd need to go to Birmingham on the Sunday. That was in two days. Obviously, my next thought was 'What am I going to wear?!'

Further investigation revealed it was originally to be called *Paul O'Grady's Britain's Got Talent*, but Paul had dropped out after the pilot. The premise was that contestants would audition for a place in the final and a prize of £100,000 and a chance to perform in front of the Queen at that year's *Royal Variety Performance*. My agent described it as being like *Opportunity Knocks* and *New Faces*, which of course after ten years with Les I was totally familiar with. I couldn't wait. I knew it would work. I had come from a marriage steeped in people I loved and admired from that background. I felt like we could finally do that genre justice again and give it back its good name.

My agent came back with a finished deal the next day. Chris, Lexi and I were all in the park, and I literally had to leave straight away and get on a train that night. I didn't have a stylist or anything and I was so grateful that Jess – now married with children – was prepared to drop everything to come and be my make-up artist. Even so, by the time I arrived in Birmingham I was extremely nervous.

I asked Simon, 'What do I do? How do I do this?'

He smiled, as always. 'Say exactly what you think. Be honest! If you can't think of anything to say, say you can't think of anything to say.'

He confided that the show was considered a risk, and that some TV executives were less than convinced about it. I was gob-smacked. 'But this is variety!' I said. 'It's what people have been asking to be back on telly for ages.'

But Simon had been told by executives that it might not work, which had only made him more determined. That, I have since dis-covered, is where we are very similar. If anyone puts us down, or we are on the back foot, we will come back fighting – it's like fuel to us. We share determination, and Simon recognises this in me. He has since said I am made of steel, but these days, I would say more like titanium!

There was some 'bad' news, however – our fellow judge was to be Piers Morgan, the former editor of the *Mirror* who had made my life such a misery when I split up with Les. I dreaded working with Piers and by all accounts he felt the same way because he told Simon, 'I turned Amanda's life upside down. She's going to hate me.'

The first thing I said to Piers when I met him in Birmingham was, 'I think you need to apologise to me!'

He fixed me with a stare and replied, 'I think you need to thank me.'

I was speechless (almost). 'Thank you?!'

'Yes,' he replied with a cocky grin, 'because if I hadn't exposed your affair you wouldn't be with your good-looking music pro-ducer fiancé and have your daughter.'

I said, 'That's true.' I laughed. 'But I'm never thanking you.'

He smiled and said, 'Well, I am sorry.'

I still hate that I love Piers. I must be one of the few people in the world who likes him. He is arrogant, charming, self-effacing, and extremely knowledgeable, which is annoying as he can be such a pompous pain in the arse. When it came to giving his opinion on an act, he never stopped talking. We'd just want a 'yes' or 'no', and he'd drone on, using up all the adjectives I'd thought of. I don't know how he was ever a newspaper editor. He needs editing himself!

On *Britain's Got Talent*, he'd start talking about the 'youth of today' when no one gave a damn and it was all going to get cut anyway. Simon would say, 'You're so dull and boring,' and then they'd have a big row about who has the best car, who has the best ratings on what show, who has the best gig. Even when they both appear wearing suits for the show's promotional shoot, they're needling each other. Once Simon said, 'This is how you wear a suit, Piers.' (Piers always wears a suit, even when we go out socially.) But I'd like to see him lighten up and try a really good tailored jacket with a T-shirt, instead of the predictable suit. He's only in his forties, but he seems so much older.

Piers has had an indecent amount of good luck. It's small wonder he's smug: he's reached mid-life without the crisis. He's got money, fantastic cars, a beautiful wife and gorgeous kids. But we have great chemistry together and I am very fond of him. While we were filming, we had a connecting door between our dressing rooms, we would leave the door open so that we could gossip and have a good old catch-up.

Completely by chance, it seemed, Simon had created what someone called the best judging panel in the world – although, of course, he would say that was all part of his master plan. I have always said that Simon is Frankenstein and Piers his monster. Simon helped create a TV career for Piers in the UK and then he put him on his show in the US, which made him a star over there as well. (Simon has made no secret of the fact that he takes the entire credit for Piers' success!)

The first day was amazing. I look back and can't believe how casual it all was! I wore jeans – can you imagine the big fat cross I would get in a magazine for that now! At least Simon would have some competition. Everyone always asks if I get nervous, doing live telly in front of millions of people, but honestly, Simon, Piers and I got along so well that up on that stage between them I felt really comfortable and natural and happy.

We complemented each other – and took the piss out of each other!

Technically, of course, I was the only one who had ever done any performing so, strictly speaking, I was the only one qualified to judge . . . Although, secretly, Piers and Simon are both softies too, the two boys pretended to be made of stone and, as a mum and a girl, I was the softie in the middle. I was always the first to start crying. I became a professional weeper and I know it was the thing that Simon and the producers homed in on a lot. Every time a child came on they'd have me introduce them, box of tissues at the ready. I'm amazed I've never got a Kleenex commercial, as during the first series I never seemed to stop. From early on, I coined the phrase 'The audience is the fourth judge' (well, technically Chris gave it to me) and it's now used so much it's practically a cliché.

Even now, eight series on, the live shows are like Christmas Day every day – I still wake up with butterflies and have a normal day until 3 or 4 p.m. (I go from feeding ducks by the river to watching ducks performing on stage!) I love my dressing room. Team Mandy (Ben, who does my hair, Jane, who does my make-up and Sinead, my stylist) put mood boards on the walls (we don't pay much attention to them but we like to have them there!) and there are always pictures that Lexi has drawn. It's filled with fairy lights, chocolates, candles and champagne – and most importantly, people. Everybody comes to my room – I've got all the bubbles for after the show! – and even Simon pops in for a cigarette during the ad break. It's always manic right up to the last minute as well – we never know what is coming up or what we're doing. It's the most amazing buzz – like getting on a rollercoaster without strapping yourself in.

On set, none of it is scripted or rehearsed, so it's edge-of-the-seat stuff and we have to think fast. We don't even make notes. All we are given is a piece of paper with the next contestant's name on it. I sometimes write a tick or a cross to show that they are through to the next round. If I'm bored I might draw flowers and hearts. Simon draws cars on his piece of paper – they look very phallic – whereas Piers used to doodle mad squares and circles. I should send them off and get them analysed!

Working so closely with Simon has been a revelation. We have a lot of fun but it's remarkable to witness in person the phenomenon that is Mr Cowell. Having been insolvent before the age of forty, he's a workaholic with something to prove to those who once regarded him as a joke. He oversees every aspect of his vast empire and has a memory like an elephant, which is a worry. With millions in the bank he has gone way beyond the desire for money or success and treats everything like a game. He rarely goes to bed before dawn and seems to exist on very little sleep. He does push-ups and has chin bars set up in his toilet, but then he drinks and smokes and loves to binge on fish and chips or Chinese takeaways.

We talk about food a lot on the show and I'll be like, 'I'm bloody starving. I'm having a jacket potato with baked beans for my tea.' He'll roll his eyes and say, 'It's *dinner*, Amanda, not tea!' before calling up Brenda, his housekeeper, and asking her to have jacket potato and beans waiting for him when he gets home, too. He tries to offset his worst indulgences by munching on raw organic carrots, drinking green slime that looks as if it's been dredged off the bottom of a swamp (apparently it's some kind of elixir of life!) or a special ginger infusion he has someone blend for him, or having colonic irrigation.

Simon has said before that Botox is 'just like brushing your teeth'. He also sprays his mouth with pure oxygen from a canister he keeps on his make-up table and offers to anyone who's passing. (One day I'll replace it with helium and see what he sounds like with a Mickey Mouse voice!) He once sent Dr Wendy Denning, the woman he calls his 'white witch', so that I could try a multi-vitamin injection. Jane said, 'Don't do it, Amanda,' but I was assured it was natural so I sat with Dr Wendy's drip in my arm, chatting to people and drinking champagne. The combination went straight to my head and I felt like I'd had eight gin and tonics. I was totally drunk!

Simon is very old-fashioned and can't stand any talk of medical details, womanly problems or toilet matters. I often say, 'Oh, I really need to go for a poo now!' just to wind him up. He'll pull a face, hold up his hand and say, 'Amanda! Amanda! Don't kill the magic!' And, after an edge-of-your-seat magic act on a live show, I said I might have to consider using Tena Lady pads. He was literally speechless, until he found his voice and told me I had ruined it for him for ever. If I want to get him off a subject I just start talking about his bowel movements, which he hates, so I'll laugh and tell him, 'Simon, I adore you and when you're old and decrepit I promise it will be me who wipes your arse and brings you meals on wheels!' I understand him and how his mind works. I know each of his alleged girlfriends. They aren't stupid – they know the score, but I am glad I am his friend only. His private life is fascinating. You can't help but be intrigued with the drama – and he wouldn't have it any other way.

Professionally I do have to give credit to Simon for allowing me to be me. It's enabled me to change some people's perceptions of me which were entirely based on what they had read. I have always said there is nowhere to hide on this show and I stand by that – of course, not everyone is going to like you but at least the audience have the chance to make up their own minds. That really matters to me. Best of all, 20 years of working my arse off and going through the agony of auditioning myself has meant I can be in a position to judge.

Doing the show has also helped me remember who I was when I left drama school, and why I went into the business in the first place. Seeing people with their dreams in our hands, their hopes and fears so close to the surface, has made me realise that *Britain's Got Talent* isn't just some reality television show but a life-changing moment that we have the power to make happen. It's reminded me of back then when I was that person on stage who also naively believed I was capable of anything.

I always had my family behind me but on *Britain's Got Talent* sometimes we judges are the first people to ever see a person's performance and that matters to me. I record every show, and have them all on tape, but I've only ever watched it back once, because I wanted to see Pudsey!

We judges were invited to dinner at 10 Downing Street by the then prime minister, Gordon Brown. (Well, to be accurate, Simon was . . .) Simon said he was 'too shy' to go alone and asked Piers and me to go with him. I thought, 'What do you take as a present for the prime minister?' I mean, you can't turn up with a bottle of tequila, can you? So I took some Moon Sand mouldable material for his boys – although I was a bit worried about getting through security, in case they thought it was Semtex.

It was really relaxed and informal. I was the first to arrive and when I got there Gordon's wife, Sarah, was reading the kids a bedtime story. I was looking at a cabinet of silverware when Gordon tapped me on the shoulder and then took me up in the lift to their private apartment. It was just like anyone else's house, with the kids' drawings pasted on the kitchen walls.

The boys had been given some cupcakes covered with glitter, and I told them that when they did a poo it would have glitter all over it. A few weeks later, at the *News of the World* Children's Awards, Sarah came over to me and told me that the following day both boys had been on the toilet checking for sparkly poo!

At dinner, there was no standing on ceremony. Ten of us sat round the table for dinner and there was a veggie dish and chicken, and we just tucked in. We were talking about a Michael Jackson impersonator dressed as Darth Vader who had auditioned for the show in Birmingham. Gordon knew all about it. He is so charming and charismatic, and looks more attractive in real life, and yet we never saw that side of him! We just saw this rather stuffy politician. I suggested, 'You two need your own fly-on-the-wall reality show.' We all had such a laugh that evening – so much so, in fact, that when I went to say thank you to the lady in the kitchen who'd cooked for us, she said she'd never heard such high-spirited laughter round the dinner table since Gordon took office. (Piers, of course, was at the other end of the table boring the arse off people.)

It was in that first series that a chubby Carphone Warehouse salesman named Paul Potts turned up at the Cardiff auditions. It was March 2007 and when he opened a mouth full of crooked teeth to sing Puccini's 'Nessun dorma', the hairs on the back of my neck stood to attention and my skin broke into goose pimples. Welling up as he rose to the final note, I held my breath and then jumped to my feet, along with every one of the 2,000 people in that Millennium Centre. Simon's face cracked into a broad grin and he said, 'I wasn't expecting that. That was a complete breath of fresh air. Fantastic!'

Piers predicted that Paul would win the competition and I told him, 'I think we have a little lump of coal here that is going to turn into a diamond.' When the show was eventually aired that summer, the footage of Paul's performance went viral on the Internet and attracted more than 100 million viewers. He's gone on to have a glittering career, sold millions of records and even had a film made about his life, starring James Corden and called *One Chance*. Needless to say, Paul did win *Britain's Got Talent* that year and, wearing a floor-length silver dress, I presented him to the Queen alongside Simon and Piers in Liverpool.

It was as we took to the stage that I first realised Simon needs to wear glasses. (He was too embarrassed to wear them at that time – he does now!) Back then, though, he muttered under his breath, 'Darling, I can't see the autocue.' 'Don't worry,' I told him. 'I'll say most of your words with Piers, and you can just say the last bit.' So Piers made a speech and I said something and Simon managed a few words he'd memorised before saying, 'Ladies and gentlemen, I am proud to introduce Paul Potts.'

Paul did a wonderful job and brought the house down. We met the Queen and then drove to the airport to fly back to London in Simon's private plane. As I sat back in the leather seats of his Lear jet, I was on such a high. I told Simon, 'This is like a scene from *Pretty Woman* except that I'm with you two! Where's bloody Richard Gere?'

He smiled and asked, 'More champagne, darling?'

'Of course!'

It was probably the most fabulous thing ever to happen to me. We had some cracking conversations en route, too. Piers is a bloodhound when asking questions, but Simon was amazingly trusting – we have been privy to some really juicy stuff mid air!

It's funny to think that *Britain's Got Talent* wasn't a huge ratings winner when it first went out on telly, but it grew every week by literally millions. Critics didn't want to like it – in fact, they still try really hard not to, but the ratings just kill them! The great British public are the best judges in the world, and the show is now quite rightly described as a juggernaut of entertainment. We get on board for a very fast ride. (I can only seem to use vehicles to describe my feelings for this show but that is how it feels.)

Every year, it seems I'm a normal mum one minute and then suddenly *Britain's Got Talent* throws me head first into the spotlight more than any other job I have ever done. The press attention the show attracts is enormous, and with Twitter, social media forums and the Internet it just gets bigger and bigger (take the week-long coverage after the egging incident in 2013, for example). I take a deep breath, close my eyes and jump into its glare. The comforting phrase 'It'll be tomorrow's chip paper' (or in my family's case if we ran out during my childhood, toilet paper) doesn't hold any more.

That first year of *Britain's Got Talent* was a strange one for me personally. It was full of extreme highs but also horrible lows. My brave, strong Nan spent most of it recovering from breast cancer and then my Papa died in June. I was on holiday in Italy when my mum rang to say Papa was in hospital having surgery on a benign tumour. I asked if I should fly home and she said no, he was stable. Sadly he later caught the superbug *C. difficile* and died, aged eighty-nine. I was gutted not to have said goodbye.

At Papa's funeral I read a poem. It was an emotional moment in a day that was a strangely sad and cold affair. My sister had flown home but she and I were still not talking. When I went to sit on the family side of the church Debbie and her friend had taken the last seats, so there was no space for me. I had no choice but to sit on the other side of the church with all the friends. Chris was really upset for me but I told him it was fine. In my head I told myself, 'I've got Chris, I've got Lexi and that's all I need.' Just the three of us.

Chapter 16

To Have and to Holden

Now we had our gorgeous Lexi, there seemed no reason to wait any longer to make me and Chris 'official'. He, however, wanted to hold off getting married until she was old enough to remember it, as he had wonderful memories of his aunt getting married when he was three. Instead, Chris gave me the most amazing surprise Christmas present. Totally straight-faced, he told me, 'Security say there's a package outside for you – and apparently it's bigger than a shoebox.' (This immediately got my attention!)

We went outside together and there, in the garage, sat the Morris Minor 1000 I'd always dreamed of: a cream convertible with a red leather interior. It had apparently taken months for Chris to source the right one, which he'd eventually found in Southampton. I couldn't believe it. I love it so much – we take it out in the summer with blankets and the roof down. ('Is it bigger than a shoebox?' has now become the standard family response to any surprise or gift!)

I also wanted us to add to our little family with another baby – but knew in my heart this would have to wait until after we were married. But with a wedding and another child in the not-too-distant future, a fabulous job on one of the biggest shows on television, and a role in a hit TV series filming on location in South Africa for six months of the year, obviously the sensible thing would have been to take the chance to kick back for a bit. So I did (kind of) – by entering the London Marathon.

Running the marathon is something I've always wanted to do – another box ticked! – and it was the perfect opportunity to raise money for Born Free. As soon as Mum found out, she said, 'Well, I'm doing it too, then.' She was fifty-nine! Doing gymnastics for all those years means I have a pretty good core fitness, but even so, at thirty-eight and with a personal trainer, I was finding the training tough – let alone my poor mum, pushing sixty, with her arthritic toe, doing it all on her own by walking the dog up and down hills in Cornwall. In the end, she ran for 16 miles and walked some of the rest, coming in at 5 hours 12 minutes, only an hour after me – it was amazing.

For my part, I took the training really seriously. In winter up in Norfolk I even ran in snow and hail – it was like having a bloody face peel! To keep up my morale, Chris cycled alongside me for one 15- or 16-mile run (it was nice to have someone to talk to). Back in London, I trained with Gareth Traves, my personal trainer, along a towpath up to Kew.

One freezing morning I saw a man in a hooded sweat top hunched over on the ground. We both ran past but then I stopped and turned back. It was cold and something wasn't right. I just wanted to check that the man was warm enough, so we ran back and I noticed some Night Nurse, a bottle of spirits and a packet of cigarettes on the ground next to him. There was a thin piece of cable around his neck – the other end was tied to a low branch of a nearby tree – and I felt my blood run cold. I couldn't look any closer.

'Oh my God – I think he's dead!'

I didn't want to see his face as I knew that it would haunt me for life, so I stayed behind him while Gareth went round the front to see if there were any signs of life. When he gravely nodded confirmation that the man was indeed dead, in shock, I ran to Richmond Lock bridge and knocked on the lock-keeper's door. When he did, I couldn't get the words out fast enough.

'We've just found a dead body!'

He looked at me closely. 'Aren't you that woman off the telly?'

I stared at him in disbelief (it really wasn't the moment!). 'Erm, yes! But did you hear me? We've just found a body. Can you call the police?'

Once he'd got over recognising me, I took him back to the scene and he radioed the police. Before long, squad cars appeared, and Gareth and I both gave statements, which the officers took very sympathetically – they could tell we were both in shock. The way the man had been found, and all other signs, were pointing to 'death by deliberate act'. Apparently a common form of suicide is to put a noose around your neck and then drink or take enough drugs to get totally out of it, when you slump forward and strangle yourself. I just couldn't take it in. It was so surreal – and so sad.

Of course, the story that I had found a body was all over the papers the next day, and not long afterwards I received a letter from his widow – it was such a warm, gracious letter, in which *she* apologised to *me* for being the one to find him. It turned out they had a young son, and I couldn't have felt worse for her.

I ran the marathon a few weeks later, and it was one of the best things I have ever done. Everyone says that having kids is the best thing you can do but for me, the London Marathon is right up there too! I loved every minute – from getting to the start on a Virgin Limousine Taxi Bike (my mum got one too!) to sprinting down the Mall. No one watching could work out where I got the energy from – but I was listening to various tracks but constantly to Robbie Williams *Let Me Entertain You* and Take That's *Rule The World* that Chris and I planned to walk out of church to after we married. I'd been tagged by the BBC so I could be interviewed on Tower Bridge, but by the time I got there I didn't want to waste time talking to them, so I just ran on. I'm very competitive!

I have never felt more elated in my life – as soon as it finished I felt like I could do it all over again. Friends who saw my TV interview straight after the race didn't believe I had done it, and they joked that I looked like I'd just been for a shop round Harvey Nicks. I was so proud with my finish time: 4 hours, 13 minutes and 22 seconds, a respectable 2,771 out of 34,000. I came back down to earth with a bump, though, when I met up with Dad, who was meant to be taking me and Mum home. It took ages to find Mum after she'd finished and then it turned out that Dad, being Dad, hadn't wanted to pay for parking close to St James's Palace and had found a spot halfway across the West End. So after running 26.2 miles we had to walk another mile and a half to the bloody car!

When we eventually got home I cooked a four-course dinner and me and my Mum polished off a bottle of wine between us with our medals still on. It was brilliant. Two days later, so sore I could hardly walk, we moved house and I spent all day moving boxes up and down the stairs.

A new series of *Britain's Got Talent* had begun in January with the usual two days here, three days there spread across a month (I'm never away for more than ten days in total) and then in June I was to start filming my last series of *Wild at Heart*. After three years, I had decided it was high time for me to leave. However much she loved the giraffes and elephants, I couldn't keep taking Lexi away for months at a time – it wasn't fair on her or Chris.

As it was their last chance to visit, I decided to fly Nan and Mum out to South Africa with me in July. As a surprise I booked a cruise for them all for that coming December. My Nan had wanted to go on one her whole life. She was feeling lost after losing Papa – they had been together for sixty-four years, after all – and I wanted to do something to try and take her mind off her loss.

I was adamant that I didn't want to just walk out of *Wild at Heart*, or leave my story open-ended – for a start, my character deserved a more dramatic end, and I didn't want to have any chance of being lured back. I quite fancied getting eaten by a lion but in the end I burned to death in a bush fire created by special effects. It was really hot and I was surrounded by gas pipes while trying to save a cheetah – you couldn't make it up. I made sure all the black make-up was glamorously placed across my face, and I was still wearing lipgloss, obviously! It did, however, tick the dramatic box and I got to scream and scream. I watched my own funeral being filmed, which was a bit weird. I'm not sure I'd want to do that again.

Back home, there was lots to keep me occupied. We had finally fixed a date for our wedding (our invitations featured a cartoon showing me dragging him to church on a lead). We booked the private chapel at Babington House in Somerset for a candlelit ceremony, which we'd fallen in love with at my friend Angela Griffin's wedding, and as 10 December 2008 approached I asked Mum, Nan and my future mother-in-law Polly to come with me to Harrods to help choose my wedding dress.

It started off as a really fun day – we all had champagne and I tried on dress after dress while they told me what they thought. It was a bit like a wedding-themed *Britain's Got Talent*, only with more outspoken judges. I was in my element – and so carried away with the moment – until, wearing a gorgeous dress and standing on one of those round plinth things, I looked at my nan and said, 'What do you think, Nanny?'

She looked up at me and said, 'As long as you're happy, dear?' (Her expression said, 'Should you even be doing this?')

I was stunned. They were all very keen on Chris, and my mother had even described him as my soulmate. I didn't know how to respond. So I said, 'Yes. YES!' That response itself made me cross with myself. Only seconds before, I'd never been so happy, and suddenly I was trying to justify it. It was normal for Nan to be outspoken, but this had sounded loaded and I was so upset. I thought, 'Why would you even say that to me?'

Meanwhile, Debbie hadn't seen Lexi in nearly three years – she hadn't even sent a Christmas or birthday card – and it was that that had bothered me more than our fallout. So I sent her an e-mail which said, 'If you can be happy for us then you are invited. If you can't, then don't come.' (Chris said it was a bit mean, but it was how I felt. I was devastated.) But Debbie never replied. Nan then refused to come because my sister 'wasn't invited' and, for a while, my mum said the same.

Jane flew over from California in time for my hen weekend. To be honest, at this stage I was so upset over the family rift that I didn't even want a hen. But Sarah Parish insisted on organising one for me, and it was fabulous. Chris went off to Monaco and did a proper stag weekend, whilst us girls went to Norfolk for a weekend. We had spa treatments and went for bike rides. (On one we stopped off at a pub, had too much to drink and had to get the lovely bike-hire man to come and pick us and the bikes up in his van because we couldn't be bothered to ride them back!)

After that, on the Saturday night, we got a coach into Norwich, had teppenyaki and then went to a nightclub where they'd cordoned off an impromptu VIP area for us all. During the meal, I had to fry an egg on the teppenyaki hot plate, slipped in some cooking oil and bruised my coccyx (the glamour!). The best bit, though, was on the way in to Norwich on the coach. We were listening to a request show on the local radio station, so one of the girls called in and made a request for 'Amanda's hens' – she didn't give my surname so they had no idea it was me. Moments later, we got a mention – I was so excited. It made my night to get a shout out on Radio Norwich!

As our big day itself approached, on the face of it, everything was perfect. All our close friends were coming. The press made a really big deal of Simon Cowell not being there, but the truth was, we didn't invite him. (There's just no point in inviting Simon to weddings; they're not his thing. He didn't even go to Piers' wedding party – so we saved him the bother of not turning up.) I asked Paul Whittome to make a speech, but there was a huge hole in my day. My sister told me later she regretted her stubborness, she had never felt so depressed about not being there, and got drunk on whisky.

In spite of that, we had a lovely day. I wore a stunning crystal-encrusted Elie Saab dress; my 'old and borrowed' was a garter from my friend Shara who started out doing my nails on *Cutting It* and became one of my dearest friends; my 'blue' was a blue bow on my knickers, and my 'new' was a beautiful diamond bracelet Chris bought me for our wedding day. My bridesmaids – Jane, Jess and Lexi – were in mink-coloured dresses, and Nobbie and Fudge were there in matching ribbons. The chapel looked beautiful and Escala, the female violinists from the previous year's *Britain's Got Talent*, serenaded our guests as my dad walked me down the aisle.

Rose Keegan read from *The Good Wife's Guide* circa 1955, which included the advice:

Your goal is to make sure your home is a place of peace, order and tranquility, where your husband can renew himself in body and spirit. Don't complain if he is late home or even if he stays out all night. Count this as minor compared to what he may have gone through that day. Remember, he is the master of the house and you have no right to question him. A good wife always knows her place. [How we laughed!]

I'd always wanted it to snow on my wedding day so we had hired a company called Snow Business to create fake TV snow all around us. As we came out of the chapel it was like a scene from Narnia and I cried, 'Oh my God – it's snowing!' Then I reminded myself! Stupid Mandy.

Everything was decorated with silver and white roses – even the arch we walked under as we left the church. We had a room for the children, set up as a Snow Queen adventure, and Father Christmas and his reindeer put in an appearance. Just over a hundred of us sat down for the wedding breakfast, and we feasted on a menu of sharing plates which included pesto pasta, shepherd's pie (with HP sauce), sea bass and lamb.

The speeches – Dad, Jess, Chris, Paul Whittome and our best man David Coulthard – were all heartfelt, hilarious (and eventful). Dad was only a minute or so into his when there was suddenly a huge crash as one of the floral displays toppled over, breaking all the glasses and plates on the table below it. A stunned silence fell over the room, with everyone looking at each other awkwardly and shuffling on their seats. I couldn't believe it. I was also – very uncharacteristically – speechless. Seconds later, another one fell, wrecking everything in its wake. It was like some kind of wrecking sequence in a sitcom – except not that amusing. Suddenly, though, I saw the funny side and burst out laughing. At that point everyone else fell about too, and my dad could continue.

His was a brilliant speech. Chris's speech went down a bomb, despite him being so nervous he didn't touch his shepherd's pie, by mentioning the running joke we have with my parents about the fact that they drive a Skoda. Then he told everybody that we'd bought them a new mode of transport. Mum's eyes lit up – until Chris produced a broomstick for her. He finished: 'To quote from Jerry Maguire: "I love my wife, I love my life, and I wish you my kind of success!"'

After Chris's speech, Piers apparently put the wind up David by telling him the rule of thumb was that there had to be one rubbish speech at every wedding, and so it had to be his. David wasn't fazed though – not only was his speech a touching reminder of how much Chris means to him (he and David are like brothers and still a big part of each other's lives), and full of one-liners, but he also brought in a barber's shop quartet to help deliver it!

Despite the notable absences in the room, I was so happy. We had the most wonderful friends, family and each other, and as we flew off to the Maldives on honeymoon, I felt calm, as though, once and for all, I was drawing a line under all the drama in my life.

Chapter 17

Boyle in the Bag

The next series of *Britain's Got Talent* was unforgettable in more ways than one and proved how this business can make or break you in an instant. That series first featured a very public 'break' and then perhaps the biggest instantaneous 'make' in television history. I was centre stage for both of them.

The *Britain's Got Talent* calendar used to start with the contracts being signed towards the middle of December, which meant we celebrated Christmas and then started the new year really looking forward to starting on the new series (now they tend to get all the contracts sorted for the following year straight after the latest series, which makes much more sense).

I've always made it clear how much I love doing the show, and how happy I am to be asked back every year. I consider myself very lucky to be a part of it. I always tell Simon, 'If you ever sack me, you tell me to my face!' The thing is, I know he'd never have the guts to do it himself – he always gets his executive producer

Richard Holloway, aka The Grim Reaper, to deliver bad news – and so I've told him if that ever happens I'll just keep turning up regardless!

But in January 2009, I came back from my honeymoon with an awful feeling of dread. I couldn't put my finger on it, but the gut instinct that has never failed me was telling me something was wrong. Then, just before I got in the car to go to Manchester for the first round of *Britain's Got Talent* auditions, I received a phone call. It was Richard Holloway, and my heart dropped to the floor. (I wouldn't be surprised if Richard hasn't ended some of Simon's relationships in the past.)

Richard began by saying, 'I do hope you had a nice holiday. I just wanted to let you know that there is going to be a fourth judge.'

I laughed. 'Oh, very funny!'

'No, seriously,' he said. 'We've booked Kelly Brook.'

I was gutted. I had nothing against Kelly – I didn't even know her – but I was really upset. The dynamic between we three judges was unbeatable. I thought we were the dream team. I was the only girl, sandwiched between 'my boys', and I liked it that way. We had all been friends from the start, but we had become even closer as the series continued. Simon, Piers and I were like The Three Musketeers. All for one and one for all. It felt as if Simon had adopted a stranger into our family on a whim, and I didn't understand why he had to change things.

It was only when I met up with everyone else that I realised I wasn't the only one who'd found it a shock – in fact, the whole team was furious. It seemed the thing people were most upset about was that there had been no warning. Richard Holloway told me that Piers didn't know yet. He was only to be told when he arrived and we all met for drinks. (Of course, I rang him and told him myself – he's my friend!) He was just as annoyed. We were all pissed off because we had no warning and were not consulted, and the show would be filmed in 24 hours.

But I had seen the relationship between Danni Minogue and Cheryl Cole on *The X Factor*, that had been created to look competetive, and I wasn't going to play the game of having two women fighting. I hate that kind of shit, so I talked to Piers and we decided to go and find her – and then we discovered she had been put in another hotel!

We all arrived at the venue the next morning and Simon was late, as always. Ant and Dec, professionals to the end, were there, and Kelly didn't get off to a great start when she went up to them and asked, 'So, what do you do on the show, then?' Whoops. It seemed she hadn't even seen the show. I grabbed her and hugged her like a long-lost friend and told her, 'You'll be amazing!' At that point, Simon finally walked in and smiled. 'Hi, kids! Have you all met?'

We could have killed him and, one by one, everyone pounced on him privately, asking him what was he thinking. He said very little and instead seemed to secretly be enjoying the havoc. He was like a cat, playing with his pet mice. Then, when we finally went out into the auditorium and looked up at our names above the crosses, I stopped dead in my tracks – Simon had placed Kelly next to him instead of me. That really stung, but I could have won an Oscar that night for my performance, even though I was dying inside.

Kelly was sweet and inoffensive, but judging isn't as easy as everyone thinks. You have to find something interesting and different to say about every act, and you can't be bland or repetitive.

On a practical level, it was also very confusing having four judges back then, as nobody had worked out a format. With three judges on the panel, the contestants knew that if two buzzers went off they were fighting for survival; three, and they were off. But when two out of four went off they didn't know where they were, which was a technicality that hadn't been thought through. Ant and Dec, who were watching from the wings waiting for it all to kick off, had to keep explaining that they needed three buzzers to guarantee getting through to the next round. And we were listening to four people's opinions. It slowed the process down, and we didn't finish until midnight. We were knackered, the audience was falling asleep – and everyone was confused.

After that first night, Simon admitted that he'd made a mistake but he said he couldn't get rid of Kelly straight away because that wouldn't be fair. But that weekend, at home for Lexi's birthday party, the papers were full of 'The Amanda-Kelly War', with photos of us both in cream dresses, trying to make out there was friction between us that simply didn't exist. I mean, if there's a massive hole with a flashing sign over it saying, 'Jump in and be a bitch', I'm not likely to fall into it, am I? It couldn't have been further from the truth, and there were no spats. It's not me. I'm a girl's girl.

I came straight back from those auditions for Lexi's birthday – I'm always given the weekend off to celebrate it with her – and as I was in the middle of her Tinkerbell birthday party, the call came through that Kelly Brook was not coming back for the next auditions in Glasgow. She was very dignified and to her credit, because of the fuss the papers had made, she made it clear to everyone that her leaving had nothing to do with me. Kelly is amazing – she never stops working – but she just wasn't right for our show.

And so the Glasgow auditions in April 2009 started with the production team in a much better frame of mind. The auditions were to be held at the King's Theatre, where I'd appeared in *Aladdin* with Les what felt like a hundred years before. Scotland is always a hard gig, and Glasgow is the toughest. Its audience is the scariest in the whole country, and fiercely loyal. They even have their own chants!

Close to the end of the day, Piers and I were, as always, full to the brim of milky lattes and burping Red Bull. Simon, on the other hand, had probably OD'd on mango smoothies. The atmosphere was so dark and black that Simon was really worried about how he would edit the show, and he was also getting bored, so we were trying to keep his spirits up.

Simon gets bored very easily and sometimes has a face on him that looks like he's just sat down for double maths on a Friday afternoon, so I'll suggest we write notes on paper, draw stupid things or play games – like the one where we have to add words into our comments (in the past I've told a ventriloquist I didn't trust him because he was 'as slippery as a moray eel', and told a woman she was like 'raspberry ripple ice cream' . . .)

Simon toys with me as well – one day he told me that the next contestant was pregnant so I asked her, 'Are you up the duff?' She didn't understand me, so I said, 'Sorry, are you expecting?' Still she didn't get it, so I said, 'Are you having a baby?' 'No I am not!' she replied indignantly. Simon laughed and said, 'Oh, Amanda – you bitch!' I was mortified. Later he told me that one contestant had been a man in a previous life and said I should ask them about it, but I knew he was trying to trick me and refused. (It is only ever me he seems to play this game with and sometimes I play and sometimes I don't!)

But on this occasion we hadn't had a chance to start any games before a thickset middle-aged woman from a small town in West Lothian walked out on to the stage – she was giddy and excitable, and to be honest, we all thought she was one of our more eccentric acts. My first hunch was that she'd be a stand-up comic and my heart sank.

I try not to judge by appearance (I mean, Paul Potts didn't exactly look great when we first saw him, and he sang like an angel) but even though she was in a favourite gold dress and had clearly made a bit of an effort, her black tights and white shoes she now admits herself were a no, no. She said her name was Susan Boyle. Simon asked her how old she was and in a thick Scottish accent she said, 'Forty-seven, and that's just one side of me.' Simon asked what her dream was and she said she wanted to be a professional singer as successful as Elaine Paige but hadn't been given the chance before. 'Here's hoping it will change,' she added. Someone shouted something and the audience began to get restless. They wanted blood, and by now were laughing at her and shouting, 'Elvis, get off Elvis.' Susan announced she was going to sing 'I Dreamed a Dream' from *Les Misérables* and I gave Piers a look which said, 'Oh God, here we go!'

But what happened next that day was unbelievable. Now, we call it a YouTube moment (until then YouTube, MySpace or Twitter hadn't really had an impact on us, but now it is a core part of the show. The first question Simon will ask a band is how many YouTube hits they have had). Susan's singing was something else. I had goosebumps – in fact, I've got goosebumps now just thinking about it! Even that toughest of Glasgow audiences jumped to its feet and started cheering within a few seconds of her opening her mouth. I joined them, leaning back against my chair, hands behind my head in shock. (When I look back at that clip that went global, I just think, 'Thank God I waxed those pits!') As I watched Susan, I had tears in my eyes. I felt ashamed of myself for judging her – she was amazing.

Piers told her that she was the biggest surprise of his three years on the show. He said people had laughed at her when she'd said she wanted to be like Elaine Paige. 'No one is laughing now,' he added. 'Stunning. An incredible performance. I am reeling from shock.' I told her, 'I am so thrilled, because I know that everybody was against you. I honestly think that we were all being very cyn-

Me and Chris on
our first date

Chris with 'Mr Greedy'

Chris, Me and Lexi when she
was three minutes old

All cleaned up

Me, Chris and Lexi
in South Africa

Me and Lexi say 'hi' to our
South African neighbours

Simon Cowell, Me and
Piers Morgan meeting Her
Majesty The Queen at the
Royal Variety Show 2009.
The first that *Britain's Got
Talent* was involved in

My Norfolk hen weekend
(L–R: Shara Walsh, Lucy Jo
Hudson, Jane Wall, Me, Sian
Reeves, Sally Haynes, Sarah
Parish and Angela Griffin)

Our Wedding Invitation!

Karen Minier, Chris, Me and Best Man,
David Coulthard

Jane Wall, Me and
Jessica Taylor

Me, Lexi and Chris
say 'I do'

In something a little
more comfortable

The only way Piers can shut me up

Me with Ant and Dec
backstage at *BGT*

Me and Chris attend the *Brit Awards*

Me and My Simon

Not a lot of things go over
my head, but this did! *BGT*
Winners 2010, Spellbound

Chris, Lexi and Me at home

Lexi's first day at school
(I was a wreck!)

Maldives Holiday, 2010, where Lexi got the
happy news. I love this picture.

ITV Midwife documentary *Out of my
Depth* where I met my three 'white
witches'. This is Pippa Nightingale

Me pregnant with the
little boy we lost

My Happy Happy place – Shutters On
The Beach, Santa Monica, LA

Me as Princess Fiona in the original West End cast of *Shrek* doing the 'Rat Tap'

Me, Richard Blackwood as Donkey and Nigel Lynsay as Shrek.

The Princess finally got to meet her Prince

Me and Chris at the *National Television Awards*

Me as host of ITV's *Superstar* with Sir Andrew Lloyd Webber and Melanie Chisholm

Our first family pic with Hollie

BGT Judges: Alesha Dixon, Simon Cowell, David Walliams and Me

Me and Alesha, cackling!

Uncle Simon gives me a bear hug for Hollie

(L–R: Melissa and Angela Griffin, Hollie and Me, Martha and Lucy Gaskill, Sarah Parish and Nell, Lexi and Tallulah)

Larking around on set at *BGT*

Lexi's first shot of her at home with her sister

Lexi with beloved Muffy

Circle of Life! Lexi and HRH

Hollie does it 'her way'

Lexi and HRH at Mels Diner, LA, 2013. I could eat them!

ical and I think that is the biggest wake-up call ever. I just want to say it was a complete privilege listening to that.' Simon, of course, claimed he could tell the minute Susan walked on to the stage that we were going to hear something extraordinary and added, 'and I was right!' Cheeky bugger.

Her performance really struck us all that night, but none of us could have imagined what would happen next. Later, Chris phoned me and asked if we found anyone, and I simply said, 'Yes, I think we had a Paul Potts moment.' I didn't even have Susan down to win! She was definitely in my top five, but we had some strong contenders for the final – she was up against Diversity and Flawless.

When the Susan Boyle audition show aired, the world went nuts. Piers called me the next day and said, 'Have you heard about Susan Boyle?' (Can you believe I replied. 'Susan who?') I had no clue what he was talking about so I put the news on. It was on the news. She was on the news. *I* was on the news myself! The video went viral around the globe and she must have almost brought YouTube to a standstill. (I was wearing a hideous green satin dress on the clip – typical that was the one that went worldwide!) Chris put her on Google Alerts for me but had to turn it off because of the input. When you flicked channels, you would just hear Susan Boyle/Susan Boyle/Susan Boyle. It was the first time the public had seen something like that. It was mad, huge and life-changing – for all of us.

But it was America that *really* got her. She epitomises the American dream, that it doesn't matter what you look like or where you come from. Demi Moore and Ashton Kutcher tweeted about her and her story took off from there. I tweeted Demi back and said, 'Why don't you come to the finals?' Swiftly, Susan became known as SuBo. News crews from all over the world flew to

Scotland to interview Susan at her modest little house. Within hours, I had news crews turning up at my house, too, and the next few weeks were crazy as I did live feeds to NBC, Fox, CBS in the US and other TV shows all over the world. Interviewer after interviewer asked me, 'How did you feel when you first heard her sing? How do you feel now?'

After watching me and interviewing me, CBS asked me to be their 'special British contributor', which meant presenting live shows and being a news correspondent, covering anything from the Afghan war to fashion bargains. They wanted me to comment on anything and everything, and suddenly I was spending most of my time back and forth to their studios in New York. I couldn't believe it. All those fruitless years of traipsing around LA for pilot season and it took an unassuming unemployed singer from Scotland to start my career in America. All of a sudden I was introduced as, 'Live from London, here's Special Correspondent Amanda Holden!' Everyone knew who I was and wanted to know what I thought, what Susan would be wearing for the finals, how she was doing or how I thought she'd cope with future fame as she had learning difficulties. I told them she was tougher than she looked. 'She's been singing in Glasgow bars! She's a tough cookie.' Weeks later, Susan was still on every news channel in the US. There was a major plane crash, and even that was still second to the Susan Boyle story, nearly two weeks after it had first broken.

CBS asked me to go to the States and anchor a show for a week's holiday cover. Bear in mind that, up to this point, my presenting skills stretched as far as shiny-floor shows – or what the industry calls light entertainment. So there I was, with my male co-presenter, interviewing (for example) a woman who had her kids taken away from her because she was so obese. Every afternoon I would have to meet my producer, to get my 'package' and see what I was going to be talking about and what I was going to wear (you can't have too much cleavage over there – Lorraine Kelly would cause a scandal in middle America with her chest!).

When it came to the finals six weeks later, Susan seemed nervous but I was actually more concerned about the other contestants – it seemed a given that she'd win. Susan had really enjoyed all the attention but the pressure for her to come up with the goods again – this time with the whole world watching – was massive.

Backstage, I asked if she was okay and she told me she was going to be sick. 'Oh, that's normal,' I told her. 'Barbra Streisand is sick every time she goes on stage.' She went outside and had a cup of tea with my motorbike taxi driver, Rhys, who'd just dropped me off, and they had a poignant conversation about how she knew her life would change.

The vote came in and Susan was named as the first act in the top three. Saxophonist Julian Smith and dance troupe Diversity were named too, as Susan stood stony-faced and bilious. Eventually Ant and Dec announced that Julian was out, leaving Susan and Diversity as the final two. It seemed as if all the predictions would come true. Then the announcement came that Diversity had won – which, on the face of it, was a huge shock, but of course the demographic of voters is mainly young. None of us know the result beforehand, and it was like a moment frozen in time.

Susan put on a brave face and smiled and clapped but I could tell she was gutted, as if her world had ended. I felt so sorry for her. Once she left the stage her façade crumbled – she thought it was all over – and she was spirited away with the other contestants to a hotel in Wembley near to Fountain Studios where *Britain's Got Talent* is filmed, while as on previous shows, us judges all went to The Dorchester for post-finals drinks . . .

It was in her hotel that Susan had what can only be described as a bit of a breakdown. I think the pressure became too much for her and she buckled under it. It had been her only option, and she thought her dream had been snatched away. She thought her life was over and the whole thing a cruel gimmick. Fortunately she has a very sensible brother who looked after her well and, with his help, the producers got her into The Priory clinic to have a rest. Of course, she made worldwide headlines again. I was flown to CBS to appear on their breakfast show and was also invited on to *Larry King Live* on CNN to comment. Treading carefully, I quoted her brother as saying she was in a clinic and was very much looking forward to coming out and seeing what work was on offer to her when she felt better.

'*Britain's Got Talent* is a very loyal show and all the contestants are extraordinarily well looked after,' I told Larry King. 'We love Susan and she's getting the best possible support.' I told Susan's American fans that if she was a loser then she was 'the biggest and best loser in the world' and coming second was no bad thing.

On CBS's *Early Show* I sat against a backdrop of Union Jack cushions with tea and cakes, and chatted to their anchors. Later, they encouraged me to come up with my own ideas so I had breakfast at Tiffany's, took a horse carriage ride around Central Park and auditioned people to see if I could find 'a new Susan Boyle'. Thanks to Susan, I went on to host a series of magazine slots for CBS, including red carpet interviews at events such as Elton John's Academy Awards party (Victoria Beckham told me she'd been touched to see me 'looking amazing' in one of her dresses a few weeks earlier!) and interviews on their sofa for stars such as Leonardo DiCaprio, Johnny Depp, Cate Blanchett, Anne Hathaway, Tim Burton and Keira Knightley. I covered the Royal Wedding and the exhibition of Princess Diana's dresses at Kensington Palace, but turned down covering the Olympics for them because I was going to LA that summer with Chris and Lexi. I even interviewed Simon at his home. The Beatles had just gone on to iTunes and so I asked if he would have put them through if they had auditioned on *The X Factor*. He said he'd put three of them through and get rid of the drummer, which caused a huge uproar.

Over this time I appeared on just about every chat show sofa in the UK, too – except Jonathan Ross's, that is. Years earlier he'd made a cheap gag about me at the Comedy Awards during my affair with Neil (even the audience had booed him!), and I'd vowed I'd never do his programme, especially after he continued the gag for three consecutive years. I've never regretted it, either. After he and Russell Brand got the sack from the BBC, he moved to ITV and included me on his wishlist of guests for his last BBC show. He wrote me a letter telling me I was on it. Over the years, Jonathan had made countless cheap gags at my expense and although he had indirectly apologised, it was great to say no. 'I'd rather go on a new couch than a stinky old one,' I wrote back. (I may guest in future though – I'm over it now!)

The first time I heard Susan's album *I Dreamed a Dream* I was at Simon's house in Los Angeles with Chris and Piers. It was very dark and Simon had fire torches burning all around his swimming pool. He put 'Wild Horses' on and said, 'Listen to this.' Susan's voice rang out into the night, and it was an ethereal, spiritual moment. What a voice! I thought even Simon might cry. Chris said it would be the biggest selling record in the world, and in 2010 it was – it's still the biggest selling debut of all time.

One of the reasons I love *Britain's Got Talent* so much is that it constantly reminds me of why I got involved in the business in the first place, and there's no better story to illustrate that than Susan's. She has proved that talent wins out, and that anyone from anywhere can make it. She has released four albums, sold more records than anyone else in the world over the last four years, netted over £22 million and she's now a showbiz legend even though her career has only just begun. She has truly dreamed her dream, and she's inspired the rest of us to never give up on ours. The words Susan Boyle and global phenomenon are now forever entwined – whenever you search one you'll get the other – and I became central to that phenomenon too. I was and still am so proud to have been a part of it.

The only question now was, how the hell was *Britain's Got Talent* going to top all that?

Chapter 18

A Bumpy Year

The worldwide focus on *Britain's Got Talent* meant work offers came flooding in, and when ITV asked me to train as a midwife and front a documentary *Out of My Depth*, I was immediately intrigued. Midwifery was a subject I was really interested in, and now, having done it, something I really believe I could do for a living. And so, with our second baby still not on the agenda, I focused on the next best thing – other people's babies!

Putting on my uniform and starting my training at West Middlesex Hospital was terrifying and amazing, but I felt right at home, and I loved and adored every minute of it. Under the expert eyes of Pippa Nightingale, Natalie Carter and Jackie Nash, I spent five weeks doing my basic training of scrubbing beds, holding hands, hugging tearful mums and dads, sieving poo out of birthing pools (yep!) and – best of all – delivering five babies, including twins in a Caesarean section (although I only watched that one ...). The best thing about the whole experience, though, was meeting the three women, who not only became close friends but my 'guardian angels' in the months and years to come.

It was in Norfolk during a break in filming in May 2009 that we had a call from Los Angeles telling us that Mike, Chris's dad, was critically ill in hospital. He'd been hit by a UPS truck which had been left parked on a hill with a faulty handbrake. It rolled down the hill soundlessly (the engine wasn't on) and into his side, and he'd been rushed to hospital in a coma. Chris was distraught, especially when he heard more about the circumstances. Mike had apparently just nipped out to buy a newspaper, and was carrying no ID so the hospital had called him 'Charlie Trauma'. Through some nifty detective work based on a business card in his pocket the police finally found out who he was and called Chris. The doctors told us that they didn't know if he would survive or that, if he did, if he would ever walk again.

We flew straight out to see him. Poor Mike had suffered multiple injuries and looked terrible. His body was black and blue, they'd had to insert metal plates into his face and he'd broken several bones. Luckily he made almost a full recovery.

When we were packing up Mike's room to take him home weeks later he wouldn't let Chris take his bag. Chris, being a gent, was insistent he carry it for his dad. They were having a bit of a tussle when the bag fell open and a load of hospital booty fell out. It turned out Mike had been stashing every pair of socks he'd been given, along with every plastic knife and fork, eye mask and disposable bottle. His defence was, 'You never know when you might need this stuff!' (A year to the day later, I was making a beach picnic for us when I opened a drawer in his house and found all the stuff – napkins, forks, the lot. There was everything we needed for the picnic except the food – even salt and pepper. He was right – you do never know when you're going to need stuff!) Later, Chris's dad successfully sued UPS for all the trauma caused.

I came back home from LA to carry on filming with my mid-wives and then was asked to star in *Big Top,* a new BBC television comedy series. I played Lizzie, the Ring Mistress of Circus Maestro. It was produced by the talented John Stroud, who I'd worked with on *Kiss Me Kate.* I loved John, and it was a great cast, but there was an air of sadness over the whole production. John had been struck down on the ski slopes and subsequently diagnosed with a brain tumour. He was fighting it throughout filming, but sadly died later that year. We were all devastated – he was a great producer and a good man.

Meanwhile ITV had asked me what I might like to do next, and I had said, flippantly, 'I'd love to be a stuntperson!' So, almost as a joke, we came up with the concept of *Fantasy Lives* – a three-part series in which I lived out my fantasies of being a country singer in Nashville, a showgirl in Paris and a movie stuntperson in Hollywood. Each episode was better than the last (the stuntperson role was the best, though!). I got to play a police officer chasing a villain, I leapt off buildings, did some hand-to-hand combat, rode a horse and watched my own (fake) skin go up in flames.

Whilst I was doing my training one of the girls on the crew found some kind of pea-sized growth in her tummy. A doctor came on set, and I asked him to check out a tiny lump I'd felt in my breast a couple of days earlier. He was really worried, and advised me to go in for a scan straight away. This, of course, transformed my mild concern into panic, and for the twenty-four hours until I could get to see a consultant, I carried on practising my crash land-ing, jumping 60 feet on to mats, which I was loving, with the prospect of some awful diagnosis in the back of my mind. In the event, the scan didn't show anything up, and I was given the all clear. It turned out that 'lump' the doctor had felt was actually my rib. Only in America! (I still think it was worth checking out, though.)

As it turned out, it was just as well I got all that action out of my system, because with my next big news it became clear I certainly wouldn't be throwing myself off the top of buildings for a while. At last, I was pregnant! Chris and I were both thrilled to be expecting again and the timing seemed perfect, for us and for Lexi, who was *desperate* for a brother or sister. After my first scan (with my new midwife friends at the West Middlesex Hospital) I relaxed into my pregnancy. By Easter 2010, I was sixteen weeks pregnant and feeling great. (I always seem to be pregnant at Easter – it must be when my eggs are ready!) But one night, I was sitting at the dinner table when I had the overwhelming feeling of wanting to be sick. I went to the toilet and found that I was bleeding.

I panicked, and got straight in the car and drove to the West Middlesex Hospital for a scan. The scan showed there was nothing wrong with the baby, but I still didn't feel right, and I was advised that the best possible thing would be to rest. Chris wanted me to stay at home, but I longed to be in Norfolk where I knew I would properly be able to unwind, and drove there to have a few days' peace and quiet while Chris stayed in London. Once I got there, though, it became clear that actually there was something very wrong. I knew my baby wasn't going to survive. I called Chris straight away. He was upset, and worried, and frustrated that I was so far away when I needed help – and when I needed him.

'I told you not to go on your own!' he said. 'I'm coming up.'

The trouble was, we still hadn't told anyone I was pregnant and we certainly didn't want anyone outside the family to know what was happening. Chris called his mum. She was unavailable, so a close friend looked after Lexi while we went back to London. I remember looking out of the car window and trying not to cry as we got closer and closer to the hospital. I tried not to show it, but inside I was crumbling.

The hospital confirmed what we didn't need confirming, and Chris stayed with me throughout. I was crying my eyes out on my way to theatre, because there were teddy bears just everywhere. (Afterwards I suggested that they get rid of them because not everyone is in there for happy stuff.) When I came round from the anaesthetic, I was groggy but my doctor tells me the first thing I said was, 'I need a glass of champagne.' Obviously, that was the last thing I needed, and so instead I got an orange Calippo lolly.

A week or so later I went back to my doctor and I looked at my notes and saw the words 'male foetus'. A little boy. My heart broke again. Chris, of course, was devastated, too, but we agreed that we had no choice but to get on with life. We had to go on, for us, and for Lexi's sake. There was nothing to be gained from moping. For me, that meant trying for another baby as soon as possible. I was almost forty and time was running out. I desperately didn't want Lexi to be an only child. I just had to persuade Chris, who didn't want to see me heartbroken again.

We kept the whole event private – no one knew anything about it and that suited us fine. Chris took me away to a spa to recover and the cottage he rented wasn't far from my nan's house. My relationship with her was still strained over the wedding debacle, and she still wasn't over the fact that Debbie and I had fallen out and that Debbie hadn't been at my wedding. I have always had an especially strong bond with my nan and I was gutted that all this had happened so, since she knew that we had lost the baby, I told Chris, 'Let's do this. Let's go see my nan.' I knocked on her door and as she opened it, she stood there like Elsie Tanner with her arm across the doorway. I said, 'Nanny, we were just in the area and I thought it would be nice to come and see you.' But she didn't seem to feel the same way – in fact she looked at her watch pointedly and said; 'How long are you staying? Your Auntie Vivienne is coming over to take me to the carpet shop.' She didn't even suggest we wait and see my Auntie Vivian! So, we left. I even tried to make excuses for her, until later Mum rang me and told me that Nanny had rung to confess that she'd been awful to us. She wasn't apologetic though – it was almost as though she was proud of how she'd behaved. Mum said; 'You're both as stubborn as each other,' but I didn't feel stubborn. I felt that she had let me down badly. She had always been such a huge influence on me, but when I really needed her, she cut me down. So, in order to protect myself from any more heartache, I decided that I had to divorce myself from it all for a while.

I was so unhappy. I was so down about the rifts in the family. I obsessed over my miscarriage, and what I could have done to prevent it. I started to drink. A lot. We went to a dinner party at Piers' house with some of his close friends including Rebekah Wade, then chief executive of News International, and I made a right arse of myself, rambling on about my family, my ex-boyfriends and my life – I mean, everything a husband doesn't want to hear. I was majorly depressed, and Chris said it was clear I was bereft, and blamed my family.

Yet, I still had to finish the latest series of *Britain's Got Talent*. We were about to go live with the finals in May. The next few weeks were among the toughest of my life as I had to go back and pretend nothing had happened. I didn't want anyone knowing. I am not a victim and did not want sympathy. I like normality. So, I did what I had to do. I had my hair and make-up done, fixed a smile to my face and stepped into the spotlight as if my life was perfect. To this day, anyone watching that series – won by Spellbound – wouldn't know anything was wrong, except perhaps that I may have cried a few more tears than usual. Inside, though, I was a wreck.

It was then that Frank, my biological father, decided to contribute to yet another article about me – this time in the *Daily Mail* (he'd made a public plea the previous year asking for my forgiveness). The headline was: 'Amanda Holden – my daughter is one of TV's most famous women but she's a stranger to me.' I was photographed shopping in downtown Los Angeles weighed down with bags in the same week that he was snapped working on the Torpoint Ferry in his fluorescent jacket. Frank admitted that he knew that giving another interview would wreck any 'slim chance of a reconciliation' but said that he'd had enough of being portrayed as a 'sperm donor' or 'an ogre who abandoned my children'. This latest reminder that he existed only left me feeling cold. He had never been a part of my life, so it was just as if a stranger was saying those things about me. A part of me felt betrayed, but another part hoped he made good money out of it – I really meant that. Either way, I decided I'd never speak to him again.

Around that time, Chris was on the internet and found a clip of me performing *Thoroughly Modern Millie* at the *Royal Variety Performance*. I watched it over his shoulder and was like, 'Oh my God, look! I loved doing that!' 'Well, you bloody moaned a lot when you were doing it!' he said. I did! But still loved every minute. All actresses say, the best thing about getting a job is the call, and then after that's it's just hard work. *Millie* was no different, and when I told Chris then that I'd love to do another musical, I meant it.

The next time I spoke to my agent, Sue, I told her the same: I wanted to do another musical. I should be careful what I wish for!

She laughed. 'Well, it's funny you should say that because *Shrek* has come up as a possibility . . .'

That was it – I knew I *had* to be Princess Fiona! It was a dream role for me, and *Shrek* is Lexi's favourite film.

Sue sent me the script. Hollywood film director Sam Mendes was supervising the show as creative producer for DreamWorks and Neal Street Productions, and there were around twenty people up for the role of Princess Fiona. Lexi was beside herself when I told her Mama was going to see a man who was doing *Shrek the Musical* – to sing in front of him! 'If I'm good enough I might be Princess Fiona,' I said. Normally I wouldn't mention anything to her, but I was so excited myself I couldn't help it.

Auditions aren't something I do very often any more and when I do it is terrifying. It takes me right back to the days when I was straight out of drama school waiting in line with my 'words' clasped in hand, nervously listening to better singers than me inside the audition room, watching better dancers and hearing better actors. When I look back, I can't help but think I loved every minute of them really. I can remember getting ready on audition mornings in my bedroom, dressing to character and asking Jason, 'Do I look enough like a teacher?' or 'Do I pass for seventeen?' 'God, my roots are showing!' 'I don't think it matters that I'm not Spanish, do you?' 'Could I be a goat herder?' And I'll never forget the buzz, the terror, then the joy of the phone call or answering-machine message from your agent to let you know you had a call back or had even got the part! There was nothing better.

So, I put myself back in the zone and prepared myself for *Shrek*. I sang the songs for days, practised the script and honed my US accent. On the day, I wore a green blouse but opted against a Princess tiara (you can imagine how the conversation at home went: 'Do I look like a potential ogre, Chris? Don't even answer that'). Then I got on my Virgin Limobike and sped off to the audi-tion. 'Keep the engine running, Rhys,' I said as I legged it into the offices of Neal Street Productions. 'I may be out of there really fast.'

With my crash helmet under one arm and script in the other, I walked into the room and straight into Rob Ashford, who had been my (very patient) choreographer on *Millie*. Until that moment I had no clue he was involved in this production. He had been brought in at the last minute to help direct, and I couldn't have been happier! His career was doing brilliantly and he deserved it.

Even though I knew him I started to ramble, like I always do when I'm nervous, and the next thing I heard myself saying was that I had had a special wax (down there) for the role as I was 'method' and I believed Princess Fiona would have a tidy garden! Lucky for me, they found it amusing and that put me at ease as I sang, acted, never stopped talking and then left. As I walked back into the reception area the PAs gave me a round of applause. I was gobsmacked and shocked – they had heard it all and were so kind. I felt like I was in a movie. Rhys was downstairs with the engine turned off, a coffee in hand. 'It went well then,' he said, pointing at his watch. I was on a high.

A few auditions later I got the call. Very glamorously I was in LA doing a show for CBS with my agent Sue and Daniel Radcliffe when she told me. (Dan was such a lovely boy, and unbeknownst to Sue he had knocked on my door for some Touche Éclat before facing her that morning. She has represented him from day one on Harry Potter and is like his adopted mother. At twenty in the US he wasn't supposed to be out on the lash, but of course like every good son he had snuck out of Sue's clutches and needed me to cover the evidence with some make-up!) When I heard the news, I could hardly believe it. I was going to be Princess Fiona! Lexi would be thrilled. *I* was thrilled. Even though it was only 10 a.m., we all drank champagne and toasted the future. Dan was also going to be doing a musical and then it was a big secret. We were so happy!

My excitement, though, was tempered days later by the devastating news that our lovely friend Paul Whittome, inimitable host of The Hoste Arms in Norfolk and the man I called 'Lord Mayor of Burnham Market', had finally lost his long battle with cancer. Paul had been such a friend to me for so many years. He loved life and he lived it to the full. Just a month earlier, I'd thrown a surprise party at the hotel for him and 140 guests, starring my all-time favourites from *Britain's Got Talent*, the Greek dancing duo Stavros Flatley and Signature, who kindly did it as a favour. We all knew by then that Paul wasn't going to make it but he remained so cheerful in the face of his illness that we could only be inspired. He was just fifty-five when he died, and I couldn't believe he was gone. I flew home straight away to be with his wife Jeanne.

The funeral took place a few weeks later, and there were so many people that they showed the service on plasma screens in the village green and outside the church. The night before, I went into the Hoste for a drink and a local friend came rushing over to me. 'Les is here,' she said. 'He asked me to tell you not to approach or go up to him in any way tonight or tomorrow. He doesn't want to see or speak to you.' I had no idea whether that was what he wanted, but if so, I thought that was so sad. Les, by now, had married a life coach called Claire who – by all accounts – takes very good care of him, and I had been looking forward to seeing him again and to meeting her. But there we both were, attending the funeral of a dear mutual friend, and once again, it was all about him.

The day of the funeral was an amazing sunny day and the service was wonderful. I gave a speech, and at the end I said what Jess always says about people which is 'There are radiators and drains in this life – Paul was a radiator.'

I spotted Les from a distance but at the Hoste later he and his wife sat in the conservatory at the back and spoke to no one. As we all celebrated Paul's life with drinks and laughter in the marquee in the sun, they sat stony faced, miserable and completely alone in the empty pub.

Later that summer we were at our home in Los Angeles and I realised I was late. We were on our way to Las Vegas and stopped at Bristol Farms to buy a sandwich for the journey. Their deli is amazing and they make up everything from scratch – so whilst I was waiting I asked to use their staff toilet, where I nipped in and did my pregnancy test. It came up positive, so barely containing my excitement I collected the sarnies and went outside where Chris was waiting in the car park for his lunch, which I delivered with a 'side of baby'! We have a picture of me and Lexi by the sign outside Bristol Farms warning people of the hump, which in the US says BUMP!

Shrek was to open the following May. I'd have to juggle rehearsals in February to May with the fifth series of *Britain's Got Talent* and my CBS work as well as other jobs I had in the UK, co-presenting shows like 'The Millies' (the Night of Heroes military awards) with Phillip Schofield. To say it was going to be a really busy year (even without factoring in a new baby!) was an understatement. If everything worked out okay then our baby would be born in February 2011, just in time for me to start rehearsals and filming for television.

Chapter 19

The Lost Boy

That was the most secret of pregnancies. For a whole six months, we never told a soul, not even my family, but it was mainly not to tempt fate. Chris and I were anxious not to announce anything until I was past the riskiest phase, but the fear that we might lose this baby too was never far from our minds, and we were also terrified of getting too attached to my little bump. The timing workwise wasn't ideal – I'd signed my contracts for *Shrek* and it had been publicly announced. It felt like an odd time to be saying I was pregnant, too. So, still, we kept the little bundle inside me as our secret – we felt like a team.

I don't know how I managed to keep it hidden. I felt like I was showing from the start but no one suspected. I was doing the school run every day and I went to Lexi's nativity play at five months pregnant and still no one noticed. (Luckily it was easier to cover myself up in layers of winter clothes!) Chris and I brought our winter holiday forward because we knew I wouldn't be able to fly soon, and we took off to the Maldives in December. I've looked back at our own photographs of me around the pool and I was so pregnant, I can't believe no one guessed. We told Lexi about the baby for the first time on that holiday.

'What? There's a baby in there?' she asked, poking my tummy.

'Oi, missus! Careful!' I told her.

She then kissed my tummy gently and I looked up at Chris with tears in my eyes – it was such a special moment. Then, Lexi brought me straight back down to earth by announcing that she was happy about the news but not so happy as it was a sister she wanted, not a brother. 'Boys are the best, Lexi,' I said, trying to sell it to her as we all wandered down to the beach to make sand-castles. 'They won't steal your Barbies or pinch your clothes and make-up.' She thought about it for a second, and seemed happy with it.

I hadn't even told my parents I was pregnant in case they got overexcited and told someone. Eventually, I phoned Mum to tell them and then the next day made an official announcement that I was six months pregnant, but I don't think anyone believed it at first, especially the newspaper picture editors trawling back through all the recent photographs of me wondering why they hadn't noticed.

At this point, we explained that we'd kept it quiet for so long because I'd previously had a miscarriage. This sparked a huge debate in the papers and on TV and the radio about whether or not I should have worn Spanx and high heels when I was expecting, but I was too happy to care. The moment we announced it my tummy suddenly popped right out, which felt so good. I could tell everyone I was pregnant. I was over the moon.

That year's was a very different *Britain's Got Talent*. Simon was away working on *The X Factor* in the States and Piers had just been offered a job taking over from Larry King on CNN. It was weird without my boys but I had so much else going on. At a dinner party once, in front of all his guests, Simon did offer to replace Sharon Osbourne on the American *X Factor* with me. I secretly hoped he would, of course, but I wasn't going to lose any sleep over it – anyway I love Sharon and I'd almost be too scared to try and fill her Jimmy Choos. It never happened – thank God I didn't tell anybody! Instead, the new judges were Michael McIntyre and David 'The Hoff' Hasselhoff which – without Simon and Piers' egos – brought a whole new dynamic to the show. Simon was due back for the live shows but in his absence it was like the king was away and all his little courtiers were playing up – we were quite naughty!

Michael was in his element and settled in really well, loving the audience and spending his whole time trying to entertain them. We immediately bonded, and straight away he called me Mandy (only my very special friends call me after a half-mangled cat). Ever ready with the funnies, he was also sweet and kind and constantly checking that me and the bump were okay. He has two sons with his wife Kitty and was very caring – although ironically it was him who had the naps and the chocolate in the break, not me. He said it was out of sympathy!

David is also a father, and a great one at that. He has a heart of gold, and he is so well-intentioned, even if the *Britain's Got Talent* audience didn't always get his sense of humour. Mind you, he didn't always get ours, either. Michael would often go off on one telling a joke to the audience and all I'd be able to hear was David in my ear saying, 'C'mon, Michael, get on with it.' I'd be like, 'David! He's a comedy genius!' (In Europe, however, David is like the Messiah. I once stood on the grid with him at the Monaco Grand Prix, and the crowds were going mental for him.)

I invited Pippa, Jackie and Natalie, my three lovely midwife friends, to the London auditions and watch a show. We had a lovely reunion. They were so excited – they couldn't believe I'd kept it quiet for so long – and desperate to feel the bump. They assured me I could get a scan at the West Middlesex any time of the day or night, which was a huge comfort.

Our baby loved *Britain's Got Talent*. He was constantly kicking throughout the auditions. He was like a joke baby, a little alien creature rolling around inside me. I thought that everyone would be able to see my tummy moving, he kicked so frequently – so much so that I spoke to my obstetrician to check that it was normal. He reassured me by telling me it was a healthy and strong baby who kicked that much. Filming went on – two days here and three days there – but I made sure I got lots of rest in between. I was determined nothing was going to go wrong with my pregnancy.

On 31 January, our auditions were in Birmingham. Before the auditions I ate a McDonald's Filet-of-Fish with Michael McIntyre. Travelling home from Birmingham I offered to give a lift to Roycey, our warm-up man in the show. The driver dropped him off and the car took me home to our house in Richmond, where we'd moved when Lexi was two. Even though it was part of a gated community, Chris had never wanted to move there, citing privacy and safety. I argued that we'd been free of paparazzi for years and enjoyed a normal family life without hassle. Our penthouse remained as Chris's office but I had a feeling it would one day be home again. As I slid under the duvet, the bed was warm and cosy and Chris woke up to snuggle me. He wrapped his arm around my huge bump and said, 'Wow, Mandy! He's grown in the last three days!' I drifted off to sleep.

The next morning I lay in as Chris did the school run. I woke and decided to have a bath. It wasn't until about an hour later that I realised I hadn't felt the baby kicking in a while. Because he was normally so active, it was strange but I wasn't initially panicked. I decided to watch morning telly, then Myleene Klass, who was also pregnant with her second baby, on *Loose Women*. I clearly remember watching the interview and thinking I should pop down to my lovely friends at the West Middlesex Hospital who I knew would do a quick ultrasound scan, put my mind at rest and then we'd grab a hot chocolate and catch-up.

It was 1 February. I drove myself to the hospital and didn't worry Chris at work with a call. As I got nearer the hospital, I got stuck in traffic and it was then that I started to feel anxious. I moved my hand across my swollen tummy and gave it a little shove to 'wake up' my son. Nothing. Don't panic, I said to myself, he's probably sleeping after all that kicking. I was 28 weeks' pregnant.

I parked the car and Jackie Nash met me in the car park. 'Hello, love,' she said reassuringly. 'Let's get this heartbeat up on screen and then we'll have a catch-up.' We linked arms and my heart was racing but I still couldn't imagine what was coming.

Jackie took me into a small private room and went to get a scanner as I lay there on my own with my hands on my tummy, staring at the ceiling. She arrived and put the gel on my bump for the ultrasound. Looking back, I realised she'd faced the screen towards her, not to me as usual, to be cautious. She felt around and moved the scanner several times before very calmly saying, 'Sometimes this happens. I'm going to fetch someone else to have a go.'

Jackie later told me she knew immediately that our precious little boy's heart had stopped beating. She told me she walked out of that room, closed the door and collapsed against it in despair, not knowing what to say and needing support from her team. As fate would have it, the leading obstetrician at the hospital was passing along the corridor and Jackie brought her into the room. She scanned me again and then said, 'I'm terribly sorry, Amanda, but the baby's heart is not beating. He's gone.'

From somewhere in the hospital I could hear the most horrendous screams. I presumed it was from the labour ward until I realised I could hear the name, 'Lexi, Lexi, Lexi!' being shouted out animalistically. It was me. It was me wailing and making the most horrific guttural noises. 'What can I say to Lexi? What can I say to Lexi?' It was all I could think about. I jumped up and all I could think was how I was going to break the news to my little girl. Writing this now my heart is racing again and those moments are never far from my memory. I feel sick and frightened and long still to hold my baby boy again. Jackie held me tight as I started to thrash about and punch the bed I was now standing by

'Where's Chris?' she asked me. 'We need to call Chris.'

Oh my God. My poor darling husband was somewhere in London in ignorant bliss. I hadn't contacted him so as not to worry him, and now I was about to destroy his world. Ironically, he hadn't been my first thought but I now needed him with every fibre of my being. But I was also terrified. Suddenly, stupidly, I thought he would blame me. It was my fault. It was the McDonald's. It was the sip of champagne. It was the buzzers from *Britain's Got Talent*. It was me. I hadn't rested. The list was endless but it had to be my fault, right? Everything came tumbling down.

We rang him and I said as calmly as I could, 'Darling, you have to come to the hospital. I am so, *so* sorry but the baby's heart has stopped beating.' It was like a scene from a TV drama and I suddenly felt so calm, as if a director was going to say, 'Okay, cut! That's a wrap!' I almost looked around for the cameras, even though I knew this was real. It's amazing, the ridiculous thoughts you have. My mind tried to persuade me then that I was actually dreaming.

The weirdest thing in all this was that somewhere inside me I had known I wasn't going to meet my baby. I was walking upstairs to his nursery only a few weeks before when I suddenly heard a voice deep within me say, 'You're not going to meet your baby.' Of course, I'd ignored it. Most mothers have that thought. Carrying a living, breathing thing in your tummy still doesn't feel real until it's actually in your arms and even then it's hard to accept. No amount of time or preparation can truly prepare you. I also felt a stab of guilt that we had practically ignored him for six months. We had done it for all the right reasons, but now it felt like we had somehow known.

Chris told me later he thought the telephone call was a sick joke. God knows who has that sense of humour. He arrived at the hospital ashen-faced and chilled from the wind. He took me in his arms as my legs went from beneath me. We all sat and stared blankly at each other, trying to let the worst possible news sink in.

Chris started asking questions about why it had happened or what could have caused it. Neither Jackie nor Pippa, who had arrived almost immediately, had answers for us and, all too soon, the obstetrician came into the room to bring us back to the gruesome world of reality.

'Amanda, you have to think how you want baby to be delivered,' she said. 'I am advising you that a natural delivery is best.' With all that had happened I hadn't considered giving birth. Ridiculous, I know, but I wasn't thinking I had to see my baby or get him out. The thought must have been inconceivable to me. The obstetrician was still talking. 'We would give you medication to induce labour overnight and sometime tomorrow you would have him.'

'I can't,' I said. 'I cannot have him tomorrow. I do not want to feel and go through the agony of a labour to give birth to a dead baby.' I was as blunt and as matter of fact as that.

'If you have a C-section you will have a longer recovery time,' she continued softly. 'I cannot recommend highly enough that induced labour and natural delivery is the way forward.' I was terrified now and I was angry – angry with my baby for dying and putting me through this pain. Angry with her for trying to coerce me into a natural labour and angry at God, or whoever else it is you blame in these moments.

'I'm not doing that!' I yelled. Then, more quietly, I told her I wanted a C-section as I had had with Lexi. Chris was on my side. There was no way we could do this naturally. It was horrific and I could not contemplate it. I wanted to be put under completely and not know anything about it.

The obstetrician left the room as Jackie tried to calm me down. Pippa promised to help perform the C-section as Chris and I sat side by side in total disbelief. Then, ever so gently, the girls persuaded me to stay awake for the 'birth'. 'You might want to hold your baby,' Pippa said.

'I can't,' I said. I was agonised at the thought of holding a baby that was not breathing. A lifeless and limp baby was frightening. I felt angry with my baby and with myself.

I was dressed in a gown and wheeled into the theatre. They gave me an epidural and the process began. Chris stayed with me all the way through. We'd agreed that he could leave the room just before the baby was delivered as he couldn't face seeing him.

I studied Pippa's face as she helped the obstetrician. She stayed neutral throughout as she told me how well I was doing and how it would soon be over. They rummaged and pulled at the little body inside me, and Pippa later told me that my baby was very difficult to get out; she really had to pull hard. I took comfort in that. I felt he didn't want to leave me. I lost more blood and then I heard the suck and gush when they finally released him.

'I can't see him,' I said. 'I just can't.' Then I broke down in tears.

Pippa held me as I wept all over her and, silently, they began to stitch me up.

Jackie discreetly wrapped the baby and took him out of the room. She told me on the way out that he was perfect and beautiful. It was then that my mother instinct just took over. I desperately wanted to smell his hair and kiss him, just as if he had been alive. 'Please, please, give me my baby,' I begged Jackie.

They brought my baby to me and laid him in my arms as my tears flowed over him. His little face and body were perfect. He was nearly 3 lb in weight (which is totally viable, and bigger than most premature babies) and felt like a young cat in my arms. I rubbed noses with him and smelled his face and his neck and I just cried and cried. I cried for his life, for the hope and joy and expectation that had been taken from us. I felt so much anger that he wasn't going to come and live with us after all. For some reason I put my finger to his mouth to feel his slack jaw, and then I traced my fingers across his perfect eyebrows. He looked like Lexi as well as Chris, and that only made it more heartbreaking. I held his tiny fingers and kissed them all over.

It all felt so inadequate. I felt so inadequate. I wanted to do so much more. I wanted to give him my life so he could breathe again. It was a pain so searing, so deep, so hard to explain. It is still very hard to put into words the grief and torment I felt and still do feel whenever I let myself think of him. Then there was Lexi . . . it was her little brother that wasn't coming home and that thought broke my heart.

I gave him back to Jackie as they dosed me up on morphine to take away the pain. They made imprints of his little feet and gave me a photo of him snuggled in a blanket. I have kept them and occasionally get them out to look at the tiny images. (We have shared this with no one except Jane. I wanted her to see how perfect he was and almost to prove he had been born with nothing wrong with him . . .)

I was taken to a small private room and Chris and I just held on to each other. We were checked on every now and then by staff, but mostly we were left in our dark empty world. The nurses gave me morphine to help my pain and anguish. A warm feeling of numbness flooded through me and for the next few hours I slept.

There was another tiny room in my private room. There were small windows that had been discreetly covered by curtains. It was a cold room like a small morgue into which they had placed our boy in case we wanted to see him again. It was too much to bear for Chris, but on his way to the bathroom he happened to glance into the smaller room and through an accidental gap in the curtain he saw our precious angel's tiny foot poking out of his blanket. It is an image he cannot shake off, and thinks of often.

Chapter 20

Neverland

The days that followed are still painfully clear to me. The obstetrician came to talk things through the following morning. It is a meeting I will never forget as she sat there and told me that I would be going home empty-handed, like a game-show contestant. She also suggested that I should wait eighteen months before I tried again for another baby. Eighteen months? That would put me at forty-one years old. Time was of the essence.

I had already begged Chris to let us try again, just minutes after our baby was stillborn. As shocking as my request may sound, most mothers feel the same. It is part of the survival instinct. I knew I wouldn't be able to live with this if I didn't have the hope of knowing we could try again.

Chris was in shock and grieving too and he was adamant about taking things slowly. Then the doctor's dire warning about not trying again for at least eighteen months echoed around the room and Chris agreed with her. I was seething.

I knew I could never wait eighteen months. Grief would take over and I wouldn't be able to function as a woman, let alone as a mother and wife. I knew that for the sake of my marriage, and for me to survive this tragedy, I had to have another baby. She may have been saying what she thought was right medically but for me it was utterly wrong. At that moment I think I would have happily killed her. It was all I could think of until Chris took me home.

While I was in hospital the nursery we'd so lovingly prepared was quietly packed away. We had carefully re-erected the cot that once held Lexi as a baby and put it in pride of place. Now it was dismantled, I often wonder when that was done and whether Lexi witnessed it. The baby clothes Lexi and I had spent hours choosing together were wrapped in tissue and hidden away in a box. We'd taken Lexi to Harrods, where she'd chosen two blue 'Nyah Nyah' comforters, one for her new brother and a spare.

Chris and I decided that I should be the one to tell Lexi the news. All she knew was that Mama had been in hospital because she was poorly but now she was coming home.

Waiting for her to come in from school, I sat propped up in bed. I heard the front door slam and Lexi's little voice shouting happily for me. 'Mama!' For the first time in my life I dreaded seeing her. My stomach turned over and my heart pounded in terror. I had nothing planned to say.

Jackie had been through something similar twenty years earlier and her experience had prompted her to help others by becoming a grief counsellor. Ironically, when we made the midwife documentary we had covered stillbirth and loss in pregnancy, but it was something that until then I'd never thought about and found difficult to comprehend. In the documentary, we were both filmed crying as she talked me through the process. Neither of us can watch it any more. Who could have guessed that three years later it would be me she was talking to as a mother who had lost her baby?

I truly believe there are reasons for people being in our lives and that Jackie, Pippa and Natalie were in my life for a purpose. They looked after us like family, and on Jackie's advice, I knew I had to be very matter of fact to Lexi. 'Be as kind and simple and honest as you can be,' she'd told me. I didn't want any wafty talk about the baby being taken by angels. I wanted to tell her something straightforward but gentle that would help her understand that the baby brother she longed for wasn't coming back.

Lexi came running into the room and bounced up on my bed excitedly. Ever protective, Chris said, 'Careful, Bundle. Mama's still a bit poorly . . .'

I took a breath. 'Mama has something sad to tell you, Lexi,' I said.

'What is it, Mama?'

'Mama and Dada are very sad because the baby's heart has stopped beating. It means he's not coming to live with us now.'

Lexi looked confused.

'Do you know what Mama is trying to say?' I whispered, barely able to breathe, a hard lump forming in my throat. There was absolutely *no way* I was going to cry or let this moment scar my little girl.

Chris squeezed my hand. I took a massive breath.

'It's a bit like Peter Pan,' I heard myself saying. 'He's decided he doesn't want to come and play with us and would rather stay in Neverland with all his friends. What a naughty little boy he is!' I joked, and I smiled into my darling girl's green eyes.

She lifted her head. 'Okay, Mama. Can I watch children's now?' (That's Lexi-speak for 'Put CBeebies on.') It took me a second before I said, as lightly as I could, 'Go on then, Minxy-moo, and you can have some lemonade as a special treat.' She jumped off the bed and walked towards the door.

I said again, 'You understand what Mama said, don't you?'

'Yes,' she said. 'My baby brother's heart stopped beating and he's gone back to heaven. Maybe the angels will give us another baby.' (So much for the wafty angels chat.) And with that she skipped out of the room.

The days that followed are still clear to me. The midwives – or my 'white witches', as I'd come to think of them – came and told us that we had to go to a registry office and register my baby's birth and death. 'We'd go for you but you have to go yourselves,' they said. I got up ever so carefully and went in the car with Chris to Isleworth registry office to do what the law requires – writing our dead baby's name and the date on an official piece of paper – 1 February 2011.

Back at home I lay in bed or on the sofa mostly, wracked with guilt over what I might or might not have done to contribute to our baby's death. We had deliberately kept him secret for so long; we were afraid to bond with him and we'd hidden news of his arrival. I felt so guilty that he'd been ignored by us for all those months. I hadn't allowed myself to connect with him or talk to him because of my secret fears. I was so walled up about the possibility of losing him. Had he sensed that somehow?

Chris deliberately didn't release a statement about what had happened to us but I'd slipped off the media radar heavily pregnant and it was only a matter of time before the press got wind of the fact that there had been a tragedy. Sadly, within hours the paparazzi were double parked all the way along the driveway and in our neighbour's driveway, waiting for a photo of me. There was no escape. Colin Myler, then editor of the *News of the World* (which I still wrote for via my column in *Fabulous* magazine) phoned us to say he'd received some long-lens photos that had been taken of us and bought them all off the market after warning the snappers to leave us alone. (Sometimes the tabloids do brilliant things.)

For our safety and privacy we decided to move back into our penthouse. Chris packed our belongings and took care to fill the apartment with candles and flowers and everything to make us feel at home. We fled in the middle of the night. We felt safe, cocooned in our little tower away from the nightmare. I have never seen the headlines or papers from that terrible time but cannot get over the sacks of mail I received from people sending me their stories and their love.

Every day I would wake up and – for a split second – feel normal before my stomach flipped over and the blackness descended on me. I felt like there was a wicked spirit trying to hurt us, or that we'd been invaded by evil. I didn't want Lexi to go to school or Chris to go to work. I was so afraid something might happen to them too. Every day, though, I forced myself to get up, dress Lexi and make her brekkie. I then put a coat over my PJs and sat in the back of the blacked-out car with her whilst Chris drove her to school. I kissed and waved her off and looked out of the window, watching everyone else's life carrying on around me. It was amazing to me to think that the world outside was normal when we were burning up with grief and desolation.

The mothers, families and staff at Lexi's school were amazing. They arranged play dates and small chats. They offered brief hugs. There was no nonsense, which was all Chris required to get Lexi through the door. We monitored her through her teacher who said she was doing fine and had told everyone her baby brother's heart had stopped beating and he wasn't coming home.

If ever Lexi brought it up with me, I'd tell her, 'He was such a naughty little baby, he was always doing karate in Mummy's tummy, he just blinking well didn't want to come to us, which is a shame because we were really looking forward to seeing him, weren't we?'

She'd nod and talk about 'nearly' having a brother. She has never really talked about it since, other than once to Jess, when she said, 'Mama did have a baby boy and she called it something weird, but he went back to heaven!' And I said to Jess, 'Oh my God, how did she sound when she said it?' And she said she was fine, she just said it as a statement, as a matter of fact. Who knows what goes on in her head? Recently we had a little chat about Nyah Nyah. She said, 'Remember when we got that blue Nyah Nyah – where is it?' I was like, 'Oh, I don't know. I probably put it in a little box somewhere because it's special.' So she definitely remembers some things. My heart ached for her. It still does.

I spent those early days in tracksuits (Juicy Couture, mind you – still a bit stylish!). Every day one of my white witches would come and spend hours drinking coffee and entertaining my ridiculous questions about why my baby had died. Chris was out of his mind with worry – he says I was just sitting at home and going round in circles about what had happened.

We had given permission for our baby's little body to be taken away for a post-mortem. Although part of me desperately wanted a reason, I'd been warned that there is usually no explanation for a stillborn baby. I have since learned that at least seventeen babies a day are born dead. But still, I needed an explanation. It seemed to take forever as we waited for the results.

Knowing that others had gone through the same thing helped me, somehow. I would wake up in the night and search the Internet. I tried and tried to get on to the website for Sands (the Stillbirth and Neonatal Death Society), but I always found it so difficult (it was a long-winded process to get on to the forums, and then I couldn't ever tell whether my posts had gone up correctly. When you are dealing with people who are blinded by tears, you need to make things as easy as possible). Nevertheless I sent the links for bereaved grandparents' sites to my parents and Chris's. I read blogs from people who had gone on to have more children and I became obsessed with those as they were a great source of comfort. Night after night we had stayed up until 3 a.m. watching back-to-back episodes of the TV series *Entourage*. We deliberately didn't watch any news programmes or read any headlines. Chris protected me.

I even started painting. (I am rubbish at art, so this is definitely not the moment that I discovered through grief that I was the next Monet!) Chris bought Lexi and I proper easels and we stood side by side painting. She painted rainbows, while I attempted to paint the view. Along with a lot of Lego building, it was very effective therapy.

Around this time I started exchanging heart-wrenching emails with someone else in the public eye who'd also recently lost a baby. She said that at first her husband hid all the newspapers about me from her, in case it brought everything flooding back. We spoke on the phone and were able to open up and express ourselves quite darkly to each other over the ensuing months. Her hand of friendship during that time is something I will never forget. We are not really in touch now as I think we needed each other for that time only. However, one day I will share a glass of wine with her at some function and be able to give her the hug I have long waited to give.

She gave me a little necklace with the name we gave him on it (she wears a similar one with her lost baby's name on it and never takes it off). When it first arrived in the post, Chris asked if he could have it. He wore it around his neck for ages and then one day he quietly put it back in my jewellery box.

Then I received an amazing letter from Hayley Mills, which I will always keep. She is a Buddhist, and told me that because of what had happened I would now be in touch with the atrocities of the world and be far more sensitive to others. She said, 'We always think we are here to teach our children a lesson but we forget they are here to teach us one. Your last son was your greatest teacher. Learn from him.'

I came to the conclusion from that day on that I had been chosen for this because I can handle it. In my heart I always knew we weren't going to have our little boy. When I told Chris, he said that he felt the same. Chris has always had psychic dreams (my favourite ones are about property!). But after we lost our baby, he reminded me that when I was pregnant with Lexi he had dreamed we would be pregnant with a little boy but never have it. I knew I was pregnant with a girl that time, so hadn't worried. But now I totally believe that I was a vehicle for our baby to finish his spiritual life.

He is now a warrior waiting for me in another world; a good little man somewhere around me on a different plane. He never has to come back to earth because his job is done. I am so flattered and honoured to have been chosen. I totally and utterly believe that and it is absolutely right. I'm glad it happened to me and not somebody else. We are all part of a vast universe and I gave him back to the universe. I will always have given birth to my little boy even if I wasn't able to be his mother – I was his little driver.

Not long after this, someone started to follow me on Twitter who'd given birth at term to a little girl who died. Her mother got in touch with me first and I put her in touch with Jackie Nash who helped them. I told her mother how I perceived our experience and said although it was a hard thing to get my head around, I felt that my body had been a vehicle. She passed this thought on to her daughter, who adopted my theory too, and which helped her get over her terrible loss. I felt happy I'd been able to help and encourage her to try again. We met last year when I invited her to *Britain's Got Talent* and she confided she was pregnant again with a boy. He was born October 2012.

The days passed and I wished them all away. I wanted to put distance between me and the past. Fifteen days after my baby's birth, I turned forty. Any grand plans we'd had to celebrate before the baby died had melted away and I didn't want to do anything public, so Chris arranged instead for my closest friends (and honorary girlfriend Ben) to come around. I insisted that it was a tracksuit and no make-up party. We ordered Indian food from Tangawizi, my favourite restaurant in Twickenham, and David Coulthard flew over from Monaco to support Chris and be a waiter. Moments before he walked into the penthouse Chris said David stopped outside. He was frightened to come in, because he didn't know what to expect. I opened the front door and said, 'Come on in, darling! There are no more tears left in this house. We need you to make margaritas – naked if possible!'

Lexi was very excited as everyone arrived. I told them that nobody was to talk about the baby or act strangely in any way. Chris had created a funny video which featured images of me, including my *Blind Date* appearance at nineteen as well as outtakes from other shows, and it was all fine. Another milestone that had been passed.

I don't want to look like I'm trying to be a hero when I write this. I don't think I'm especially courageous but it is very important to me that everyone knows that one thing I am not is a victim. I have been criticised on social media for wallowing in my misfortune. This is something I would never do. I hate being pitied, even though I know it comes from a good place. I especially hate people who use their sob stories for sympathy or gain. All I wanted was normality. Sarah Brown, the wife of ex-prime minister Gordon, wrote me a beautiful letter about when she lost her daughter. She lights a candle for her every night, and she said after something like that all you want is to – well, I interpreted it as, what you want is to be able to take things for granted again, to carry on going and get back to normality.

Yes, I've grieved and cried and shouted in private but my mask goes on when I need it to. I have metaphorically worn that mask since I was a little girl and it has served me well over the years. It's something to hide behind in disappointment, regret, unhappiness, anger and now death. It's not denial – it's more to do with my pride. I'll always have it as I want people to feel at ease and not uncomfortable around me. I won't allow anyone to see the cracks. I want them to feel normal even in the direst of circumstances. If that is people-pleasing, then so what? I am fine with it. I will never be beaten by circumstance. I am determined not to be defined by the bad things that happen to me, but rather channel them to mould me into a better person. I've said it before, but I don't care who or what judges me. Nothing is going to stop me from living my life how I choose.

The results came back from the post-mortem and it was as we expected. There was nothing physically wrong – just some slight scarring to the baby's umbilical cord. That cord is made of strong stuff and usually bounces back. The scarring could have meant one of the three tiny arteries inside was momentarily constricted, cutting off the oxygen or blood flow to the baby, which would have caused death in less than a minute. There would have been no struggle and no pain, the experts assured me. No scan could have predicted it but my question to the doctor all those months earlier came flooding back: Could the baby's frenetic kicking have meant that he'd bashed his own cord? This was a possibility, the hospital told me, but not definite. We would never know. They reassured me that, medically, everything was healthy and there was no genetic or other reason not to try again.

Now there was the matter of the funeral. Our baby boy was born, not miscarried, as some newspapers said. If nothing else is learnt from this book I hope the differences between a stillbirth and a miscarriage become clear. Anyone pregnant with a baby that has died within them from four/five months onwards is more likely to physically give birth than take a pill to miscarry.

A born baby has to have a funeral. I could not face this. I did not want the image of a tiny coffin in my head. I wanted his tiny face, which I have. I did not want to involve family in an already tragic circumstance to endure any more. I did not want to make a fuss. I didn't want a grave to tend to or remind Lexi of him. It sounds harsh but we never knew our son. We only knew expectation and hope of him. He was already buried deep in my soul

In the end my lovely midwives stepped in again and went to the funeral on our behalf – just the three of them in a little chapel behind the hospital as a vicar presided. Jackie picked a simple casket and I gave her some clothes, his blue cashmere blanket and his Nyah Nyah comforter Lexi had chosen. Jackie dressed his little body and said goodbye for me. I went to bed and drew the covers over my head. Do not judge me for this decision. I still ask myself if it was the right one, just as Chris asks himself if he should have held him when he was born. Unless you have experienced grief like ours, you won't ever understand. A friend of mine had an eleven-year-old daughter who died suddenly from a brain tumour and she couldn't bear to go to that funeral either. It's too final – it's too much for a mother and father to bear. I completely understood. Chris and I were saying goodbye in our own way.

I asked Jackie to bring me the ashes. She handed them to me in a mock wooden box and told me the blessing was 'just right'. She also brought me the blanket he'd been wrapped in when I held him at the hospital. I'd asked for it – there was still our blood on it and she was right to think I wanted to keep it. I silently took it and held her and then she left. I opened the box and looked at the ash inside but there was so little of it. I went to my walk-in wardrobe and cradled the box and the blanket in the darkness. Chris found me there and kissed me tenderly.

We had to make a decision about what to do with that little box but in my head I knew I had to take it to my heart place – my Norfolk. To a beach where we would continue to go to as a family, and where I could think of him on happier days. It was Easter when we finally made the journey to the cottage that has seen me through the best and worst of times. The morning we decided to carry our baby's ashes to the beach was beautifully crisp and sunny.

Lexi was running around the garden being her usual, happy self. I was so proud of how she digested the news those months ago and carried on normally. We had striven to keep everything just as it was. Sometimes Mama was sad that the baby had gone back to heaven but I never broke down in front of her. We had both stayed strong and carried on for her. (I joked that I didn't want her piercing a body part and getting tattoos at twelve and then saying to me it was because she was emotionally wrecked because of our loss!) I know everyone is different, but in my opinion it is selfish to involve young children in terrible events like this. They can be dealt with when they are asleep. Our overwhelming desire was to protect Lexi and we had succeeded.

That day, she was picking daisies from the garden all morning and collecting flints she thought looked pretty. Unbeknown to her I placed the daisies in the box, along with some stones to weigh it down and make it sink once we had thrown it into the sea. At the last minute I unwrapped the box and kept some ashes so that I've always got a little bit of him. I couldn't fully let him go.

Chris was such a tower of strength. He was hard, he was brave, he was a rock (and all the clichés of hard and brave things you can think of!). In my mind he went to battle for his family. He didn't once cry but he fought to hold me up and keep us pushing forward. He battled against the darkness, taking us all by the hand and dragging us back into the light. He was amazing. I will be honest and say I had underestimated his strength in our relationship. I'd always considered myself to be the strong one; the calm one who dealt with stuff. I kept things from him so as not to worry him. But he proved to be a better human being than I could ever hope to be. I now respected him as much as I loved him.

We drove to the beach and parked. After weeks and weeks of being scared together, being emotional together and talking together we had come to this place to start the healing process.

Chris and I walked hand in hand with Lexi and Fudge in front. I kept my other hand on the tiny wooden box in my pocket. As we made our way through the dunes and over the heather we came upon the most stunning view and I knew that this was the spot where we would have to let go and put the pain and torture of the last few months behind us.

We walked across the pools of water the sea had left behind when the tide went out (Chris joked that if we threw the box into the waves we might find it back again the next day). When we reached the sea, we told Lexi we were going to see how deep our wellies would allow us to go before water came in. She, of course, wanted to join in with her little pink ones! Even so, I was confident she wouldn't get far enough to see what we were doing.

We carried on walking as far out as we could as the water lapped against our boots. We could hear Lexi behind us, moaning all the way that she was cold and the sea was freezing. Chris and I were trying to be reflective and loving in between promises of chips and hot chocolate for Lexi if she could just be quiet for a bit and see if she could find some fish! When she had occupied herself, Chris threw the box out to sea as far as he could. We held each other tight and kissed as we watched it float further and further out. It went on and on. It soon became clear that it wasn't going to sink. (I mean, if we had wanted it to float, it would have sunk!) It was endless. We joked it would probably reach Belgium by sunrise. We carried on watching it go – a little pea-green boat floating away in the distance.

We started to get the giggles and then suddenly we heard a splash and a scream. We turned to see Lexi sitting on her bum in the sea. 'Mama! My blinkin' knickers are soaked!' Chris and I lost it completely. I laughed and laughed as we ran back to pull her out. Months of heartache suddenly dispersed.

Life goes on. And so would ours.

Chapter 21

It's Good Being Green

It's no exaggeration to say that *Shrek* saved my life. Rehearsals were due to start almost six weeks to the day after we lost our baby and I told Chris that I would be there for them. He was angry with everyone who told me not to and said, 'You don't know Mandy.' He understood completely that I needed something to focus my mind, and *Shrek* was it.

DreamWorks made it quite clear I didn't have to do it if I wasn't ready, but they were exceptionally supportive of my choice. And I wasn't just doing it for me. One of the main reasons I did *Shrek* was that I'd wanted Lexi to see Mama on stage and for her to go backstage and be a part of the buzz, to see the costumes and understand about the make-up and the fantasy. I had promised and I wasn't going to let her down again! I was going to 'deliver' Fiona.

On the first day of the *Shrek* rehearsals in Belsize Park, I was very scared and Chris came with me for moral support. He was so embarrassed. Being shy of any public attention, his worst nightmare is to walk into a room where there is the whole cast and the director of a West End show standing in a line waiting to greet him! We walked into that huge, busy room together and shook hands, smiling outwardly at everyone, but I was dying inside. It was the first time I had really stepped out of my bubble, and it felt like walking out of the cinema and into the cold light of day.

We stood in a circle and awkwardly introduced ourselves – it was like being back at drama school! The introductions went along the line. Chris said he mentally was counting down – five people before him, four people, three, and then he murmured to me, 'I'm not saying anything!' So when it was my turn, I said, 'I'm Amanda and this is Chris my husband. He's here for me but he's not in the show unless you're desperate! He's also too shy to introduce himself. Oh, and he does his own ironing and is very good at foot massage.'

Rehearsals started the next day. It was the toughest thing I have ever had to do, but out came my mask and I got on with it – and dancing, singing and being painted green ended up being very cathartic for me. *Shrek* pulled me from a very dark place, and to all those people who do not understand my decision to return to work so quickly, I would say you can never judge until you've been in that situation yourself. Chris says it was like I was cured. It wasn't closure, but it did refocus me, and I definitely turned a corner that day.

Those six weeks of rehearsals were indeed the best kind of therapy I could have had. But I look back and even I am not sure how I got through the long days, trying to keep up with the talent surrounding me. I would often blush and feel myself get sweaty when I knew people were watching me do my stuff. It might surprise you to know how embarrassed I felt, but it's a hard thing to prove you're worthy when you go into a show like *Shrek*, however much you bring with you professionally. Once you're established as a television 'personality' your experience in the theatre is immediately overlooked, your twenty-year CV is forgotten and you arrive back in the West End billed as someone 'off the telly', someone who might (possibly) put 'bums on seats'. The scrutiny is harsh (life on the stage doesn't get easier with recognition and money). But the attitude and determination I learnt on day one at drama school has always stayed with me, and it was that that got me through it.

I couldn't have done it without that wonderful cast and crew, though. I told them, 'Please don't tiptoe around me, I want to get on with it. If I'm crap, then tell me. Talk to me properly and don't give me any special treatment.' They showed they cared not by outlandish gestures, but by an occasional little hug or squeeze of the hand, or a compliment thrown my way every now and then. They were the most loving, funny people with no in-house fighting or bitching (very unusual for this business!).

Before I started Nigel Lindsay, who was playing Shrek, had written me a touching letter in which he said, among other kind words, that he was looking forward to the rehearsals, a family member had also experienced what we had been through. We spoke about that privately later and it was very moving. At *Shrek*, I didn't want top billing or the number one dressing room. (Besides, I only thought it fair that Nigel should have the biggest dressing room because of the three hours he had to spend in prosthetics each day!) I didn't want any star treatment at all – I even requested that the posters were designed with my name having middle billing so the show didn't become all about me. There is sometimes a weird hierarchy in theatre and I am happy to be no part of it. I only asked the producers for one thing, and that was for there to be no gossip magazines or newspapers in the rehearsal space. I didn't want to see anything about myself, and still to this day have no idea of the newspaper coverage of that awful time.

Instead of the biggest dressing room, I chose a cosy dressing room up three flights of steep winding stairs. I had signs made up: 'This way to the tower!' I had it refurbished into a purple boudoir with a chaise longue, soft furnishings, feather boas and most importantly a fridge stacked with bubbles and my old-fashioned bowl-shaped champagne coupes. I filled it with candles and flowers and bowls of sweets. It was gorgeous. There is also a pair of small green footprints on the ceiling where Chris and I painted Lexi's feet and held her upside down – against her will! – to make her mark for ever. I hope no future Princess Fionas or Willy Wonkas ever paint over it!

During those first days I was still in moderate pain from my C-section (I realised it may have technically been a little early to go back to work one night when I was dancing and had to jump over the bed I'd just been lying on – I felt a trickle and realised my Caesarean scar was opening . . .) but it was my emotions that were really all over the place. I felt a mixture of elation, guilt at feeling happier and thinking I shouldn't be, and this weird feeling of having lost something. Whenever I remembered it was my baby, I would feel a gut-wrenching stab. I still get this feeling now. Everybody was respectful and kept out of my way, but going back to work so soon was much harder than I thought it would be. I had underestimated how much I needed head space. I lunched alone for the first few weeks, as I felt too shy to join the others and wanted to be on my own. I found a secret fire exit and cried a lot over my sandwiches there, before finally pulling myself together and arranging lunch dates with my own friends near by, my new friends in the cast, or Divs (who was written into my contract as my dresser from the off – I rescued her from *Wicked* where she'd worked since the opening night).

I never talked about our baby with anyone in the show apart from Nigel. I just wanted to put it behind me and move on. The rehearsals were going great, and the producers and choreographers would give me a pat on the back if I picked up a new tap routine. I'm not a natural dancer – I really had to apply myself – but I don't know what the word 'no' means. I exhaust every possibility before I give up, to the occasional annoyance of other people! The only problem was, I didn't think I was funny enough. I wasn't in the right place mentally for humour. That is, until one day when Ben Cooke and his friend Joe met me for lunch before a performance. I don't normally drink when I'm working but I had a glass of wine and got a bit squiffy, ran back to the rehearsal space, and did the show. I was able to let go and relax, and got a huge round of applause. It was an epiphany for me. It had given me a new insight into my character and I suddenly knew what I had to do to make Fiona funnier. (But obviously that wouldn't involve wine.)

Early on in the previews, I was doing a scene set at sunset where I turned from a princess into an ogre. I stood centre stage as a net was lowered behind me and then the 'magic lights' came on. I had to look at my hands as they appeared to turn green. As I went to exit the stage, out of the corner of my eye I saw a man standing where I was heading. Instinctively, I moved out of the way and said, 'Oh, sorry excuse me.' When I came off, I said to Davina, 'Who was that, getting in the way of stage directions when I'm meant to be leaving the stage?' Divs told me there wasn't anybody there, and looked at me as if I was going mad. The weird thing is, I couldn't describe him to her, but I was adamant there'd been someone there. Davina laughingly told me I must have seen a ghost (the Theatre Royal, Drury Lane is one of the world's most haunted theatres).

About a week later, we did the first orchestra rehearsal, which is when you first get to sing with the orchestra (it's an amazing experience). In the bar in the break, I was chatting to some of the boys and they started to talk about the resident ghosts. Stage crews and casts always love seeing one, as it is meant to signal good luck for that production or that person. The most famous one at Drury Lane is the Man in Grey, who appears dressed as a nobleman of the late eighteenth century: powdered hair beneath a tricorn hat, wearing a dress jacket and cloak or cape, riding boots and a sword. Legend says that the Man in Grey is the ghost of a man who was stabbed to death and whose skeletal remains were found within a walled-up side passage in 1848.

Apparently, there is another one, Lavender Man, who had such weeping sores before he died that he used to wear lavender tied to him everywhere to disguise the rotten smell. Now he haunts the theatre in wafts of lavender. (All cleaning products or toiletries that smell of it are banned, so that if you smell lavender anywhere in the theatre you *know* that it's definitely Lavender Man.)

Actor Charles Macklin is also supposed to appear backstage, wandering the corridor which now stands where he killed fellow actor Thomas Hallam in 1735, in an argument over a wig (he pierced his left eye with a cane, which wasn't very friendly at all!). The comedian Stanley Lupino also claimed to have seen the ghost of Dan Leno in a dressing room.

None of these seemed to match the description of the man on the stage, so I remained convinced he was a real person, until someone mentioned the ghost clown Joseph Grimaldi, who appears on stage. I immediately got goosebumps and went a bit cold. 'What kind of performer?' I asked. It turns out Grimaldi guides actors around the stage or makes them move out of his way. I said, 'Oh my God, you are not going to believe this, but I met him!' So, I can confirm that he does move people out of the way – and typical me, I even apologised to him! After that I would sit in my dressing room and be like, 'Come on, Joseph, I don't mind if you want to come in!' Mad.

Often my lovely midwives Jackie and Pippa would come over to see me, which is when we started plotting my future pregnancy. It sounds unprofessional to have been thinking about it in the middle of a job, but I knew I had to have another baby. Chris wanted to wait until *Shrek* had finished, but I had other ideas. In fact, Chris thought I was on the Pill – and I certainly looked like I was. I kept them by my bedside and I made a big show of taking them – but in reality, they were being spat down the toilet religiously on a daily basis. Meanwhile, he thought it was his birthday in the bedroom department – I couldn't stop myself from grabbing him at every opportunity. I can only now put it down to the primal need to have another baby that had overtaken me, but poor Chris had no clue.

There will be some of you reading this and thinking, poor bloke – how could she dupe him? As dishonest as it does sound, he *is* married to me – he knows better than anyone that I am a nutter and control freak, and I did eventually come clean to him. All I can say in my defence is that I could not have lived through that time without the knowledge that I would get myself pregnant again as soon as possible. I could not have done *Shrek*, I could not have been a mum, I could not have been a wife. I felt I owed it to myself. As awful as it is for griefstruck husbands or partners when a baby dies, only a woman can possibly understand what it's like to feel the baby inside you and then have it born dead. I had seen how strong Chris had been with me and for me, and I knew he would be again.

I was also getting my body in prime condition for conceiving – eating fruits and nuts, taking lots of vitamins and visiting the extraordinary Zita West, who took me under her wing for therapy, hypnosis and acupuncture twice a week after rehearsals. She advised me, hugged me, dosed me up and told me stories of families who had been through the same (not naming them, obviously) and she started to make me feel it was possible for me to become pregnant again. She was a godsend – I credit her clinic for making me believe in my body again.

The opening night of the preview shows could not have gone better. Ben Elton came backstage to congratulate me and was so over the top with his praise I didn't know what to say. It was definitely one of the best things I've ever done. On a personal level I learnt so much about myself. The reviews were good apparently (I didn't read them) and the theatre was fully booked for months to come. DreamWorks (specifically Jeff Katzenberg) said it was the best production to date and we were all euphoric. I knew I'd made the right decision to carry on.

The first song I sang every night was called 'I Know It's Today', and in my head I made it about when I would get pregnant! I had ovulation kits hidden away in Lexi's drawer where Chris wouldn't find them and peed on sticks left, right and centre. Every third Saturday of the month during those preview weeks of *Shrek* I would find out I wasn't pregnant. It was always a tortuous day, as I would also normally find out between the matinee and the evening show. Poor Divs would often walk into the room having left a cheerful Mandy applying her red lips, only to return to one looking like Alice Cooper with her mascara running down her cheeks. Normally a chocolate brownie and a Nespresso coffee would rally me, Dr Footlights would take over and I would just get on with it, but there was one Saturday when I felt I couldn't take any more.

There had been an outbreak of chickenpox and shingles. My midwives knew I'd never had either so they pumped me full of white blood cells in case it jeopardised me getting pregnant. Even

Lexi had a jab against it. Unfortunately, Chris didn't, and because he had been pushing himself so hard he came down with a serious case of chickenpox, which doctors put down to all the stress he'd been through. With him out of action, I had to do the school run and then get a motorbike to the theatre six days a week. It was a gruelling schedule. I longed to spend at least one day with Lexi and would have loved Sundays off, but I had to take Tuesdays like everyone else, so on Sundays I'd finish at five and rush off to have tea with Lexi after the theatre.

That Saturday, it all became too much, and I suppose I had some kind of breakdown. The weeks of stress and rehearsals and not being pregnant, on top of losing my little boy, finally drove me to a place I never want to go again. I would never end my life – I have too much to live for – but this day, I could see why some people choose to take that escape route. Despair doesn't allow reasoning.

Davina eventually found me in a heap in the theatre stage door, a weeping mess. I was taken upstairs. 'I just want a baby,' I wailed to director Rob Ashford. He held me fiercely and whispered, 'You will. Let's get the official opening night done and then your little one will come.' His patience and kindness, along with the rest of the cast and crew, was amazing! My agent Sue Latimer was called. Caro Newling also arrived and we all talked it through. After that, I had my coffee and two ring doughnuts (to make up for the hole), reapplied my eyelashes and went and kicked the door down on stage like I did every night. It was as if nothing had happened. In case any producers are reading this, I do just want to point out that I did always get my work done – I wasn't a neurotic hormonal mess all of the time!

Zita was away, but she recommended a hypnotist, Maureen. She had never treated me before but she immediately centred me. She had lost her son at the age of twenty-five and she told me, 'Every time I ask him something, he makes it happen. That's his job. I will ask him to bring you a baby.' I know it sounds weird, but she told me she had no doubt that I would get pregnant and, somehow, I believed her. I went back to work and back to secretly trying for my baby feeling confident and relaxed.

In the middle of all this I had to do a promo for the next series of *Britain's Got Talent.* It would be the first time I'd seen everyone since our baby died, and felt like another major hurdle to get over. I walked in with a smile and told everyone, 'It's okay. I'm okay. We can talk about it. You don't have to worry about me.'

The Hoff came up to me straight away and told me how his wife had nearly lost a baby. Obviously – as always with David – the story centred around him and how they'd been having a picnic on top of a hill when he had to do this big butch race to call the paramedics and then had to take an air ambulance to hospital. Nodding sagely, he said, 'It gave me wisdom.' (Bless him!) Michael McIntyre was much more emotional. He had been so supportive when I was pregnant and he'd felt the baby kicking. We had a big hug and he asked me if I was alright. Then Hoff stepped in (a case of 'back to me'!) and said, 'I nearly bought you a bowl.' I had no idea what to say to that! (I was quite glad I didn't have to accept a commemorative gift for my lost baby, though.)

With that, so began the litany of that day's weird and wonderful acts, one of which was a Jack Russell that was meant to skateboard along our desk. Sadly, he did it wrong and had to do it again, so his owner called him from the wings. 'Theo! Theo!' she said, over and over again. It was a spooky thing. Theo was the name we had given our baby boy. No one else knew we had called him that. It was the first time I had ever heard the name said in public – and who calls their dog Theo anyway?

After the initial shock, when I finally gathered myself together I told Michael that we'd called our little boy Theo. He was gob-smacked at the weirdness of the coincidence, and at my reaction, while I was still laughing and crying all at once. I guess the universe has a sick sense of humour too.

Chapter 22

Well, Hello Hollie!

The week before the opening night of *Shrek* was totally manic, with the week-long live shows of *Britain's Got Talent* taking place and all the build-up to the first night. That Saturday was the third of the month, and unbelievably, the inevitable didn't happen. I phoned Jackie.

'It hasn't happened!' I said.

'Don't get your hopes up,' she said, wisely. 'Stress of the show, and opening night next week may be the cause.'

I knew she could be right, but a flicker of hope was suddenly lit inside me. Opening night was the following Friday, and I wanted it to be perfect, so I didn't buy a pregnancy test in case I was wrong and ended up totally disappointed. Instead, I kept the feeling to myself – I didn't even tell Chris, who remained blissfully unaware and was just looking forward to the Friday. But with impeccable timing, it was on the red carpet with Jane – who had flown in from LA with her son Jack (Lexi's best friend) to be there for me – that

I suddenly couldn't keep it in any longer and I decided to confide in her.

'I think I could be pregnant,' I whispered to her, smiling at the paps and hissing the news through my teeth.

'Oh my God!' she said. 'Does Chris know?'

'He doesn't even know we've been trying,' I admitted, and I felt a sharp stab of fear. Jesus, what had I done – and what would he say? I pushed the worry to the back of my mind. I had a big night to get through and anyway, I could be totally mistaken.

The official opening night went well. As well as Jane, Michael McIntyre came along with Sarah Parish, Angela Griffin, Rose Keegan, Ben Cooke and Sally Haynes. My darling Jason Maddocks was there with his partner Taro, along with my old drama teacher from my am dram days. Simon Cowell sent the hugest bunch of white roses, as did Sharon Osbourne and Piers. I searched out my family whilst dancing on top of the wedding cake at the end of the show, and blew them all a kiss. We had come through so much, and this really was the icing on the cake!

Afterwards, of course, there was a big party and drinks all round, and by rights I should have been completely in the mood to celebrate, but although I was over the moon at how the show had gone, I simply didn't want to drink. It totally wasn't like me, and even Sarah and the girls trying to throw red wine down me couldn't change anything – I couldn't bear the thought of it.

I managed to last out until the following Friday, and then, when all the signs were still good, and while Jane was still staying at the penthouse, I nipped to the chemist in my Mini to buy a test. By the time I got back home, I was absolutely dying for a wee and knew I couldn't make it up in the lift in time, so I asked the concierge in our building if I could use his loo. I peed on the stick and then dashed back to read the result alone in the car. It came up positive.

Even though I'd had a strong inkling that I was pregnant, it took a few moments to sink in. I couldn't believe it. Then it really hit me. I had never felt so happy in my whole life. I couldn't catch my breath with the sudden sense of realisation. 'Oh God, I'm going to have to tell Chris!'

I couldn't bear to put him through any more pain. He had had enough. I was okay and I felt I could handle it all. But Chris ... The weeks of inevitable worry, the endless waiting for the twelve-week scan and then the results of all the tests that a woman of my age would opt to take – it would be too much, and I just couldn't ask him to go through all that again. Jane and I discussed it, and I decided not to tell him until the twelve weeks were up. 'That way,' I reasoned, 'when I do tell him I can also assure him he has nothing to worry about.'

In my head, at least, it all made perfect sense. In practice, it was a lot less straightforward. It seemed everything conspired to make things as tough as possible over those next few weeks. Chris was pre-occupied with selling our house, which meant he was perhaps less attentive than usual and helped me keep the secret from him. But we were getting ready to move back to the penthouse permanently and that, along with juggling the tiring early weeks of pregnancy with both *Shrek* and *Britain's Got Talent*, meant my schedule felt extra tough.

Every night doing *Shrek* was thrilling but felt as physically demanding as doing a marathon. I was knackered, on edge about the pregnancy itself and about keeping it all from Chris, and he accused me of being irritable.

I lasted for three weeks, but it was too tough. I tell Chris everything, and I knew I was never going to last until my first scan without sharing it with him. I'd had the tiniest scan with Jackie and everything looked fine with my little bean, so I knew I was okay – I was six weeks pregnant and it was all in the right spot.

We went to have a coffee in Kew and he was rabbiting on about the completion on the house. I watched his lips but his words were a blur. 'Just say it,' I told myself. 'Say, "I'm pregnant."' I practised it a few times in my head. Snapping back to reality I heard him tell me, 'You're not listening to me. You never listen to me.'

'Can you make sure that the completion's on a Tuesday so that I can help you move?' I said. Then I blurted out, 'I'm pregnant.'

His expression was one of horror and then he said, 'Are you joking?'

'No!' I cried. I was about to say something more but just at that moment the weather outside turned. It was like something from a film. It went from a normal July day to being incredibly dark, with giant hailstones hammering against the windows and the roof. It felt prophetic, and apocalyptic. As I watched the hailstones bouncing off the pavement I tried not to think of it as a sign.

'I've lied to you,' I said once the flash storm had passed. 'I haven't been on the Pill.'

He looked confused. 'But I've seen you take it!'

I felt so ashamed explaining that I'd been spitting it out afterwards, and he just couldn't understand how I could have been so deceitful (I can't blame him!) I leaned forward and took his hand in mine.

'I'm telling you now that if I hadn't been doing this you would no longer have a marriage and you would not have had me,' I said. 'I would have been in an asylum if not for this. You think I am so strong and battle on but I could only be that person because of my cunning plan.' He pulled a face, but I carried on. 'I would have gone under, Chris. This was the final straw for me.'

He shook his head, and asked how pregnant I was (six weeks) and I told him Jackie and Jane knew, and how I was going to try and wait until the first twelve weeks were up so had to confide in them. Taking one of my hands in his, he attempted a little smile and, running his hand through his hair, he nodded and said, 'Okay, okay.' That was all I needed to hear.

As it turned out, *Shrek* would cure me for a second time – but this time, of morning sickness. This pregnancy was the first time I had suffered from it, and I was constantly nauseous – I even had to tell everyone I had a bug and the stage manager put buckets on the side of the stage, just in case! In the event, they weren't needed as, weirdly, I always felt absolutely fine the minute I walked on to the stage. I was constantly shattered, though, and the staircase up to my tower dressing room was suddenly a killer. I felt every one of those twenty-five steps and I was always puffed out when I reached the top.

Looking back, my pregnancy had to have been the worst-kept secret ever – everybody must have known, but no one said anything, and I was so grateful they all kept quiet and left me alone to rub my tummy in hope. (A weird thing happens to me when I'm pregnant. I seem to develop some sort of inner ability to know if things are going to be okay or not and, this time, I felt as though me and my baby were going to be fine.) But once we felt comfortable telling the cast and crew, everyone was thrilled for us.

Girls Aloud's Kimberley Walsh was lined up to replace me as Princess Fiona in the October, the press were respectful and delighted once we broke the news, my family were beyond thrilled, it seemed everyone was keeping their fingers crossed for me. (I guess there were so many pictures of my previous pregnancy that no one needed any new ones!) However, I knew that the first time I left the theatre after I returned I'd be papped, so I made sure I was mentally prepared. I came out smiling with my hand on my tummy and signed autographs for all the waiting well-wishers. Jill, who'd worked at the stage door of the Theatre Royal for thirty years, told me she'd never seen such crowds. 'We never needed three barriers before, not even for Rowan Atkinson!'

Once my sickness passed, I felt amazing and I carried on the show in great spirits, now really enjoying my pregnancy. My midwives were always around, seemingly whenever I needed them, keeping a close eye on me. They scanned me every time I felt doubtful and Pippa even lent me a Doppler foetal heart detector so I could hear my baby's heartbeat whenever I wanted.

I tried not to be too neurotic about it, but I checked it every morning. If I felt panicky I'd use the Doppler, which I was quite practised at thanks to my midwife course, and her little heartbeat would boom out of the speaker reassuringly. (I drove Chris mad with it. I thought I was being quite subtle, but I've since discovered he could hear everything and would feel sick with anxiety until he could hear the thud thud of the heartbeat, too. Jane, my make-up artist, was pregnant one month ahead of me, so I'd do it for her baby as well, and Lexi was always asking me to test it on her – we even tested the cat!) One day she asked me, 'What if the angels want to take this baby back too, Mummy?' That really threw me, and I told her, 'Mummy is really hoping that this one is staying.' (Again, blinkin' angels!)

Prince Charles came to see the show and later asked me to become patron of one of his charities, The Prince's Foundation for Children & the Arts. A few months later I was invited, along with the other patrons, to Clarence House for lunch.

Andrew Lloyd Webber also came to see *Shrek* and popped backstage to tell me he might have a project for me. He was putting together a talent show for 2012 to find the right actor to play Jesus for his rock opera *Jesus Christ Superstar*. I remember thinking he probably wanted to see me so I could play Mary Magdalene and then I realised Mary wasn't blonde, but I thought I might as well go and see him anyway. I had lunch with Peter Fincham, the Director of Television for ITV, who told me about the project and was very excited. I was over the moon about it, but I made sure I consulted Simon about it – I wasn't sure how he'd feel about me doing another talent show.

'They want me to be a judge!' I told him.

He was unmoving. 'No, darling. You must host it.'

I went to Andrew's house for yet another meeting, and in the end it transpired that I was indeed asked to host it – he said that he wanted somebody relevant to the West End. I was over the moon. For me it was another full circle, because when I was at drama school he was like God! To go from singing *Cats* back at Mountview to having lunch at his house was just incredible. 'Jesus Christ Superstar' was also Chris's favourite musical.

The auditions would take Andrew and the judges all over the country before the finalists were invited to 'Superstar Island' (a little piece of land off Essex called Osea Island), and then to Andrew's villa in Majorca. I would host the live shows in London later on with a judging panel that was to include Dawn French, who was a total revelation – I loved her! – Melanie Chisholm, who was a fantastic judge and was to play Mary Magdalene, and Jason Donovan. It was a fantastic experience, and both Peter Fincham and Andrew told me they were really pleased with my perform-ance. I loved it. Ben Forster won the role and was magnificent in the part.

By September that year, I had almost finished *Shrek* and was four months pregnant when I went to fetch Lexi from school. On the way, driving behind a lorry in Kew, I must have momentarily lost concentration and I slammed into the back of it at 30 mph. The airbag went off and there was smoke everywhere. My car horn sounded and it wouldn't switch off, but I didn't care about any of that – I was calm, but obviously concerned for the baby and just wanted to phone Chris, but my phone had slipped under the seat and I couldn't find it. I climbed out of the wreckage and a van driver behind me came up and asked, 'Are you alright, love?'

My Mini was a write-off but even though I felt fine once the shock had worn off (I didn't even make a dent on the lorry!), I still went straight to hospital. An auto repair man who happened to be passing moved my car to the side of the road and gave me a cup of tea in the back of a van while I finally phoned Chris, then the school, to let them know what had happened and that our friend would collect Lexi.

The van driver then offered to drive me to the hospital. He was so lovely and chatted non-stop all the way there about his wife and four kids. Then he looked at me and said, 'You don't half look like Amanda Holden!' (funny he should say that . . .!). I confessed and asked for his name and address. Later, I arranged for a chauffeur-driven car to collect him and his family to see a performance of Shrek and then come backstage afterwards, as a thank you for their dad's amazing kindness.

After another scan at the West Middlesex it turned out the crash hadn't harmed the baby, but that night I decided to give my understudy another chance to be Princess Fiona. I was taking no chances! I finally left *Shrek* in early October and was overwhelmed as the cast and crew threw me a farewell tea party and baby shower to wish me luck. I left the theatre clutching a bouquet and told waiting reporters, 'Let's hope I get a happy ending too!'

There was more sadness to come though, when we lost our beloved Fudge the dog. It was the first time Chris had cried since he was fourteen, and I felt relief. The tears were about more than the pain of losing our faithful family pet – I felt that he was finally grieving for our lost baby.

A month later, I developed a sharp pain in my side. It was bloody painful and I couldn't take a deep breath. If someone made me laugh it was agony. I thought I must have cracked a rib somehow, so I went for an X-ray, only to be told I had pleurisy (which is fluid on the lung). I couldn't take painkillers or antibiotics so I just had to stay in and keep warm until it passed.

And there were to be even more hospital visits after that, when the doctors told me at my next scan that I had something called a placenta accreta, which meant my placenta was growing into scar tissue from my previous C-section. I was constantly monitored and after a more detailed scan they assured me they could work around the problem and go in another way to get my baby out, but I became more and more worried as her due date, 14 February, loomed.

I also had something called a succenturiate lobe, an extra part (or lobe) of my placenta which was attached to the main part of the placenta. The baby's umbilical cord had implanted itself into the smaller side of the succenturiate lobe; this could also increase the risk of infection or haemorrhage after birth. There is only a 1 in 4,000 chance of this happening! Honestly I really must start doing the lottery . . . !

Pippa had just got a job as Director of Midwifery, which meant working with incredible people, including a placenta accreta expert at Queen Charlotte's in Hammersmith and after due consideration I moved my pregnancy over to her. It felt like it was all meant to be, and that the entire chain of events had led me to this point. The loss of my first baby had helped me with my stillbirth, and doing the midwifery TV show had helped me with both events. Everything happens for a reason, and every disappointment prepares you for something you have yet to face. I've learnt always to try to find lessons in what life throws at me.

With these new developments, I was told I'd have to have a Caesarean – which was fine by me! I met the expert obstetrician Dr Sailesh Kumar – I called him 'Slash' because he was due to give me a C-section – and fell a little bit in love. He smelled gorgeous (Hermes aftershave, ladies!). A scan confirmed the placenta was stuck, so Slash examined me, I had something called a VQ scan, and he told me that it was actually stuck in three places. I was immediately worried about the effects of radiation on the baby until I found out it was less than you'd get on a plane. My bump and I had been on a few of those together, so I felt a bit better! Everyone reassured me the birth would be well-prepared for and that my baby was perfect.

By January 2012 I was about to burst, but on the judging panel for *Britain's Got Talent*. Simon was back, and not too alarmed by the sight of me with a swollen tummy. The previous series had ended on a rather flat note, and when Michael's tour commitments prevented him returning, Simon shook things up by introducing four judges. When it was announced that we would have *two* new judges – the divine Alesha Dixon and lovely David Walliams – I was firstly just anxious about how the logistics would work. There had been so much publicity surrounding Kelly Brook that 'Four judges don't work' had practically become a *Britain's Got Talent* mantra – and now we were being told the opposite!

But the first day I cannot tell you how happy I was to meet them. It felt right and I felt total relief. I'm not sure why, but I suppose it meant I could sit back and relax and enjoy the show more – rather than try and run it, which I had done the previous year with David and Michael. I knew David Walliams would be funny, but I worried his humour was pretty near the knuckle for a family show (*Little Britain* is an acquired taste and not to everyone's liking). But having swum and drunk most of the Thames for Sport Relief he was also now considered a national treasure, and he turned out to be hysterical. He gave the show the reinvention it needed. His ability to push but not topple over the edge with innuendos really works and he has famously, of course, brought out the smutty, funny side to Simon that I have known about for years but which, until now, Simon has never let the world see. David also has a soft, thoughtful side – he is someone you could go to and chat about anything. Although he loves a name-drop (don't we all!), he is not at all intimidating to speak to. I am really fond of him.

I wanted to meet Alesha before we started the show so I arranged to meet her and her manager Malcolm in the Wolesely for breakfast. We had a good old chat about the show and life in general but I was there because I was very anxious to point out that the press would, without doubt, try and spin it so that we were enemies. I wanted to let them know I would publicly condemn any negative articles or questioning. I didn't want any part of it, because I am a girl's girl. Not only that, I now have two baby girls and I want them to grow up with nothing but positivity about other females in their life. There is no way their mama is going to be perceived as a bitch just for ratings.

Even though I had expected it, I was relieved when they openly said the same thing. Poor Alesha has had to deal with so much similar nonsense after replacing Arlene Philips on *Strictly Come Dancing*, and has told me some hideous stories about the stuff that has been written about her. There is so much negativity in this business, but I refuse to be part of it all. I find it utterly depressing how many female celebrities are damning and bitchy about other girls, and how much also comes from female journalists, who seem to want to fuel it all rather than join the sisterhood and promote women. It's a tough business for all of us.

So there we were, Alesha and I, sisters-in-arms over our

scrambled eggs and coffee. I was just in awe of how bloody pretty she is – striking to say the least! She also has the softest skin in the world, but then when she opens her gob it belies her beauty. Sarah Parish once said of me, 'face of an angel, mouth of a trucker!', and I would say the same of my fellow judge. Alesha is such a good person – down to earth, on the money, fun, very sweet and very thoughtful. Her beauty lies beneath, and it shines through. I am aware this all sounds a bit gushy but I love working with another woman who not only likes women but is actively pro-women. I have never felt intimidated or threatened by her. How can anyone even begin to compare us? We are on the show for completely different reasons, and she is eight years younger than me, for a start! We both laugh about it and try not to look at any publicity describing our 'fashion wars'.

During *Britain's Got Talent*, I had another scan which revealed the baby weighed 6 lb, so Slash asked if I wanted her early. I told him I'd have to work out the dates and would book in for two or three weeks' time. I didn't tell a soul other than Chris and Jane, my make-up artist about the potential problems. My pregnancy was healthy – it was always the delivery we had to worry about. Privately, we picked the date to have my baby – Monday 23 January – three days after Lexi's birthday, ironically the same date we picked for Lexi before she came early. I instructed Alison to release the news on the Wednesday when I was safely back at home. We wanted it to be secret until then.

It all seemed very straightforward. But in the early hours before the due date, Chris found me in Lexi's bedroom, looking at Lexi fast asleep. I was quietly crying. Silently, uncontrollably weeping.

'What's wrong?' he asked.

'I don't want to die,' I said. (My gut instinct was kicking in again.)

'You won't,' he said, folding me into his arms. 'Don't be ridiculous, Mandy.'

I tried to tell myself he was right and that I was being overdramatic. But then I felt a sudden tug of emotion at not having seen Mum and Dad for so long. I made him promise that if anything happened, he'd get in touch with them. (I had no idea how prophetic that would prove to be.)

When I arrived at the hospital the next day, my midwife Jackie was waiting and told me that she'd sneaked a jug of margarita mix into the fridge for me as she knew I'd been craving one for my entire pregnancy (now, that's what I call a girlfriend!). More importantly, the medical staff assured me they also had pints and pints of my blood. They wired me up for every eventuality and Dr Kumar told me, 'If anything happens or if you bleed out in the worst-case scenario, we'll put you under and get the baby out,' but they kept repeating the phrase 'worst case scenario'. It felt relaxed and under control, but I was still nervous as they began the C-section, and I needed Chris to stay right where I could see him at all times whilst I tried hard not to think about the last time I'd been in this situation. Mercifully, all went well, and adorable little Hollie Rose Hughes was born. As they showed me all 6 lb 1 oz of her, I couldn't believe how beautiful she was. She cried and I cried, with joy and gratitude and relief – it seemed so wonderful and unreal after what had happened before.

But just as Pippa was checking the baby over – she was fine apart from a little fluid in her lungs – I suddenly felt myself draining away and I gave a little sigh. Dr Kumar very calmly came straight up to where I could see him and told me, 'Amanda, you're bleeding quite heavily so we are going to put you under now, okay?' I looked up at him and across at Pippa and said, 'Don't let me die!' That's the last thing I remember.

Chris said later he could feel liquid splashing about at his feet and thought someone had kicked over a bucket of water. When he looked down he realised he was standing in pools of my blood. Within about 10 seconds my head shrank to half its size – as if the life had been sucked from it. I looked like a corpse, and in that moment, he thought I had gone. Unbeknown to everyone, and not in the VQ scan, my placenta had attached itself to my bladder, and when they lifted it out, it snagged a large artery and ruptured it. I had haemorrhaged and was bleeding to death.

They bundled Chris out of the operating theatre and he stood the other side of the door, holding Hollie and watching helplessly for a full seven minutes, not knowing if I was alive or dead. As I lay unconscious they couldn't get blood into me fast enough – as much blood as they were putting into me was going out. It just would not clot. Dr Kumar was packing my stomach with wadding to soak up what I was losing, using what they call 'trauma medicine' learnt specifically at Camp Bastion in Helmand Province (thank God for the experience doctors get on the front line). All of a sudden, my heart stopped beating. For forty seconds I flatlined.

Pippa smashed my chest with her fist and my heart started beating again. At one point there were more than thirty medical staff trying to save my life as Chris stood outside watching them running in to cope with the trauma, fearing the worst. They eventually stemmed the bleeding but left me open and unstitched in case it happened again.

Just as Pippa came out to see Chris and tell him I was going to be okay, the emergency buzzers went off and it started happening all over again. She and Chris watched a whole new emergency trolley being wheeled in, and when Pippa followed it she found me bleeding once more. They had to put some sort of balloon inside me which they filled with air to put pressure on the torn artery, but my blood still wouldn't clot and the doctors weren't sure I was going to survive. They had emergency motorbikes arriving at the hospital bringing extra blood for me and I had 15 litres in three transfusions as they practically threw it into me. (I always knew how important it was to give blood but until something like this happens you don't take on board how vital it is.) But when they realised that wasn't working, as a last resort to clot my blood they tried using vials of 'Factor 7' man-made blood (so I guess I've definitely got the X Factor!). But in the end, that is what saved me. Fake blood. They had to operate then and I almost lost my bladder but they managed to save it, thank God, or I'd have had a 'Prada handbag' for life, as my midwife joked later. Hollie was looked after in Neonatal as a precaution but was doing well.

Poor Chris – he had me critically ill in one room and Hollie on another floor of the hospital. He says he felt numb. Apparently it made him feel like one of those guys on The Big Reunion who talk like they've just come back from Vietnam. 'Yeah, I just felt numb.' Except this, of course, *was* a bit more serious.

Nine hours after they'd first started operating, they finally stitched me up and took me to the high dependency unit, where I remained in a coma under general anaesthetic for another three days. The doctors told Chris they didn't know if any of my organs might pack up because of the blood loss, and they had no idea how my heart might react. I was wired up to a ventilator but Chris didn't trust the machines, so he insisted on staying with me in case anything happened, and he grilled every doctor who came in to see me.

Jackie, Natalie and Pippa were there too, and helped him enormously. Pippa especially kept it very unemotional and straight, which is what he needed, and whenever he asked her to tell him the truth she did. He sat by my bedside in a chair for three days and barely slept – he was so exhausted that he actually temporarily lost the hearing in both ears, though he reckons it was down to all the beeping in the room! The doctor said it was stress that caused hearing loss. The nurses were worried about him and eventually persuaded him to go home and sleep. He reluctantly agreed and left at about 1 a.m. He left his mobile on, of course, and at about 5 a.m. it rang. It was the hospital.

'Mr Hughes?'

His heart was in his mouth. Immediately, he was thinking the worst. Why else would they have called so soon? 'Yes?'

'This is the ICU at Queen Charlotte's Hospital.'

By now he was well in the zone. Why were they taking so long to tell him? It had to be bad news. 'Yes?'

'It's about Amanda.'

(You can imagine.) 'Yes?'

'Just to let you know, she's awake, and asking for you . . .'

Finally, it sank in that the receptionist just had an unfortunately long-drawn-out manner and they weren't ringing to tell him that I had died. He says now that all he could think of was how he would tell Lexi.

Heart still pounding, adrenaline coursing round his body again, he dressed and rushed to the hospital, only to be told by the doctors that what was actually happening was that they were gently bringing me out of the coma they'd put me into. I was semi-conscious at one point, and had asked for him, but had gone back under by the time he arrived. He got there at 6 a.m. and embarked on his second bedside vigil. Just to rub in that it was his fourth sleepless night on the trot, it was 3 p.m. that afternoon before I woke up again!

I was really groggy and confused, but when I became more fully aware I thought it was the same day as the birth. I couldn't move my legs, and was scared I was paralysed. They were enormous and I had big hands like the prosthetic ones I wore as Princess Fiona in *Shrek*. My whole body was swollen with fluid and was three times its normal size. I couldn't sit up or breathe easily, I had a hacking cough with fluid on my lungs and was in excruciating pain. I was also heavily sedated on morphine, but just about conscious. However, the drugs made me feel like I was being tricked. I became aggressive – which is apparently a side effect of morphine – and paranoid and thought everyone was playing around with the time. I got annoyed with Pippa and told her to stop clicking around in her heels.

The nurse fed me a few mouthfuls of Complan and then the doctor came in and asked, 'Did she eat anything?' and the nurse said no.

I said, 'She's lying!' I was hideous.

Chris tried feeding me Complan too and I spat it out and told him, 'That is effing bollocks!'

I was still under the spell of morphia when I heard a man on the ward shouting, 'No! No! No!' and then an animalistic cry. I didn't know where I was or what was happening. I thought someone had died having a baby and got very upset. I found out later that some-one had died in intensive care. His shouts will haunt me for ever.

I kept asking, 'Where am I?'

Eventually, I came to enough to understand exactly where I was, and was finally able to take in everything that Chris was telling me. Almost. He kept saying, 'Do you know what happened? Do you know you almost died?' I could hardly believe it. (I joke that when I died I saw God and it was Simon Cowell. In truth, I don't remem-ber what happened. There was no white light or anything, just a void.) As I was coming out of my coma, the TV was on and I appar-ently began to shake my shoulders in time to the music of *Deal or*

No Deal. Dancing in bed! Chris said he knew I was going to be alright when he saw that.

Once Chris knew I was going to make it, he finally called my mum and dad. He said, 'Judith, this is Chris. I want you to keep your mouth closed and don't interrupt.' (He wasn't being rude – my mum is terrible for not listening and talking over everyone else!) He said, 'I have to speak to you. I have to tell you something. It's about Amanda.' For the first time ever, she did listen (miracles were coming thick and fast that week), and she listened as he told her how they'd nearly lost me. Finally, she broke down, thanked him for letting her know, and asked if she could come and see me. Chris told her I'd been asking for her, and then she dropped the real bombshell. 'Debbie is staying with us at the moment – can she come too?' It was over six years since we'd spoken, but Chris said yes without hesitation.

When I was awake and more *compos mentis* my desperation to see Hollie was overwhelming. I was just so weak. I couldn't sit up – I could barely hold myself together. I also couldn't wait to see my Lexi. Knowing how close I had come to never seeing her again is something that makes me want to be physically sick every time I think of it. Again, she had been protected. She knew she had a lovely baby sister but she also knew Mama was poorly and a lot of blood had fallen out of her!

She was coming to visit, but I was adamant that I didn't want her to see me in a hospital gown lying down in a hospital bed. The nurse looking after me was incredible (the NHS has nothing but my praise and gratitude). She and another nurse helped me get up out of bed and into a chair, since my legs were so swollen that I couldn't walk. I couldn't even put them together, so I sat there like an old man, legs akimbo! I was totally helpless as she tenderly brushed my matted hair, helped me wash my face and changed me into black PJs. She set about hiding the wires and IV lines that were coming out of my body. And we used make-up to try and cover two puncture marks on my neck from IV lines that were black with dried blood – I looked like I had been bitten by a vampire. I told them I was ready.

My heart ached for Hollie, and finally I was told she was on her way down from the baby ward. The door of my room was kept open so I could see her coming from my chair, and I waited anxiously, butterflies in my tummy with every bump of a trolley and every footstep, my arms aching to be filled up with baby. But as it turned out, the first footsteps I heard running up the corridor were those of my lovely Lexi.

She stopped in the doorway, slightly overwhelmed with the sight that greeted her. Shyly she came up to her mummy, Chris behind her and she gently hugged me before immediately asking, 'What's that on your neck, Mama?'

'Daddy did a bad neck attack,' I said with a smile. (Her daddy pins her to the floor and snuffles her neck with his stubble to shrieks of laughter on a regular basis.)

Then quietly, and without warning, my parents and sister walked into the room. My parents were emotional as they hugged me but best of all (and I mean this sincerely), my little sister walked over and silently hugged me, her voluminous hair soaking up my tears of joy. It had been such a stupid, ridiculous situation between us and yet it dissipated in seconds. Neither of us spoke at that moment. We didn't have to.

Then finally, Chris wheeled in Hollie, in her little portable cot. He gently handed her to me and at last my beautiful perfect baby was in my arms. My family and I were all meeting her at the same time.

Hollie stared up at me sleepily and my heart swelled with joy and unconditional love immediately. She was utterly gorgeous. I couldn't help but notice she had the same features as her brother and the same defined little eyebrows, as well as a thick mop of brown hair. I said a silent 'thank you' to the universe and to Theo for this moment. It felt very surreal. The people I love most in the world were all in the same room looking down at this most precious gift. If my life was a movie (and bloody hell, it was beginning to feel like one!), this was the moment when the director would say, 'And that's a wrap.' The end!

A huge, humbling lesson was learnt by us all that day. Life really is short. Who knows what comes after it but, Oh My Goodness, was I determined to start living again. As I put my arm around Lexi's waist, her eyes wide with wonder at her baby sister, I studied the faces of my mum, dad, sister and Chris, and I felt such relief and happiness. My children were lucky to be part of this loving, pain-in-the-arse, horribly stubborn but wonderful family! I knew that Hollie's birth signalled a new beginning for us all.

Chapter 23

Still Holden on

Beyond the hospital, 'Amanda's Fight for Life' was headline news in every paper and on the news programmes. Twitter was all over it, David Walliams made a speech wishing me better at the National Television Awards and people were even praying for me! In our little bubble in the hospital, I had no idea about any of it. There wasn't even any telephone signal (which was a good thing!) and I was just focused on getting better.

I'm never one to pity myself. I push myself to get over things, to get on with it. But this time it was Chris who gave me an ultimatum. He was like a sports coach – I think he knew I needed someone else pushing me and he told me, 'I want you out of this hospital by Monday.'

'Bloody hell, Chris!' I said. 'I don't know how I'm going to do it!'

That would be just a week after I had nearly died, but as I thought about it, I realised that being safely home with Hollie was what I needed – what we all needed. It was a deal. 'I'll try. I'll really try,' I said.

I'd been moved out of intensive care into a private wing, the Stanley Clayton wing, which Mum always got wrong and called the Stanley Kubrick Wing, but I couldn't walk without a Zimmer frame, I still had massively swollen legs and feet and some of my stitches hadn't been taken out yet. Everyone thought I was crazy. Pippa told me, 'It's too soon!' I still hadn't even had a shower, and was desperate for one, so one of the nurses arrived to help me. Mum was there, too, and I just looked at her and said, 'Will you wash me, Mum?'

She hadn't seen me naked in forever, and we hobbled into the disabled shower together and she said, 'I'm going to wash your hair.' I was like a vulnerable little girl again – it felt so lovely to have her take care of me. She washed me and dried my hair, and I have never felt so appreciative of her (or of water!).

Chris came by every day, on what became known as Mandy Watch, and was so supportive that I put a lot of my speedy recovery down to him. He did, however, keep wanting to talk about what had happened to me – he'd had a hell of a shock, and needed to get it all out of his system, but I couldn't listen to him. It was too frightening. It sounds mean, but I told him to talk about it to Pippa, because dwelling on it was the worst thing I could do. Instead, I needed to focus on getting better. Otherwise, we made it as fun as possible.

Hollie was in the room with me most of the time, and Lexi came in with my mum and dad every day between shopping and cinema trips with my sister. The only time I ever felt devastated about the situation I was in was at the end of Mandy Watch. Everyone would stay as long as they could (Chris would always be last to go), after which the nurses would leave Hollie with me in her little crib. The cot bars would be up as I was still too weak to hold her, and one night she was a bit sick after having some milk. I couldn't even gather the strength to lean over and grab her muzzie to wipe her – instead, I had to press the bell for the nurse. I wept then – I felt utterly shit and useless. I couldn't even look after my baby – I was in there to be a mother and I couldn't do it.

That was when I really started to pull my act together. I stopped taking painkillers, I stopped taking the antibiotics that were making me throw up and I asked every doctor, 'What do I need to do to get out of here?' A physiotherapist came in every day to help me walk again. At first, I could barely stand but I practised walking a bit further every day and eventually they took the catheters out. Until that point I hadn't been sure I'd be able to walk or laugh or sneeze or have sex again!

One by one, the midwives and the physiotherapist checked and double-checked me. Chris promised them we would have family help with the baby and that my mum would take care of Lexi. Everything else would be done for me – I would just be at home in bed or propped up in a chair instead of in hospital.

I was very poorly, but I did it. The following Monday, a week after Hollie's birth, Chris wheeled me out of a back door of the hospital in the middle of the night, away from prying eyes. I was still in pain when I left hospital, I had this stuff on my lungs and every time I coughed I had excruciating pain through my scar – it felt like I was being stabbed with knitting needles. But he was right: the minute I got home I started to feel better and look better.

Two days later, on 1 February, Theo's first birthday, I hugged Hollie tight and wept tears of joy at having this tiny precious life to cherish for ever. Chris and I still checked on her all the time to make sure she was breathing and, of course, she was perfectly well. There was nothing to worry about and I had to try to let go of my anxiety.

Surrounded by such loving care I improved by the day. Now I

was desperate to get back to some sort of normality and no longer be an invalid. I took inspiration from my family. Lexi is a hard taskmaster like her mummy – she was thrilled to have me home, but when she came back from school the next afternoon she was really shocked to find me still in my pyjamas. (It's hardly like I normally hang out at home in full make-up, but I usually at least manage to get dressed!) I swore then that she wouldn't see me like that again, and she never did.

Not only that, the Edinburgh auditions for *Britain's Got Talent* were coming up in three weeks. Poor Carmen Electra, my stand-in, was getting it in the neck from all sides and I wanted to go back to work. I kept looking at the dates – Edinburgh was just one day and then there was a ten-day break until the auditions at Birmingham, so I told Chris I wanted to try to be there. I just wanted not to think about death, not to feel like death and be able to show Lexi everything was getting back to normal. Most of all, I wanted to have something to aim for.

I spoke to my surgeon and admitted that I was still a bit swollen and weak but he said, if I was determined, then I should go for it. He added, 'I have only ever seen one person in my whole career who has rallied as quickly as you after what you went through!'

Richard Holloway came to see me, to see how I looked (and of course to hold the baby!). He was keen to make me realise there was no pressure to return to the show, but I had made up my mind. My mum and my sister would look after the babies, so there was absolutely no reason not to. I wanted to do it for me, for Chris, for Lexi and for Hollie. So I tried even harder.

I rested. I started eating well (it was all in the food!). I had reflexology. My lovely Cath, who comes round to my house to do my waxing, massaged the fluid out of my legs, my shoulders and my hands. In the end, as I wasn't allowed to fly, Chris and I got the train to Edinburgh together, and I really enjoyed the journey itself. It was nice being quiet and feeling like a normal couple, like nothing had happened, and I slept a lot of the way.

I woke up in Edinburgh to find a bit of a commotion outside. There were a few paps, so I took a deep breath, stood tall and tried to walk normally. Everything was painful but I just ignored it and smiled through my painkiller buzz. (The painkillers made me feel woozy and I said to Simon, 'Tonight, Simon, I'm going to be Paula Abdul!') When we reached the hotel there were more cameras and reporters. Chris dashed inside first – even in those circumstances he still leaves me with security! – leaving me to walk in and find that everyone was there waiting. They were all so gorgeous to me! Ant and Dec were there, too, grinning away.

'Oh, for fuck's sake!' I cried and hugged them both.

'You back to normal then, pet?' Ant asked.

Not everyone was so happy for me, sadly, and almost immediately people on online forums started to criticise me for going back to work so soon and accused me of abandoning my baby, which was bollocks. Women on Mumsnet judged me especially harshly, some saying that I couldn't have been very ill if I came back to work so soon. How bloody dare they! But for the most part, I felt nothing but support from so many people I didn't even know.

The next day, the crowds that had gathered outside for us judges were just beyond amazing. Leaving the hotel, I felt like one of The Beatles (the police even had to stop the traffic!). I felt so buoyant and supported and happy. Everyone wanted to know about Hollie and it was just the best feeling to be able to say. 'Yes, she's fine, she's with my mum.' (Although sometimes I couldn't think of Hollie's name – I think something in me still couldn't believe I had my baby.)

I walked into the theatre and Simon was already there, which was unusual in itself. He gave me a massive hug and I said, 'You know I'm going to milk this!' He sat me down and started to hand me cards and gifts for the baby from Ant and Dec (a toy dragon), Alesha and David. The presents got bigger and bigger, until from behind his chair he pulled out a teddy bear as big as me 'with love from Simon'. It now lives in Hollie's bedroom.

Later on that day I received an award for best actress for *Shrek*, which Simon had to present to me in the afternoon via a live videolink of me accepting it, and I just kept thinking, 'Every moment of my life feels like a movie either ending or starting.' I always say about that time that if I was a character in *EastEnders* you would think, 'That is so far-fetched – give this character a break!'

The big moment for me, though, came when it was time to walk into my first auditions in months. The routine is always that Simon walks in last but the producer said, 'No, this time Amanda comes in last.' As I walked into that auditorium, it was, without doubt, one of the most incredible nights of my life. The audience gave me a standing ovation as Ant and Dec announced, 'She's back!'

Afterword

Yes, I am back. And I am looking forward, not behind me. That year, at the Birmingham show, I took Hollie too. That was the theatre where I last felt Theo kick me, and finally, I felt like I'd come full circle. It was very important to me to take my baby back there with me.

I took the plunge and sold our little Norfolk hideaway to a friend (on the condition that he sells it back to me if ever he doesn't want it any more). I had gone through so much in that cottage. I will always have my memories of dinners at the Hoste with Paul and Jeanne, and of family picnics and noisy Sunday lunches. We had cast Theo out to sea in his little pea-green boat on a windswept beach not far from there. But it was time to let go and start anew. Chris and I bought a thatched cottage in the Cotswolds instead and are creating wonderful new memories there.

That summer, me and Mum took a motorbike taxi to see the Opening Ceremony of the Olympics. Then, a week or so later, we went back to LA, to the beach, to my happy place, with my complete perfect little family. Jane says her fondest recent memory of me is there then, carefree and unencumbered for the first time in years – a girl with a boogie board and wetsuit, without a care in the world, on a Malibu beach. Whilst the rest of them sat and relaxed on the beach, I was apparently like a child, returning again and again into the waves and being washed up unceremoniously on to the shore with a massive grin on my face!

But tragedy inevitably leaves a legacy in its wake. Mine is that I occasionally panic that I'm going to die and not see my children grow up. I have been made painfully aware of my own mortality, and other people's. Having been fit and well all my life – and rarely in hospital since I had my tonsils out.

I finally gave in to therapy this year. It was only when I got on to the *Britain's Got Talent* set that I realised the extent of the press coverage whilst I'd been in hospital. They run clips from the previous year to entertain the audience and suddenly all the Amanda Holden headlines, and television news coverage including the Ten O'Clock News and Sky News was all over the screen. I was so shocked.

I never had a problem with therapy but always felt able to deal with things on my own – in fact, I prided myself on it. It was hard to accept that my family and friends were no longer enough to help me. But I am also proud of knowing when to ask for help.

I found a lovely lady and offloaded my worries. Speaking to someone – a stranger – for a few weeks, to get me back on the pace, left me rejuvenated. We spoke about the immediate stuff and then eventually we talked about my family and the dark days of their animosity towards me. I told her that I felt I had to almost die to get everyone back together, and I truly believe that's why it happened. It was like I was a human sacrifice! There was no other lesson to learn for any of us, except to put the pettiness and crap behind us and realise family is the most important thing.

My own little family comes above everything, of course. But now I had MY family back, after a fallout that started with nothing ... A weird comment from my nan that she emphatically denied which led to trauma and heartache and accusations of lies. A moment from my sister who refused a simple favour. My mum seizing on pieces rather than seeing the whole picture. It was a spark that ignited an entire bush fire, and absolutely the most hideous time. I know families who argue about far more serious issues but all eat around the same table within hours! My family, however, are all stubborn and have shown how these things can quickly escalate out of control. I know my sister has spoken to my mum about the time she lost with Lexi and how ridiculous it has all been, but I told Debbie Hollie meant a new start for all of us – that she had her fresh out the oven, and that getting to know Lexi aged six was just the best age.

The process of creating this book has reminded me of what I have experienced over the last forty-two years and what is now important to me. I have never lost my curiosity about life and still feel an ever-present sense of discovery. I only hope I can pass that on to my children. Aside from delving deep into your memories (some of which are firmly buried!), I think one of the most notable things about writing a book is looking back on all the photos. You see yourself all those years ago and cannot believe who you are looking at. Who was that girl having such a life? We all groan, of course, at how time ages us. We all have horrid photo albums. What is interesting to me is looking at how my life has been recorded, or 'captured', by the media. The last twenty years all played out so publicly, but I look at my eyes in the pictures and they are what tell the truth. ('The eyes never lie,' to quote Al Pacino in *Scarface*.)

I have absolutely no clue what my name means to you now. A

judge on *Britain's Got Talent*? Actress, maybe? West End lovey? Ex-wife of TV game show host? Naughty minx? Annoying? Irritating? A name synonymous with baby loss? Regular winner of the annual Git Awards (at a private ceremony held at our house only!). Who knows. And who bloody cares? To be honest, these days I am just glad to still be here. To me, I am Mrs Chris Hughes. Mother to Lexi and Hollie. The two little fairies I was always meant to have. They fill our hearts with so much love and laughter. No one prepares you for the immensity of that. Or how complete it makes you feel.

I barely recognise myself as the person I was, but only my face and body have changed over the years (and no – not from Botox or surgery!). My integrity and the person my mother brought me up to be are the same. I am still intact. Battered, bruised and tougher than I had hoped for. But essentially, I am still that little girl hiding in the wardrobe ...

Acknowledgements

Firstly I would like to thank my publisher Carly Cook at Simon & Schuster. You have been like a Super hero. Thank you for dealing with all the baddies! This book wouldn't have happened without all your support and ball busting.

Mountview Theatre School and all who graduated in 1992. It was bloody hard work. It wasn't like 'Fame', but we learned a lot! In sweat! Years that I will treasure and remember forever! Jason Maddocks. Flatmate. True friend.

To Jane Lehrer, Patrick Hambleton, my agents when I first left drama school. I owe you so much. Not least your faith in me and starting me on the road to . . .? My dreams! Patrick you once said it would be a path covered in brambles but you both helped clear the way. Along with Amanda Howard Associates and much later the great Sue Latimer. Thank you.

To so many people who believed in me and gave me a chance: Tony Charles (softest beard in the biz!), Richard Parker, Wendy Toye, Stephen Dexter, David Tomlinson, the late Geoffrey Perkins,

Sally Fincher, Nick Symons, John Bishop (not the comedian), Spencer Campbell, Stuart Harcourt, Jed Mercurio, Duncan Weldon, Sam Mendes, Andrew Lloyd-Webber, Peter Fincham, Andy Harries, Damien Timner, Michelle Buck, Gareth Neame, Jed Mercurio, Harry Enfield, Charlie Pattinson, George Faber, Debbie Horsfield, Elizabeth Binns, Sally Haynes, Laura Mackie, the late John Stroud, Marcus Mortimer, Jed Leventhall, Michael Mayer, Richard Holloway, Shu Greene, Nigel Hall and Amelia Brown.

Special thanks to Rob Ashford, Jeanine Tesori, and To Caro Newling for her tireless understanding and support. A massive 'mwah' to DreamWorks.

Thank you to Simon Cowell. I owe so much to you. Not least *all my success* (at least that's what you keep telling me!) X

Piers Morgan: Thanks – you are still a git though.

To my Girlfriends: Jane Wall, Jess Taylor, Sally Haynes, Rose Keegan, Sarah Parish, Shara Walsh, Angela Griffin, Vikki Hayward and Lucy Gaskill. We've been through everything together and come out the other end – slightly more worn but no less glamorous! With the help of Touche Éclat and false lashes. Your friendship means everything to me. I love you all.

To Team Mandy: Jane Tyler, Ben Cooke, Sinead Mckeefry, Christian Vermaak, Michaela Drake and Paula Cahill.

The support I've received from my fans on Twitter has been incredible. So thank you #Holdenites.

Angie Blackford: for all the advice and sherry!

Alison Griffin: you have known me all my 'non' private life! I literally couldn't exist without you!

To my Witches of West Mid and Hammersmith; Pippa Nightingale, Jackie Nash and Natalie Carter! Thanks aren't enough for what you all did for us for during the happy and sad times. Will never forget the Mick Jaggers! (You know!)

To my Mum: I never really fully appreciated what a great child-hood you gave Debs and I until I had my own children. You dealt with so much and kept all the nasty stuff away. You gave us the absolute best you could. I know we have had our differences but thank you for allowing me to write honestly about our family and 'dig up' some old history. I love you.

To my 'Step' Dad Les; Step is such a small pointless word. It doesn't cover how I feel about you and what you have done for Debbie and I. Taking us on and loving us like a proper Daddy made the gaping hole seem infinitely smaller. We belong to you.

Nanny Win: as I read this book back there's not much mention of you, but I want you to know how lucky Debbie and I were that you totally accepted us as your own, spoilt us and loved us. Your cooking is the stuff of dreams, and memories of country walks in our wellies, picking blackberries, still makes me feel so happy. Thank you so much

Debs: we've been through an awful lot together and faced some of the same stuff, but our stories will always be different. I am glad you have been a part of mine and look forward to our happy ending. I love you. x

Nanny: you were so influential in my life. You were a feminist without realising it. Strong, stubborn, opinionated, fair, loving and fun – with the best laugh ever! We have had our differences but that's because everyone says we are the same. I'm not sure about that but one thing I know is that I will love you forever.

And lastly to my husband Chris . . .

I honestly don't know how you put up with me. This book has been 'trying' to say the least! But as with everything, you made it work. THANK YOU, THANK YOU.

Your love, sense of humour and ability to see what is REALLY important in life has got us through so much! I catch myself looking at you everyday and loving you a little bit more. How is that even possible?! I am so glad (and relieved!) you agreed to marry me and have children! Our girls are incredible! Mostly due to you!

I LUB a lot!

Amanda Holden
Professional Resume

2013 Judge on ITV's *Britain's Got Talent* (Series 7)
2013 Judge on ITV2's *Britain's Got More Talent* (Series 7)
2013 Herself in Danone Oykos TV Advertising Campaign
2013 UK Correspondent for America's CBS network
2013 Presenter of ITV's *A Night of Heroes*

2012 Presenter of ITV's *Superstar*
2012 Herself in Danone Oykos TV Advertising Campaign
2012 Judge on ITV's *Britain's Got Talent* (Series 6)
2012 Judge on ITV2 *Britain's Got More Talent* (Series 6)
2012 Presenter of *the Sun*'s Military Awards for ITV
2012 Presenter of ITV's *Lorraine*
2012 UK Correspondent for America's CBS network

2011 Judge on ITV's *Britain's Got Talent* (Series 5)
2011 Judge on ITV2's *Britain's Got More Talent*
2011 UK Correspondent for America's CBS network

2011   Presenter of ITV's *A Night of Heroes*

2011   Princess Fiona in *Shrek the Musical*, Drury Lane Theatre, London

2011   Weekly Columnist for News of the World's *Fabulous* magazine

2010   Judge on ITV's *Britain's Got Talent* (Series 4)

2010   Judge on ITV2's *Britain's Got More Talent* (Series 4)

2010   Presenter of ITV's *Amanda's Fantasy Lives* (three part Series)

2010   UK correspondent on CBS America's *The Early Show*

2010   Presenter of ITV's *The Door* game show

2010   Presenter of ITV's *Children's Champions Awards*

2010   Presenter of ITV's *A Night of Heroes*

2010   Penelope Belcher in Tesco TV Advertising Campaign

2010   UK Correspondent for America's CBS network

2010   Weekly Columnist for News of the World's *Fabulous* magazine

2009   Judge on ITV's *Britain's Got Talent* (Series 3)

2009   Judge on ITV2's *Britain's Got More Talent* (Series 3)

2009   Lizzie in BBC1's *Big Top* (x 6 episodes)

2009   Presenter of ITV's *Out of my Depth* midwife documentary

2009   Presenter of ITV's *Celebrating the Carpenters*

2009   Presenter of ITV's *A Night of Heroes*

2009   Weekly columnist for News of the Worlds *Fabulous* magazine

2009   UK Correspondent for America's CBS network

2008   Judge on ITV's *Britain's Got Talent* (Series 2)

2008   Judge on ITV2's *Britain's Got More Talent* (Series 2)

2008   Sarah Trevanion in ITV's *Wild At Heart* (Series 3 x 8 episodes)

2008   Presenter of ITV's *When Britain First Had Talent*

2007   Judge on ITV's *Britain's Got Talent* (Series 1)

2007   Judge on ITV2's *Britain's Got More Talent* (Series 1)

2007   Sarah Trevanion in ITV's *Wild At Heart* (Series 2 x 10 episode)

2007   Presenter of ITV's *Really Wild At Heart* documentary

2007   Presenter of ITV's *The National Television Awards*

2006   Sarah Trevanion in ITV's *Wild At Heart* (Series 1 x 6 episodes)

2005   Mia Bevan in BBC1's *Cutting It* (season 4 x 6 episodes)

2004   Mia Bevan in BBC1's *Cutting It* (season 3 x 6 episodes)

2004   Alice in BBC's *Mad About Alice* (x 6 episodes)

2004   Lucy Eyelesbarrow in ITV's *Miss Marple – 4:50 from Paddington*

2003   Mia Bevan in BBC1's *Cutting It* (season 2 x 7 episodes)

2003   Herself in BBC1's *Comic Relief 2003: The Big Hair Do*

2003   Presenter of ITV's *The National Music Awards*

2003   Presenter of ITV's *Greasemania*

2003   Millie Dilmount in *Thoroughly Modern Millie*, Shaftesbury Theatre, London.

2003   Millie Dilmount in *Thoroughly Modern Millie* for *The Royal Variety Performance*

2003   Amanda Holden' in *Ready When You Are Mr McGill*, Working Title Productions for ITV.

2002   Mia Bevan in BBC1's *Cutting It* (season 1 x 6 episodes)

2002   Debs Bloke in BBC1's *Celeb* (x 6 episodes)

2001   Louise Slaney in BBC1's *Hearts and Bones* (Series 2 x 6 episodes)

2001   Geraldine Titley in ITV Granada's *The Grimleys* (Series 3 x 6 episodes)

2001   Sarah Campbell in ITV's *The Hunt*

2000   Jessica in SKY One's *Now You See Her*

2000   Geraldine Titley in ITV Granada's *The Grimleys* (Series 2 x 10 episodes) –

2000   Mel in BBC1's *Kiss Me Kate* (Series 3 x 9 episodes)

2000   Louisa Slaney in BBC1's *Hearts and Bones* (Series 1 x 7 episodes)

2000   Alice in BBC1's *Happy Birthday Shakespeare* (two part drama)

2000   Geordie's girlfriend in BBC1's *The Nearly Complete and Utter History of Everything*

1999   Geraldine Titley in ITV Granada's *The Grimleys* (Series 1 x 6 episodes)

1999   Mel in BBC1's *Kiss Me Kate* (Series 2 x 7 episodes)

1999   Actress in Channel 4's *Smack the Pony* (x 4 episodes)

1999   Shoe Shop Assistant in ITV's *Virtual Sexuality*

1999   Nurse in *Don't Go Breaking My Heart,* Bill Kenwright films

1998   Mel in BBC1's *Kiss Me Kate* (Series 1) (x 6 episodes)

1998   Actress in ITV's *Hale and Pace*

1998   Various Roles in BBC2's *Goodness Gracious Me* (x 4 episodes)

1998   Petra in BBC1's *Jonathan Creek* (x 2 episodes)

1997   Various Characters in Channel 5's comedy sketch show
        We Know Where You Live (x 12 episodes)

1997   Camilla Barker in ITV's *Thief Takers*

1997   lead Actress In ITV's *The Bill*

1996   Pamela in *Intimate Relations* , Boxer/Handmade Films

1994   Carmen in BBC1's *EastEnders* (x 5 episodes)

1993   Alice Meadows BBC1's *In Suspicious Circumstances*

1992   Liesl Von Trapp in *The Sound of Music*, touring theatre
        production.

Pre-1992   Cecily Cardew in *The Importance of Being Earnest*,
            theatre production

Pre-1992   Eliza Doolittle in *Pygmalion*, theatre production

Education

Mountview Academy of Theatre Arts, Graduated 1992

Picture Credits